A FORGOTTEN

GROWING UP IN THE JEWISH PALE

*Based on the recollections
of Pearl Unikow Cooper*

LISA COOPER

PENINA PRESS

Jerusalem • New York

A Forgotten Land
Growing Up in the Jewish Pale

Published by Penina Press

Text Copyright © 2013
Cover Design: Shani Schmell
Typesetting: Ariel Walden
Editing and Production Director: Daniella Barak

Soft Cover ISBN: 978-965-524-129-7

First edition. Printed in Israel

Distributed by:
Urim Publications
POB 52287
Jerusalem 91521, Israel
Tel: 02.679.7633
Fax: 02.679.7634
urim_pub@netvision.net.il

Lambda Publishers, Inc.
527 Empire Blvd.
Brooklyn, NY 11225, USA
Tel: 718.972.5449
Fax: 718.972.6307
mh@ejudaica.com

www.UrimPublications.com

For my parents

Contents

PART III: 1914–1919

PART IV: 1920–1925

A Note on Transliteration

THE 'CH' in Yiddish and Hebrew is a hard sound like the 'ch' in the Scottish word loch, rather than the soft sound of the English word rich. I have not transliterated it consistently, preferring to choose the English spelling that feels most natural, sometimes using 'ch': Rachel, Chaya, challah, tichl, Chava; and at other times, just 'h': Hassid, Hanukkah, Hana, happers, heder, Haskl.

For Russian or Ukrainian words with the Cyrillic letter 'X', which is also pronounced like the 'ch'in loch, I have used the most commonly used Russian to English transliteration: 'kh', e.g., Khodarkov, Makhno, Kharkov.

The pronunciation is identical in all three sets of words.

Note that the words dacha and tachanka are of Russian or Ukrainian origin. The 'ch' represents the Cyrillic letter 'Ч', which is pronounced as in the English word rich.

Prologue

THIS BOOK is my grandmother's story, written as she would tell it. She was an inveterate storyteller and my father and aunt grew up with these tales of her early life. So much so, in fact, that the inhabitants of a distant Russian town – many of them long dead – seemed more real to them than those of the Canadian city in which they spent their childhood.

In the late 1970s, when my grandmother was an old lady, my father decided to record her telling some of her stories. By then he was a social historian at the University of East Anglia in Norwich, England, and wanted to know more of the world in which she had grown up. He probed her for further information. Over the course of the next twenty-five years, some of the audio tapes became distorted, broken, lost or accidentally re-recorded with pop music (my brother and I were teenagers; we wholeheartedly apologize), but enough remained to ensure that my grandmother's stories were not lost.

Until 2004 I had not listened to these cassettes. They were recorded in Yiddish, a language I don't understand, and as a youngster I was never sufficiently interested to ask my father to translate them. I had no idea what a rich and fascinating history they would reveal. Even Dad had not revisited the tapes for years.

When my father reached his 70s, I began to fear that the stories would be irretrievable, for who else would be able to translate Grandma's words and know enough of her background to make sense of them? It was a labor of love for Dad and me to listen to the cassettes one by one and piece together a story. Hour after hour Dad translated while I typed. The result was a couple of dozen A4 pages of fragmented, disordered recollections, often repetitive and riddled with contradictions.

With this as a foundation, I have supplemented these stories with information obtained from endless questioning, historical research and background reading. I have verified facts with other family members wherever possible and added large helpings of imagination, conjecture, speculation and guesswork to fill in gaps and bulk-out sketchy outlines. I have occasionally borrowed ideas and imagery from other writings on this period. Nevertheless, despite my best efforts, there are no doubt instances where I have erred, and I hope that my forefathers would forgive me for any mistakes.

As I wrote this account of my grandmother's life, it took some effort for me to comprehend that this was the same person that I had known in my childhood as Grandma. By the time I knew her, she was a tiny, fragile, stooped old lady with walnut-wrinkled skin. She lived with her sister Rachel in a small, but comfortable, apartment in the West Hollywood district of Los Angeles on the second floor of a three-sided block built around a swimming pool.

Los Angeles is a long, long way from Norwich, where I grew up, and we visited only every few years. I don't remember Grandma telling me stories. Mostly my memories of her involve food – intricate dishes that we never ate at home: blintzes and knishes, cinnamon rolls and poppy seed cookies. And when my stomach was full to bursting, I recall being entreated, "Eat! Eat! You must eat some more!" in an insistent, foreign-sounding voice as my plate was piled high again.

Back in Norwich we remembered her by the regular parcels of chunky hand-knitted sweaters and strangely shaped woolen slippers that the postman delivered year after year, and by Hanukkah cards written in mysterious Yiddish squiggles that Dad had to translate. Sometimes the cards took months to arrive because Grandma had written the address down incorrectly – she had never learned to write English properly.

Discovering Grandma's stories of her early life in Russia, I often found it hard to believe that we could be related. How could she and I, just two generations apart, lead such different lives? But looking at photos of Grandma in her youth, the close family link is abundantly evident. From her I inherited my unusually dark eyes and petite stature. I also inherited something of her strong will and determination. Although, in both our cases, those who have known us best might call it stubbornness.

Grandma bore witness to many terrible events that took place in Russia in the first part of last century: war, pogroms, famine, disease and emigration not only tore families apart, but also seared the heart out of Jewish communities like the one in which she grew up. And after she and most of her family were safely in Canada, the Nazis would do the rest. The Jewish Pale became a forgotten land, a once vibrant community whose people had all emigrated or died. So many of Grandma's contemporaries did not live to tell their tales and I am grateful that she delighted in recounting her stories and that we, in later generations, can still enjoy them.

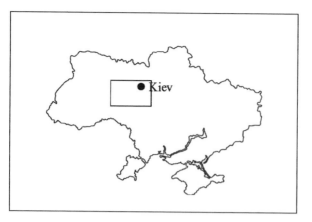

MAP OF UKRAINE

MAP OF
PAVOLITCH
AREA

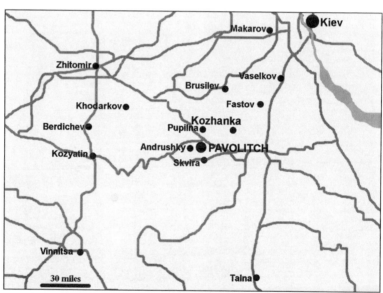

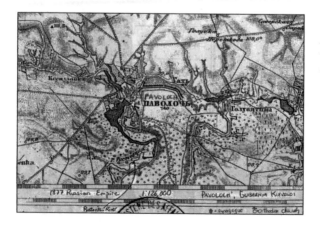

MAP OF PAVOLITCH
(dated 1877)

Abridged Family Tree

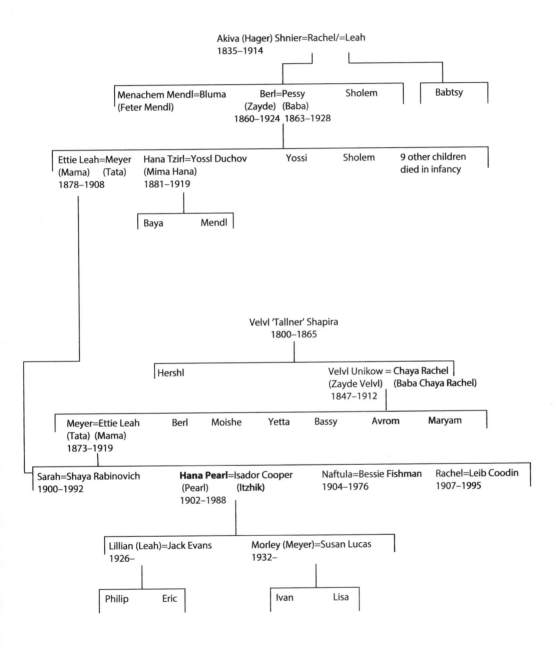

Akiva (Hager) Shnier=Rachel/=Leah
1835–1914

Menachem Mendl=Bluma
(Feter Mendl)

Berl=Pessy
(Zayde) (Baba)
1860–1924 1863–1928

Sholem

Babtsy

Ettie Leah=Meyer
(Mama) (Tata)
1878–1908

Hana Tzirl=Yossl Duchov
(Mima Hana)
1881–1919

Yossi

Sholem

9 other children
died in infancy

Baya

Mendl

Velvl 'Tallner' Shapira
1800–1865

Hershl

Velvl Unikow = Chaya Rachel
(Zayde Velvl) (Baba Chaya Rachel)
1847–1912

Meyer=Ettie Leah
(Tata) (Mama)
1873–1919

Berl

Moishe

Yetta

Bassy

Avrom

Maryam

Sarah=Shaya Rabinovich
1900–1992

Hana Pearl=Isador Cooper
(Pearl) (Itzhik)
1902–1988

Naftula=Bessie Fishman
1904–1976

Rachel=Leib Coodin
1907–1995

Lillian (Leah)=Jack Evans
1926–

Morley (Meyer)=Susan Lucas
1932–

Philip

Eric

Ivan

Lisa

PART I

1835–1905

My Great-grandfather Akiva

MY FOREFATHERS have lived in several countries without ever leaving their home town. Pavolitch is a rural community on the Rastovitsa river. Today it is in western Ukraine, but when I lived there in the early 1900s it was in southwest Russia, and before that, in eastern Poland. Earlier still it was in southern Lithuania. The area was in flux throughout the centuries with armies endlessly fighting, invading, occupying and retreating. The name of the town changed, too, depending on who was talking about it. Poles and Ukrainians called it Pawolocz or Pawolotsch and Russians knew it as Pavoloch. In Yiddish it was Pavolitch and that was what we called it.

As a little girl, Pavolitch was all I knew. It was a *shtot* – a small town – surrounded by fields of rich, dark earth and hugged on two sides by a large lake. The house where I grew up belonged to my grandfather. It was handsome and imposing: a large, double-fronted, red-brick property that bordered the Jewish and Ukrainian quarters.

I grew up speaking a mixture of Polish, Ukrainian and Russian, as well as Yiddish, my mother tongue, which we spoke at home. Pavolitch was a melting pot of different nationalities and religions. Two square, brick synagogues rose from the grassy mound at its center – the town's highest point – and a further three prayer houses were scattered across the Jewish quarter above the stream. Walking from the synagogue to the Jewish quarter we passed the grand Russian Orthodox church with its five silver domes. And high above the lake stood a Roman Catholic church.

Only the local officials and civil servants in Pavolitch were Russian. Ukrainians made up the majority of the population, easily distinguished by their wide faces, plump cheeks and flaxen hair, as well as their coarse, unkempt clothes. There were few wealthy Ukrainians. They tended to work for people like my grandparents as servants, warehouse managers or coach drivers – or they worked for the Poles.

The Poles were the landlords and the factory owners; many of them claimed to belong to the nobility and they turned their noses up at everyone else. For this had been their land for over one hundred years, up to the late eighteenth century. The Poles were a proud people and still smarted from the fact that their country had been taken away from them and cut up like a cake by the surrounding nations. Russia took her first slice of Poland in 1772, in the time of Catherine the Great, and helped herself twice more before the century was out until there was nothing left at all for the Poles. Pavolitch was in one of the portions that passed to Russia in the so-called "second partition" in 1793 and, even though this had taken place more than one hundred years before I was born, I can recall my grandmother's Polish friends still talking about it with resentment, as if they remembered a time before the partition.

Jews never chose to come to Russia: it was Russia who came to us, for the areas of eastern Poland that she swallowed up had a large Jewish population. Seen as strange and unwelcome guests in the Russian empire, the tsars set about containing these new subjects. They imposed restrictions on all spheres of Jewish life, from the schools we attended to the jobs we held and, most of all, the places we lived. Barred from St. Petersburg and Moscow and the other cities of old Russia, we were forced to remain in the Polish and Lithuanian lands on the western fringes of the empire, a region known as the Pale of Settlement. In the Pale, as a whole, just over a tenth of the population was Jewish. In Pavolitch when I was a little girl, it was more like a third – about thirty-five hundred people.

When I was growing up, it was as if the country were split in two: the Pale, where everything was familiar, people spoke Yiddish and we could travel freely to visit our numerous relatives who were scattered across different towns and villages; and the rest of Russia, which was an unknown world of cities we knew only by name, written in an alphabet that few of us could read, and where we knew nobody.

My great-grandfather, Akiva Hager, had belonged to only the second generation of Pavolitch Jews to be born into the Russian empire, entering the world in 1835. Akiva was a great storyteller. When I was a little girl, my siblings and I would sit motionless for hours at a stretch, riveted by his tales of times long gone. He was an old man already by the time I was born and it was hard to believe he had ever been a child. When my great-grandfather was little, he told us, Russia was ruled by a most repressive tsar, Nicholas I, a military despot who maintained a huge army to fight in the numerous overseas skirmishes in which he entangled his country. Pavolitch lay far, far away from any battlefield, but still the notion of war and the whims of the war-mongering tsar loomed large in Akiva's childhood. Almost every parent in the town had given up a beloved son to the army; some had lost a whole succession of boys to the recruiting officers and many of them were never seen again.

"I was so terrified of the *happers* that I couldn't sleep at night," Akiva would tell us. "They were kidnappers," he continued in a conspiratorial tone. "Like hungry wolves they circled around towns and villages gathering up recruits for the tsar."

Tsar Nicholas chose to target Jews especially. Not because they were great fighters – just the opposite, ours was a peace-loving people – but to help whittle down the number of what he considered unsavory subjects in his empire. The happers sought out anyone aged between twelve and eighteen. But if they couldn't get their hands on enough youths, they would take small children, some as young as eight or nine, until they had fulfilled their quotas.

Akiva spent his entire boyhood attempting to evade the happers, for the stories that made their way back to Pavolitch from the army were awful beyond belief.

"Twenty-five years they'd take you for. Can you imagine that?" My great-grandfather looked me straight in the eye and said, "I was barely older than you are now, Pearl, and if they'd caught me, I'd have practically been an old man by the time they let me go."

But few survived that long. It took only days for the Jewishness to be squeezed out of the recruits like water from a sponge. They were barred from following the kosher laws or keeping the Sabbath, or even from speaking Yiddish. Anyone who insisted on holding fast to the dietary laws – refusing to eat pork or soup made with lard – was beaten with a rod or forbidden from drinking. But however firm their Jewish resolve, there was no way the boys could avoid marching or performing drills on the Sabbath. At the end of a ten-hour march, having eaten nothing but dry bread, the young recruits would arrive exhausted at their destination and be forced to kneel until they agreed to convert to Christianity. If they continued to refuse, they had to kneel all night. What boy could remain steadfast under such terrible pressure? But there were rumors that some youngsters refused to sway and paid the ultimate price, taking their own lives rather than agreeing to adopt the Russian Orthodox religion.

I was horrified by the stories my great-grandfather told me and found it difficult to understand that they were real, not fairy tales like the books I read. He described to us how his neighbor had died of grief having had her precious young son ripped from her arms. A ten year old boy with a runny nose and tears rolling down his fat cheeks, he was bundled into a soldier's uniform meant for someone twice his age, then forcibly marched halfway across the country, beaten and starved until his pitiful body was ravaged by fever and exposure before he had even set eyes on a battlefield. He never came home again.

It was hardly surprising that parents would take any steps possible to prevent their sons from becoming victims of the happers. Akiva's parents decided that they must change the boy's surname so that the military authorities would fail to find any record of him through official documents. It was a very difficult decision to make. From as early as I can remember I have always been aware how distinguished our family is, and all because of the surname Hager. For Akiva was distantly related to the Hager rabbis of Viznitz[1], one of the most famous and revered dynasties within the Hassidic sect of Judaism. Even though nobody could actually put their finger on the blood link that connected us to the esteemed rabbis, the mere fact of sharing the name Hager meant that our family commanded respect among Jews throughout the Pale. Akiva's parents hated the idea that their distinguished family name would not live on after them. But if it saved their son from conscription, the sacrifice would be worth it.

Akiva's new surname was Shnier. He was never sent to school or to any other institution that could provide written evidence of his existence, as it was well known that Jewish boys who tried to enroll in a Russian *shkole* could find themselves offered up as recruits for the army. And so Akiva grew up living safe and sound with his parents, but unable to read or write. Despite their reputation as doyens of the Jewish community, this

---

1. A town in the far southwest of Ukraine.

did not trouble his family too much. In those days there was little need for education, after all, as long as one had faith.

By the 1850s, when Akiva had reached his late teens, Russia upped its forced conscription rate still higher as it headed toward the Crimean War. Wealthier families attempted to bribe the conscription officers to let them keep their boys at home, but there was no guarantee of success. Some even offered up all the money they had put aside for their daughters' dowries in an attempt to save their sons from service. But it was not unheard of for officers to accept the money, yet take the boy as well.

"My friend Froike cut off his finger to avoid going to the Crimea." I stared at my great-grandfather, my mouth agape, the first time he told me stories of self-mutilation. I wasn't sure whether to believe him or not. "Oh yes," he continued, "Cutting off fingers and toes was common. So was wielding a red-hot poker to the face." My great-grandfather urged me to look closely at the hands of the old men I saw around town. It turned out he was right – there was a whole generation of Jewish men in Pavolitch who couldn't count as high as ten on their hands. Others were blind in one eye or half-deaf or walked with a limp as a result of the damage they had done to themselves to gain exemption from military service. Akiva couldn't do it, though. He had recoiled in horror at the thought of sawing through his own flesh and bone to sever a finger, and the idea of losing his sight was beyond the bounds of his imagination. At night he lay awake sweating in panic at the idea of falling into the hands of the recruiting officers to end up a corpse on some foggy Crimean battlefield.

At last his mother came up with an idea, a way out that Akiva might be able to tolerate. It would be horribly painful – for there was no anesthetic – and alter his appearance for life, but it was guaranteed to keep him out of the army. He would visit the dentist to have teeth extracted. The tsar wouldn't accept soldiers that didn't have a sufficiently full complement of teeth and Akiva ensured there could be no argument by demanding that the dentist pull out every single one.

"I thought that if I clamped my eyes shut tightly enough, then I might be able to squeeze out the pain. But it was all I could do to keep from howling," my great-grandfather recalled, describing how his teeth dropped with a chink, one by one, into a glass jar at his side. When at last it was over, Akiva was shaking so violently that the dentist was unable to move him from his chair. There he sat for the rest of the day sobbing and holding to his face a large handkerchief, stained deep red and filled with chunks of ice.

Akiva's ruse proved successful and he avoided conscription, but at the expense of his looks. He was a tall, bony man with sparkling eyes and an unkempt beard that reached down to his chest. When his mouth was closed, his whiskers covered the whole bottom part of his face and his lack of teeth wasn't noticeable. But Akiva loved to talk and his mouth never stayed closed for long. As soon as he opened it, he took on the appearance of an overgrown baby, with a gummy smile that sat strangely with his deep-set eyes and knobby features.

Akiva's disfiguration probably saved his life. The Crimean War brought carnage for Russia's soldiers. Vast numbers were killed or horribly wounded by British and French troops in murderous man-on-man battles. Others froze or starved on the frontlines for lack of supplies. Tsar Nicholas himself died before the fighting was over, his war culminating in humiliation for his country.

With the war-mongering tsar in his grave, Akiva could at last concentrate, without fear, on peacetime pursuits. He had inherited a mill for grinding millet close to the center of Pavolitch and now devoted himself to his new trade. To assure himself of the same esteem and good custom his relatives had always enjoyed, he retained the distinguished Hager name for the business.

As a Jew, Akiva was forbidden to own land and till the soil himself, so he ground millet that was brought to him by grain dealers and the agents of local landowners. And after the serfs were emancipated in 1861 (which left us Jews the only citizens of the Russian empire denied the right to own land) much of his business was with local peasants who had been freed from bondage and started to grow crops for themselves.

Grain grew abundantly in the rich Ukrainian soil, which was so lush that, around Pavolitch at least, it was the color of stewed kidney beans. In summer mile upon mile of the flat, fertile land where I grew up rustled with the sound of swaying stems of rye, wheat, corn, barley and millet. Our region grew so much grain that it could feed the whole of Russia and more besides. In fact, the land was so productive that the Ukraine became known as the Breadbasket of Europe.

Grandfather Berl the Grain Trader

AKIVA'S THREE sons, Menachem Mendl, Sholem and Berl, came into the world in the late 1850s. From an early age it was clear that the youngest, Berl, was quick-witted and possessed a sharp mind. Berl was my grandfather. As a boy, he had been unusually serious and cared little for the games and childish pranks of his peers. He and his brothers were sent to *heder*, Jewish school, enabling them to enjoy the education that their father had been denied. As well as the scriptures and Jewish ritual they received a foundation in reading and writing Yiddish and, when they were older, Hebrew. Learning about the Torah was one thing, but what Berl loved most of all was arithmetic. Sadly, mathematics wasn't considered important for Jewish boys so everything he wanted to learn, Berl had to teach himself.

As he grew older, Berl spent more and more of his spare time at his father's mill. All Akiva's prices and accounts were calculated using an abacus that hung on the wall of his warehouse and beside it he would scratch into the crumbly red stone little chalk marks that were meaningless to anyone but himself. Berl spent hours deciphering and transcribing onto paper the scratched marks along the wall, placing his carefully drawn figures into neat columns, as if they were troops lined up for inspection, and tallying totals in his head. And, as Akiva was illiterate, Berl dealt with all his correspondence for him. Even as a small boy, Akiva would call him over to read letters that he had received and write replies in his schoolboy hand. Not having been to school, Akiva had never learned to read properly.

Once he had mastered arithmetic and basic accountancy skills, Berl set about learning to read and write both Ukrainian and Polish, and then became fluent in spoken and written Russian, too, which was very rare for a Jew in Pavolitch. By the age of seventeen he showed signs of developing into a successful businessman.

But first there were more pressing issues to attend to. Berl's two older brothers had already married and his parents decided that it was time for their youngest, too, to take a wife. Berl was quite a catch for any young woman, with his respected family background, educated ways and money-making potential. The matchmaker knew of no suitable bride in Pavolitch and was forced to look further afield. She settled on a girl called Pessy Rabinovitch. Pessy came from a good family: her parents owned a *kretchma* – a pub and store – in a nearby hamlet and her older brothers were showing themselves to be bright and resourceful, as Akiva hoped his new daughter-in-law would prove to be, too. One brother was training to be a lawyer (one of the few professions open to Jews), while another had opened a bookshop and would later set up the first movie theater in the town of Fastov.[1]

Pessy was slight with high cheekbones and the darkest eyes Berl had ever seen. Her lips were thin, but her smile pretty. She was just fourteen years old on her wedding day and still looked like a child. Although Berl was only seventeen himself, he called her Pessy Tochter – Daughter Pessy. The nickname stuck and even in her old age I remember my grandmother's friends and relatives still calling her Pessy Tochter.

Once Berl was married, his father Akiva bought a large plot of land straddling the Jewish and Ukrainian quarters of Pavolitch and employed a brigade of Ukrainian builders to erect a large, double-fronted, brick property that his three sons could share. This was the house in which, much later, I would grow up. It was split into two sides, one large and one small, divided by a third, lower section. But when the building was designed, Akiva had failed to take into account how it would be shared between the three men, all of whom were married by that time, and the two eldest already had families of their own. The brothers bickered with one another over who should live in the largest part of the house. Menachem Mendl's wife insisted that, as the oldest, it should be his by rights, but Sholem and Berl refused to give up their claim. Their father shook his head in despair. There was only one solution: as with any trouble-

1. Halfway between Kiev and Pavolitch.

some issue that couldn't be resolved within the family, he would have to ask the rabbi.

"You should draw lots," the rabbi told Akiva. The three young men could not argue with the decision of a rabbi and so each gave his trust to God that the house would be divided up as He wished by drawing a piece of paper from a hat. Berl was the chosen one and received the larger side of the house – a full seven rooms. Menachem Mendl got the smaller part while Sholem had the middle section.

But this arrangement didn't last long. Within mere months of the house being completed, Sholem had died. Even during the period of ritual mourning, discussions were underway about the fate of his section of the house. Berl was expanding his father's grain business, selling the millet as well as grinding it, and desperately needed a warehouse to conduct his trade. He was not a heartless man and mourned his brother deeply, but practical concerns were always at the forefront of his mind. Eventually he persuaded Sholem's bereaved wife to return to her parents' home in a neighboring village, and his oldest sibling, Menachem Mendl, to abandon any claim to Sholem's part of the house, and he set about converting it into what he called the *klet*, his warehouse.

Millet was brought to the klet by horse and cart and from there it would be transported all over Russia. The mechanics of trade became Berl's passion and he created a network of Jewish dealers in far-flung places – Riga, the Caucasus, Ekatarinaslav[2] and Konigsberg.[3] Despite the wide reach his business had achieved, Akiva never learned to speak – let alone read or write – Russian, the language of trade in the region, and Berl made this part of the enterprise his own.

Berl was a natural entrepreneur and developing trade on Akiva's behalf was not enough for him; he wanted something of his own. Millet was in his blood, but he had started to expand into other grains, too: wheat, rye, corn, buckwheat and barley, then pulses: peas, beans and lentils. Any dry goods that he could find a market for, and that wouldn't go bad too quickly, he bought and sold.

His network of agents, dealers and shippers expanded swiftly, multiplying as quickly as the number of long, yellow envelopes of coarse paper

2. Now Dnepropetrovsk.
3. Now Kaliningrad.

containing samples of his wares that disappeared from the klet into the maze of the Russian postal system. His goods could be found in markets right across Europe – as far west as England – and throughout Central Asia.

On a busy day, a solid flow of carts streamed into the klet hour after hour carrying excess grain grown in the peasants' plots nearby while local villagers dropped in, too, demanding small sacks of wheat that they could grind to make flour or requesting dried beans in winter when few fresh vegetables were available.

The klet was piled high with great pyramids of wheat and rye, as well as walls of coarsely woven, sand-colored sacks, full to bursting point. This was also where Berl kept his array of instruments and implements: special shovels and funnels of all shapes, sizes and materials used to ensure that not a single grain or pulse was spilt. All goods had to be weighed out meticulously using the most treasured possession of all: Berl's precious scales. A tiny shovel of wheat would be removed here, a bean or two added there, so that the customer received not a drop more or less than he paid for. Berl's business relied upon the precision of his scales and he guarded them with his life.

I grew up knowing the klet as a mysterious, forbidden place. My siblings and I were not allowed anywhere near it, especially if customers were around. But once or twice I snuck inside when my grandfather was away and it was like entering another world. While our house was always spot-lessly clean, everything in the klet was dulled by a layer of sand-colored dust and, through the cracks in the big wooden doors, the sun beamed in rays of light that were infused with tiny particles of grain. Everything was solid, functional and masculine.

As well as buying from the peasants and the itinerant Central Asian merchants who passed through the town, dealing with local landown-ers, or pritzim, constituted a large part of Berl's routine business. One particular poritz, a dark, burly man from the Caucasus by the name of Baskakov, employed Berl as his agent. Baskakov was a former army officer and a convert to Judaism. He owned a large estate at Andrushky, ten versts or so from Pavolitch, as well as much of the land and the lake around our town. Andrushky became the main source for the wheat that Berl sold across the country and beyond. Baskakov's estate was also home to a sugar factory and he assigned Berl the task of sourcing the best sugar beet in the region. Importing white beets from Galicia,[4] in exchange for Ukrainian rye, and selling the refined sugar on the international marketplace, became some of his principal and most lucrative trades.

International commerce, in an era before telephones and without established rates of exchange, was a complex and time-consuming affair. Every day Berl's *balagula* waited with a coach and horse to take him to the train station at Popilna, a small town twelve versts from Pavolitch, where he would await news from each train that passed of the prices currently being paid for different products further up or down the line: market rates in Kiev and export prices in Odessa, the region's major port.

The railway station was a daunting place for outsiders. When I was little, I occasionally travelled to visit relatives by train with my parents. I remember dodging between the swarms of traders from all over the area who congregated to discuss prices and close deals with travelling businessmen. My father would scoop me up in his arms so I didn't get lost or trampled and the noise was so loud, with frenzied shouts and hand gestures from all sides, that I couldn't understand how anyone was able to follow what was going on. As I grew older, my grandfather tried to explain it to me: The station was like a stock exchange, he said; market prices went up and down depending on the time of year, or how bountiful the last harvest was, not just locally, but all around the world. Even day by day the price of grain would fluctuate. A good deal of the trade was conducted by a process of barter so that a sack of sugar beet might be worth two sacks of rye one day, but could (theoretically, at least) change hands for one sack or three the next.

Berl also passed the hours drinking tea with his fellow traders discussing prices and agreeing complicated speculative contracts based on the potential production of various grain producers months or years ahead. He even put his signature to sophisticated deals that allowed him the option to buy or sell shipments according to future supply and demand.

While the railway station provided a daily price-list for goods and exchange rates, most of Berl's major business contracts were actually sealed in Kiev. He took the train to the city sixty miles away about once a week. And, from the end of February to late March each year, Berl would spend

---

4. Part of the Austro-Hungarian empire, which today straddles western Ukraine and southeast Poland.

a month in Kiev visiting the annual commodities exchange that was held there. Like most other dealers from out of town, he had to stay with friends or relatives while he was in the city, for Jews were barred from hotels unless they had a valid residence permit, and those were extremely difficult to obtain. As we lived in Europe's principal grain-producing region, the Kiev commodities exchange was a major international affair. Agents and dealers from all over Europe congregated in the city to examine the quality of produce, meet suppliers and negotiate prices. This was where the majority of Berl's international business was conducted. He would take with him a small quantity of each of his goods so that dealers could run their hands through the plump grains of Ukrainian wheat and rye, smell their freshness and break open the husks to chew on the kernels and test their quality. He also kept with him a supply of his long, yellow envelopes to fill with samples of his wares so that dealers could take them away to consider at their leisure.

Having spent all day at the commodities exchange, Berl whiled away his evenings in cafes in the company of travelling salesmen, brokers, money-lenders and other merchants. Over beer and bread and hard-boiled eggs they discussed their successes and failures and the business news of the day. The men swapped information, fostered deals and bargained prices. Amid the discussions of his friends' gains and losses, Berl negotiated lucrative deals to supply traders in Czechoslovakia[5] with rye and to purchase numerous varieties of dry goods including oats, barley, rye, wheat and pulses from some of the biggest landowners in Ukraine and Poland. He would return to Pavolitch just as winter was fading, always jubilant at the money he had made in Kiev and bubbling over with the energy that the city imbued him with.

---

5. Then part of the Austro-Hungarian empire.

My Grandmother's Torment

IN THE first year of their marriage, my grandparents led a charmed life. Berl's business was expanding fast and it seemed that every venture he embarked on brought success. And Pessy proved herself to be a fine cook and efficient housekeeper, as well as being able to play a role in the family business. She could read and do sums herself and helped her husband with his paperwork. She was also resourceful, coming up with ideas of her own and finding safe hiding places in the house for the, sometimes large, sums of money that her husband received. A happy and prosperous future seemed assured.

When Pessy became pregnant with their first child, both she and Berl were ecstatic. Even the fact that their first-born was a girl didn't bother them unduly, whatever the neighbors may have said. Normally the birth of a daughter to a Jewish family was little cause for celebration, but Berl and Pessy were thrilled. The baby, who would grow up to become my mother, was named Ettie Leah and my grandparents looked forward to filling their large house with a multitude of brothers and sisters for her.

Pessy was overjoyed to discover that she was soon expecting again. But this was when things started to go wrong. Normally up with the sun to feed her hungry daughter and prepare breakfast for her husband, Pessy struggled to rouse herself from bed in the mornings. She suffered cramps, shooting pains and constant tiredness. Sometimes she didn't even have the energy to attend her baby girl, the light of her life, and Ettie Leah cried for hour after hour desperate for Pessy's attention. Just as her nine months' confinement was finished, Pessy felt herself deaden inside. She knelt on the kitchen floor and prayed, "Please God! Please God! Please God!" But inside she knew that not even God could help her. Her baby was stillborn. From the pit of her stomach where her dead baby had been, Pessy felt an uneasy sensation, a premonition that her life would never be the same again. Despair threatened to engulf her, but she pushed it away and determined to carry on as normal.

Ettie Leah was relieved to have her mother back again with her usual unbreachable energy and Pessy devoted herself to the little girl as never before, sewing her tiny dresses trimmed with lace and tying ribbons in her fuzzy blonde hair. She began calling Ettie Leah My Miracle of Life. Soon she was pregnant again and the large house, which had so many empty rooms to fill, was imbued with an aura of hope. Although she suffered none of the lethargy of her previous confinement, one morning Pessy awoke with tremendous pains in her stomach. She curled into a ball and watched a deep red stain spread quickly across her crisp white linen. Her baby, so longed-for, fell to the floor no bigger than a stone. By the time Berl returned from his warehouse the blood had turned the color of the soil. He found his wife asleep, still cocooned on the bed, coated in dried blood and tears, Ettie Leah's head by the bend in her knees.

At last a second healthy baby was born. To her and Berl's overwhelming delight, Pessy brought into the world a little boy. A tiny purple slither of squalling life, he was the most beautiful creature his parents had ever seen. They decided to call him Sholem in memory of his uncle, Berl's brother, who had died a few years earlier. As a mark of their gratitude to God for allowing Sholem to live, eight days after the birth, Berl and Pessy held one of the biggest circumcision parties Pavolitch had ever seen. Pessy hired helpers to prepare platters of sweetmeats and Berl ordered dozens of bottles of whisky. He proceeded to top up the glass of every well-wisher until the guests lost all sense of decorum and spilled onto the street singing at the tops of their voices.

Much to Pessy's dismay, Sholem screamed throughout the ceremony. In fact he had screamed almost without cease ever since he was born. Clearly, Pessy believed, somebody must have cast the Evil Eye against her son and she resolved to have him blessed against the unknown ill-doer.

Reb Moishe was the local expert when it came to expelling the Evil Eye – which was, in my grandmother's day, the greatest fear of every Jewish mother – and he was kept busy by the intensely superstitious womenfolk of the town. Sometimes they would blame their enemies for setting the Evil Eye over them, in which case the remedy entailed tearing a thread from the perpetrator's clothing without his knowledge, and burning it in an earthenware pot over red-hot coals. If, as in Pessy's case, the culprit was unknown, Reb Moishe would recite a concoction of throaty incantations and spit three times. This should stop little Sholem from crying and help him grow up to be strong like his father.

Before long Pessy was pregnant again. But the hope that had infused the house in the early years of her marriage had started to dissipate. Usually so tough, Pessy found herself unable to shift from her mind an image of tiny coffins piled neatly one on top of another. She was always tired and tired of thinking about death. How many tiny coffins could she amass? Her next baby died within days of his birth and that brought the total to three.

At last, when Ettie Leah was a big-eyed five year old child, and Sholem – still painfully red-faced and not yet walking – was two, Pessy gave birth to another baby girl. From the day she was born she had a mass of black hair, bright eyes and a sunny disposition. Her name was Hana Tzirl and her parents were enraptured. Perhaps, Pessy reasoned, it was even worth suffering the heartbreak of the succession of tiny coffins to experience the ecstatic miracle of a healthy baby once again.

*

On the very day that Hana Tzirl was born, a bomb exploded far away in St. Petersburg. Pessy was too preoccupied with her new daughter to be aware of the events that everyone in the town was talking about. But, baby or no baby, her husband continued to read the newspaper every day and to discuss events with his neighbors at the synagogue.

"Ha, that'll serve the man right," were Berl's first words when he heard of the explosion that had killed Tsar Alexander II. Although the tsar had achieved a reputation as a great reformer for freeing the serfs, Berl grumbled that he hadn't done so much to emancipate the Jews. It was true that our people gained some limited freedoms under his rule. Forced conscription of children was halted; more Jews were able to attend Russian schools and universities; a select few had begun to work in state service. Jewish merchants, artisans and university graduates were allowed to settle in Kiev, which had previously been barred to Jews even though it was inside the Pale. A small handful of wealthy merchants had even gained residence permits for cities outside the Pale altogether. But emancipation this most definitely was not.

Berl was soon eating his words, however, for the events that ensued rocked the lives not just of my family, but of every single Jew right across the Pale. After the tsar's assassination, rumors began to spread. To begin with, the Jews weren't aware of the gossip and whispering; it took place surreptitiously inside houses in the Christian parts of towns. But then it spread to the shops, the markets and the train stations. The rumors were everywhere: it was Jewish revolutionaries that had killed the tsar and it was time for revenge. For a limited period, the rumormongers murmured, Christians would be allowed to loot Jewish homes and properties and the police would remain under orders not to interfere. The date was set for Orthodox Easter, which fell shortly after Passover in the year 1881.

By then Pessy was all too aware of events and, even decades later, she turned pale when she talked about how inebriated mobs had pulled down market stalls, smashed shop windows and kicked in doors in towns and cities across the Pale. Velvet dresses and woolen shawls, picture frames and broken chair legs, cabbages and bottled plums, all were trampled underfoot or piled up in grotesque mountains of mud. And everywhere there was screaming, running feet, fearful faces trying to stay out of sight. A snowstorm of white feathers cascaded out of windows and hovered in the air having been ripped from the confines of mattresses and pillows. Some of the rioters dressed themselves up in new outfits stolen from the ready-made clothes stores, piling one layer over another, shirts over jackets and underwear over trousers, until they looked like characters in some absurd stage play. How to count the cost? How many honest traders and merchants bankrupted? How many families bereft of all they had spent their whole lives working toward? How many children so traumatized that they would forever relive the fear in their dreams?

Berl visibly shook when he heard the news of a wheat merchant who had been robbed of eighty thousand rubles worth of merchandise. Despite being up half the night feeding her baby daughter, Pessy was unable to sleep, gripped by the fear that her family's kretchma might suffer the fate of so many others. For in towns across the Pale, Jewish taverns were being torn apart, the whisky and vodka bottles smashed by drunken louts who ended up on their knees in the mud drinking from streams of spirits that trickled down the street and from the pungent puddles that settled in hollows in the pitted roadside. The tavern-keepers could only watch in silent horror and wonder what would become of them now.

Any Jews found on the streets were trapped and humiliated, forced to submit to having their faces daubed with paint or their trousers pulled down and torn from them. Worse still, in one town two frightened girls threw themselves from the balcony of a two-story house onto the street below, choosing in a split second life as a cripple or possible death over rape by the rabid mob. In Kiev, the heathen crowd tore down the door of the central synagogue. They smashed into pieces the religious objects and tore up the holy books they found inside. To the rabbi and worshippers, there could be no greater evil than this.

In Berdichev the Jews fought against the hordes and held them back at the train station. Incensed by the initial defeat, the Christians returned in greater numbers and, not content with looting, they set upon their victims with whatever weapons or instruments of torture they could lay their hands on until the streets were awash with blood and littered with severed body parts.

The pogroms continued for hours and days, for as long as it took for the screams to die down and for the drunkenness to wear off. Yet still the police did nothing. Another massacre took place in Odessa, where around fifty Jews were murdered, some on the streets, and many in their own homes. But the Jews of Odessa refused to submit and friends and relatives of the dead fought back against the mob. And then, all of a sudden, the police decided to charge. Scores of Jewish fighters were arrested, some exiled without trial to the furthest reaches of the empire. Their adversaries, the *pogromchiks*, just walked away – such was the tsar's justice.

In the synagogue people talked of little else. Berl came home each evening and recounted to his wife the day's news, the stories from the newspapers and the gossip gleaned from his fellow worshippers. They held hands and prayed that the riots would remain within the confines of the larger towns and cities of the Pale as they had so far; that they and their families would be spared.

Pavolitch remained free of the pogroms that continued intermittently over the months that followed, but everyone knew that when Orthodox Easter came around again, they were likely to intensify. As the spring days lengthened, the Jews became more fearful. Gossip and tittle-tattle were circulating once again. But Berl and Pessy had other things on their minds. One bright morning Pessy entered the nursery to find her little boy Sholem cold, white and glassy-eyed. She held his body close and howled; she howled so loudly that her daughters awoke with startled cries and watched as their dear mother fell to the floor in a faint, still clasping her dead son to her chest.

The Christian holy days once again passed without incident in Pavolitch. But other towns hadn't been as lucky as theirs. Berl sat at the kitchen table reading the newspaper out loud. His voice cracked with emotion: "'Twelve hundred houses or shops in Balta[1] destroyed; fifteen thousand Jews reduced to poverty; forty killed or seriously wounded; twenty women raped; hundreds of Jews left with minor injuries.' Why are we trying to bring children into this world, Pessy Tochter? Why?" he demanded.

But Pessy knew the answer to that. Having a big family meant everything to her. It meant that she was fulfilling her obligations to God and her duty as a woman. It meant joy and laughter would fill the house and it would no longer feel like a mausoleum as it had since Sholem's death. It meant that she and her husband would be supported in their old age. It was everything she had dreamed about her whole life and it would break this awful cycle of sorrow that had somehow intertwined her own personal tragedy with that of her people.

Little more than a year after the loss of her first son, Pessy hoped the tide might finally be turning. What ecstasy she experienced at the birth of another baby boy! But Yossi was a sickly baby from the first, pale and unnervingly silent. Unable to bear the idea of another death in the family, Pessy dressed him in a white robe that looked like a shroud believing that she might be able to fool the angel of death into thinking he had already passed away and thereby save him. Around his neck she hung a tiny, inscribed amulet to ward off the Evil Eye.

More than ever before superstition came to rule Pessy's world. She became paranoid about everyday sights and sounds, seeing symbols and portents everywhere around her. Close to the front door of the big, double-fronted house lay a pool of dirty water that she called the *kaluzha*. For Pessy, this fetid puddle came to represent her family's misfortune. The dark, red soil of Pavolitch may have been rich, but it lacked a stone base layer and turned to glutinous mud in spring and autumn, sucking the boots off passers-by and disabling any coach that tried to pass. And the area in front of the house was worse than anywhere else. Rain and

1. Around 150 miles north of Odessa; a town with a large Jewish population.

melted snow settled in a hollow right outside the door, attracting rodents and farm animals; the air was often rank with the stench of stagnant water and livestock.

If only the puddle would dry up, Pessy thought, her babies might stop dying. She believed she could see the Evil Eye reflected in the kaluzha. Unblinking, it watched each new child that she brought into the world just waiting for the right moment to take its soul away. She begged Berl to get rid of it. But no matter how hard he tried the pool of water remained. He carted earth home from the fields to level the ground so the water couldn't settle. He bailed it out with wooden buckets on a scorching hot day so that the ground would dry out. The civil authorities even arrived one day with planks of wood to place over the puddle so that people could walk over it. But nothing could be done to make the filthy water go away.

As a small child I would sometimes play by the edge of the kaluzha, but if ever my grandmother saw me anywhere near it she would dart out of the house as fast as a rabbit and pound into me that I should never, ever go near it again. The kaluzha still symbolized a curse that had been with us since long before I was born.

*

Talk of pogroms continued to rumble around the Pale and still Pessy's traumas continued. Yossi never gained the rosy cheeks and puppy fat that a baby should. His constant coughing seemed to prevent him from feeding properly. And all Pessy's attempts to counteract malevolence with shrouds and amulets did little to convince anyone that Yossi would ever grow up to be fit and healthy. But Pessy refused to let herself believe that she could lose another little boy. She kept Yossi close by her side at all times and sang the most cheerful songs as she nursed him. Hana Tzirl, who had turned into a boisterous little girl, wasn't allowed near him. In a rare moment of reflection my grandfather much later admitted that he had wished he could have stopped time, to prevent what he could see was inevitable and to save himself and Pessy more sorrow. But as time marched on, Yossi succumbed to consumption. He wheezed his last shallow breath in the arms of his bereft mother before he had even learned to say "Mama".

"How we've aged, Pessy Tochter, how we've aged," Berl sighed as he held his wife close. They were only in their twenties, but the trials they had suffered already made them look much older. Berl noticed how thin Pessy had become, how the years of sadness had weathered her. The tracks of her tears seemed to leave permanent marks on her face and she wore her sorrow like a scar. But rather than weakening her, her desperation for another child made her stronger and more resolved. She would work hard, devote herself to her daughters, her husband and to God, and surely one day He would reward her. But time and again Pessy's waist thickened and she experienced the sensation of a new life stirring within her. Year after year she suffered the agony of childbirth and, one by one, she watched her babies die. Never again would she and Berl celebrate the joys of a circumcision ceremony in their house, nor would they fulfill the excited wishes of their two young daughters by providing them with more little sisters to play with. In all, Pessy gave birth to no fewer than thirteen children. All but her precious two girls were either stillborn or died as infants and the nightmare of their tiny coffins haunted Pessy's dreams for the rest of her life.

A Talmudist

My MOTHER, Ettie Leah, and her little sister Hana Tzirl spent their childhood in a cocoon of lavishness. Berl and Pessy insisted that their daughters should want for nothing; all their sorrow at the sequence of deaths they had suffered transmuted into determination that their daughters should lead a charmed life and grow up like little princesses. For starters, they must be the best dressed girls in town. Even as infants they wore posh dresses rather than everyday frocks and never bought them from the tailors in Pavolitch but travelled to the big city of Berdichev to get their clothes fitted and sewn by the best dressmakers in the area. They were sent to school – unlike many girls of their era – and were brought up to be modern and forward-thinking like their father. Pessy vowed that her two precious daughters would never see their hands grow rough and coarse like her own and refused to teach them to cook or sew or clean; they would hire servants for that.

She and Berl were particularly careful to shelter Ettie Leah and Hana Tzirl from the prejudice and violence that surrounded them and the girls grew up unaware that almost every year, around the time of Passover, fictitious rumors continued to drift around like smoke. The words "Christian blood", "ritual sacrifice" and "Jewish Passover" that wafted in the breeze and weaved in and out of people's consciousness were firmly locked out of the double-fronted house when the girls were present. Theirs may have been the only family in Pavolitch whose Passover remained a happy celebration untainted by the gossip circling outside: that Jews use the blood of a young Christian boy in their Passover rituals. Berl was convinced that the Ukrainians of Pavolitch knew full well that such talk was nonsense, but nevertheless, the rumor-filled air settled heavily over

Jewish districts until Orthodox Easter, the anniversary of the pogroms, had passed. Then the Jews felt safer, for another year at least.

Berl and Pessy couldn't, however, shelter their daughters from the malevolent fate that imbued their childhood. From as early as they could remember, the girls were aware of the presence of death. They watched one sibling after another appear and, shortly afterwards, die. While their mother continually took them to be blessed against the Evil Eye and sewed amulets for them to wear around their necks, they witnessed their father becoming sad and bitter as the likelihood of him having a son and heir receded.

Sometimes Berl would be away from home for days at a time consulting with the rabbi over his family's misfortune. The famous Rabbi Twersky lived in the town of Makarov almost a day's journey away. Berl thought that, if anyone could help, it would be him. For while the rabbi of a small town like Pavolitch was adequate to resolve less significant issues, trying to prevent a sequence of childhood deaths called for a greater authority. Berl travelled northwards along bumpy, potholed roads, muddy in spring and autumn, dusty in summer and chillingly cold in winter. Whatever the time of year, his journey was long and exhausting. Through Kornin and Brusilev he passed endless plains of wheat, divided occasionally by streams and lily-strewn ponds, and rising now and again into a gentle slope. Dogs chased his carriage as it passed and chickens scuttled away to avoid falling under the wheels as the balagula beat the horses on.

Berl became one of Rabbi Twersky's most loyal followers, frequently staying to dine with the rabbi's family and his closest associates. Although the rabbi's advice – that he should pray more fervently and never question God's will – failed to stem the continual flow of deaths, Berl never lost his faith in Rabbi Twersky, nor, indeed, in God.

Eventually he was rewarded – not with a healthy son, but with a father's joy of another kind. An agreement was sealed that his eldest daughter, Ettie Leah, would marry Meyer, the first-born son of the religious scholar Velvl Unikow, who was tutor to the rabbi's sons.

Ettie Leah had grown into an attractive young lady. She was small and slender with a pale, oval face and wavy, light-brown hair – rare among the dark-skinned, black-haired Jews – and, of course, a wardrobe of elegant dresses. But she screwed up her face and stamped her delicately-shod foot in disgust when her father told her that Reb Velvl wanted to meet her to check that she would make a suitable bride for his son.

"Tata[1], I won't see him! I'm not having some old man come and gawp at me as if I were a cow in the market!" Ettie Leah screamed at Berl as she tried to wriggle away. But her father gripped her arm and shook her so that her dainty earrings rattled.

"I didn't bring you up to be an old maid, my girl, and I'll **see** you under that wedding canopy if it's the last thing I do."

Ettie Leah knew that becoming an old maid was the greatest misfortune a girl could suffer. She also knew that there was no arguing with her father. And although Meyer's family had little money to its name, she realized that everybody would consider this a good match. For Meyer was a scholar and, being descended from a line of illustrious Talmudist forebears, he would command considerable respect.

She skulked away to her room to reflect on the end of her childhood, the meeting with an old man who would become her father-in-law and the prospect of a future spent with someone to whom she would always rank in second place behind God. This was far from the destiny she had dreamed of. As well as the latest fashions, Ettie Leah enjoyed modern books and devoured all the novels she could get her hands on. In the world of fiction pretty maidens married rich, handsome princes, not penniless religious scholars. But the world of the late nineteenth century *shtetl* and that of the novel were two very different places.

Pessy was more sympathetic to her daughter's feelings and stroked her long, fair hair reassuringly.

"I was only fourteen when I married your father," she recounted. "I'd never set eyes on him before the wedding day and I was petrified. But I learned to love him, just as you will learn to love your husband, too."

Although she had still only seen her betrothed from a distance, and had certainly never spoken to him, Ettie Leah's position softened gradually in the months leading up to her wedding. Every few weeks she would receive a letter from Meyer inscribed with neat Hebrew script, charming turns of phrase and quotes from the Bible. She tied up her letters with ribbon and kept them in a little wooden box under her bed, copying the heroines of the novels she read, and sat by the window daydreaming about her romance and turning over sentences in her mind as she decided

1. Father (Yiddish).

how best to reply to her betrothed. I still have the letters my parents wrote to one another, their faded ink now illegible in places on the yellowing paper.

At last the wedding day dawned. When it was time for Berl to conduct his daughter to the wedding canopy, Ettie Leah's hands, holding on tightly to his forearm, were moist with a nervous sweat and inside her heart was racing. As she stepped up to her groom, Meyer shot her a nervous glance and then turned his gaze back to the floor.

Oh God, he must be able to hear my heart beating, she thought as she stared at Meyer's shiny, black shoes. She still hadn't dared to take a good look at his face and dreaded the moment when she would be forced to turn toward him. But when the time came for her to stand opposite her husband as the marriage was solemnized, she couldn't stop staring, straining to see what lay beyond his dark beard. He had the skin of a man who had rarely seen the sun and deep, serious eyes. Most importantly, she didn't find his face repellent; in fact, he was almost attractive.

Pessy watched the ceremony enraptured, her heart almost bursting with pride. Her eldest princess, who had been born in happier times, had grown up and would soon, she prayed, be having children of her own. Pessy's bottom lip quivered as she raised her eyes toward God and beseeched him to spare Ettie Leah the sorrows that she herself had endured. She held her breath, hoping fate would not be tempted, as glasses were raised in endless toasts to the bride and her unborn sons and daughters. Ettie Leah blushed furiously beneath her heavy veil.

*

My parents could not have been more dissimilar. My mother was modern, educated and European in her appearance and outlook. My father was a rabbinical scholar who dressed in the traditional black coat of the Hassidic sect and a square, black skullcap. He wore a long beard and grew his sideburns downwards into little *peyes*, even though Jews in Russia had been banned from wearing their traditional side-curls almost thirty years before he was born. He cared little for business, or even for money; his only real interests were prayer and studying the Talmud – the book of Jewish laws.

Many women would have congratulated themselves on landing a scholar for a husband and willingly accepted a destiny as breadwinner, child-bearer and housewife, allowing their spouse to devote himself to the Talmud – but not Ettie Leah. As soon as the ordeal of the marriage ceremony and the embarrassing fumbling of the wedding night were behind her, she set about transforming her husband into the kind of man she would have wanted to marry. She relentlessly bullied and badgered him to take an interest in the world around him – not just the world of holy scripts – and to modernize his ways. To placate her, he reluctantly abandoned some of the external vestures of his faith, including shaving off his side-locks.

In fact, the matter of hair was one of the most troubling issues for the newly wedded couple. Hassidic custom dictates that when a woman is married she must shave off her hair and cover her bald scalp with a scarf or wig. Although Pessy always wore an Orthodox white scarf, a *tichl*, over her shorn locks, she and Berl were determined that their own daughters should not be bound by what they felt was by then an outmoded custom. Their girls did not wear the finest dresses in all of Pavolitch just to be capped with the headdress of an old woman. Ettie Leah was horrified at the very idea of shaving her head and although her new husband tried to assert his authority, he was too gentle by nature to hold sway. Ettie Leah's curls remained both in place and on show. And, to top it all, his own precious peyes had to go!

Nevertheless, however mismatched Meyer and Ettie Leah were in terms of their character and appearance – and certainly both were initially disappointed by their allotted spouse – their union was a successful one. Meyer believed that marriage was a sacrament and that to rear a family was to serve God. For her part, Ettie Leah's whole life had been dominated by the deaths of her eleven siblings and her mother's despair at being unable to raise a large family. She was petrified to her core by the idea of childbirth, which she associated only with pain and sadness. But she knew that outsiders would judge the success of her marriage on the swift arrival of a first child, preferably a boy, and on a succession of children thereafter.

Throughout Ettie Leah's first pregnancy Pessy prayed for hours every day, willing God not to inflict her curse onto her daughter, and she dragged Ettie Leah to a weekly appointment with the now elderly Reb Moishe to expel any Evil Eye that may have been cast on her. God bestowed His grace on Ettie Leah, whether thanks to Pessy's supplications nobody will ever know, and as the twentieth century began, so did Meyer and Ettie Leah's family life together. A short, sharp cry emitting from the bedroom revealed that their first child had entered the world alive and healthy. No matter that she was a girl, to her mother and father, Sarah – as they named her – was exquisite, with big brown eyes and a thin down of fair hair.

Two more children would follow in quick succession. I was born in 1902 and two years later my parents' dreams were complete: my mother gave birth to a baby boy. The arrival of a son was cause for celebration and all the friends and relatives who had made their way to Pavolitch for the wedding of Meyer and Ettie Leah returned for the joyous circumcision prayers and naming ceremony of baby Naftula eight days after he was born.

*

One of my earliest memories is sitting at the big kitchen table in my grandfather Berl's double-fronted house and listening uncomprehendingly as my family discussed serious matters that I wasn't supposed to know about.

"It's absurd! The whole story's absurd!" shouted my grandfather, thumping his hand on the table, making everybody jump.

"What's absurd, Zayde?[2]" I piped up.

My grandfather scowled at me so I turned to Mama and looked at her expectantly. She shook her head sternly. This meant that I shouldn't ask questions. My aunt Hana Tzirl winked at me and took me into the other room. She pulled funny faces at my sister Sarah and me and tickled us to make us laugh while the rest of the grown-ups sat in the kitchen discussing the scandalous news: the Russian newspapers had run an article claiming that the Jews had formed an alliance with the Japanese!

"What do we want with the Japanese?" Berl was arguing. "They're supposed to be our enemy, after all." For Russia had been sending vast numbers of soldiers east along the newly built Trans-Siberian railway to fight the Japanese army far away in distant China. If the Jews were siding with the enemy, it was certainly news to Berl. Soon word was going around the synagogues that it was a plot aimed at fomenting resentment

---

2. Grandfather (Yiddish).

toward the Jews. Could pogroms be about to spread like wildfire around the Pale, just as they had back in 1881?

Certainly something was up. Trouble was brewing in the larger towns and cities. Berl's relatives in Kiev warned him to keep away. Travelling merchants arrived with incredible tales. They had seen workers marching in the streets waving red banners. Songs slandering the tsar had echoed around the neighborhood. Strikes, uprisings, revolt . . . what would it all mean for us?

Berl discussed events with his fellow traders at the train station and studied the Jewish newspapers. He tried to explain to the rest of the grown-ups how the revolutionaries were succeeding in persuading Tsar Nicholas II to agree to a constitution and proper elections to a duma that Jews would be allowed to vote in. He recounted how lots of Jews were joining in the marches and demonstrations, together with students from the university in Kiev, scoring a victory over the discrimination that had dogged their people for centuries. Meyer shook his head. All this was beyond his comprehension. His world was ruled by God, not the tsar.

Ettie Leah couldn't understand it either. She was too young to remember the pogroms of 1881 and her parents had brought her up in ignorance of the fear and bloodshed that her people had suffered when she was a little girl. Having always been able to have whatever she wanted, the plight of the Jews meant little to Ettie Leah. She had led a sheltered life, with a mother and father who doted on her, and now a kind husband and three healthy children. She didn't know how to cook or clean or mend clothes. She didn't need to work or go shopping for food. Everything was provided for her just as it was when she was her father's little princess. Whereas most little girls are forced to grow up, my mother remained a princess well into adulthood.

Now, for the first time in her life, Ettie Leah was becoming aware of the outside world beyond the safety cordon of her family. The city was starting to mean something other than outings to buy dresses. She was afraid, just like most other Jews in the Pale. It was October 1905. The tsar had granted a constitution and the Jews should have been celebrating the new freedoms that this would mean for them. But there was a backlash. A few weeks earlier Ettie Leah had never even heard of the Black Hundreds, now those two little words were enough to send waves of panic shivering down her spine. The Black Hundreds were said to be the tsar's vigilantes and they were attacking Jewish homes and businesses from one side of the Pale to the other.

Berl stopped going to the train station because it had become too dangerous. Instead all his news came from the papers, which were several days old by the time they reached Pavolitch. Sometimes more up-to-date information came from the synagogue, for stories travel quickly in times of terror.

"If you hear anyone singing God Save the Tsar, run home immediately and hide," Berl warned his family, for the pogroms were being carried out to the tune of the Russian anthem and the singing would undoubtedly be followed by the Black Hundreds' rallying cry, *Bei Zhidov!* – Beat the Yids!

All the grown-ups gathered around the table each evening to discuss the latest events. Not even Meyer could ignore all the talk in the synagogue and turn his back on the plight of his fellow Jews. Ettie Leah clasped his hand as Berl recounted what he had heard about the latest attack:

"They've been travelling at night, the Black Hundreds, arriving when everyone's asleep. They've broken into Jewish shops and private houses, taking food, money . . . whatever they could find." Berl dropped his voice and drew out his words, "They have killed people in their own homes."

He recounted the stories that everyone had been talking about in the synagogue: how the Black Hundreds had beaten Jews with clubs until they fell to the ground bleeding. Some they didn't bother to beat, but shot with their guns at point blank range. The oldest and most respected men, the patriarchs, they hacked to death with axes. Women and children were not spared. The news that a pregnant woman had had her stomach slit open sent Ettie Leah into a faint and she had to be put to bed, clutching her own belly tightly. Hearing that a baby had been stabbed caused Pessy to let out an involuntary scream.

The tales were so terrible, so unbelievable, that once Berl had told the day's news, nobody spoke. Sarah and I were waved away to play on our own. My baby brother, Naftula, was left to cry. Hana Tzirl no longer left the discussions to keep us company, but remained at the table. These evening counsels continued day after day and always with fresh reports of horrific deeds and new towns added to the list of those attacked. One evening Berl related how Jewish shops and houses had been sacked for food, money and clothing and then set alight. On another he told how the mob had kicked down a synagogue door and ransacked the holy objects inside before burning the sacred building to the ground. Entire streets burned and towns choked for days under the suffocating stench of smoke. At last, soldiers and Cossacks had appeared in the streets and the Jews ran toward them, the relief visible in their eyes. Now the madness would stop, order would be restored and they would be able to return to what remained of their homes in safety.

"Save us!" cried the bedraggled, blood-stained Jews, throwing up their hands. But the soldiers hadn't come to save the Jews, they had come to join the fight. As the terrified men and women approached them, the tsar's men stabbed at them with their bayonets while the Cossacks rounded the Jews up to face the mob once again, rearing up their horses, trampling under their hooves anyone who tried to break free.

So far the pogroms had been restricted mostly to larger towns and villages and Pavolitch remained untouched. But the local townsfolk were taking no chances. To keep themselves safe from attack, Catholics drew white crosses on their doors in chalk as an indication of their faith while the Russian community placed icons in their windows. Jews stayed indoors as much as possible. When they did go out, they crept around cautiously. The weekly Jewish market dwindled to a handful of desperate traders.

The grown-ups were careful to keep us children well away from their daily discussions of pogroms, but we knew that something was gravely wrong. A sense of unease had enveloped the house. It was rare to see Hana Tzirl without a smile on her face, but now she seemed permanently gloom-laden. My mother had an unfamiliar air of concern about her and even my father appeared worried. And with good reason: nearly seven hundred pogroms took place that October. Across the Pale more than three thousand Jews were killed. Fifteen hundred children were orphaned.

The Twersky Court

W HEN I was little I was taken once a month to Makarov to visit my paternal grandparents. My grandfather, whose name was Velvl, would sit me on his lap and sing me a song.

"*Reb Dovidl, Reb Dovidl der Vasilkover, voynt shoyn yetst in Talne* (Reb Dovidl, Reb Dovidl of Vasilkov, now lives in Talna)" he chanted softly while jigging me up and down on his knee in time with the rhythm. It was a well known folk song that paid tribute to Rabbi Dovidl Twersky who was stolen away from the town of Vasilkov, which lay between Kiev and Pavolitch, one dark night in the year 1854 to become the great rabbi of Talna.[1]

"And do you know who Reb Dovidl took with him to Talna?" my grandfather quizzed me.

"Yes! Alter-zayde![2]" I would yell. For Zayde Velvl's father, who had died many years earlier, accompanied Reb Dovidl to Talna to be his chief advisor. My grandfather explained that he was so clever, and so good at his job, that he, too, became famous. People began calling him Velvele Tallner – Velvl of Talna – adding an extra syllable to his name to honor his authority and humility. He was born plain Velvl Shapira in Vasilkov in the early 1800s. Even as a young man he was already recognized as an exceptional debater of theoretical issues based on rabbinic wisdom and the learned commentaries on the holy books that he wrote made him well known, not just in Vasilkov, but across the whole region.

Reb Dovidl Twersky was several years older than Velvele Tallner. One

1. Talnoye in Russian. A town about 100 miles south of Kiev.
2. Great-grandfather (Yiddish).

of the leading Hassidic rabbis of the time, his reputation stemmed from the fact that his own grandfather had been a disciple of the Besht.[3] Everyone knew of the Besht – he was second only to God – the holy man who had founded Hassidism. His disciples and their descendants were rebbes – teachers or rabbis – the leaders of Ukrainian and Polish Jewry from the eighteenth century onwards.

"They say," my grandfather whispered to me, "that the apostle Peter came to Talna during his visit to Kiev." Some believed that was why Reb Dovidl had chosen to settle there. Others claimed that he was attracted by the views from a hillside overlooking the river that flows through the town where he would be able to greet the sunrise each day.

My grandfather Velvl was just a boy when his father uprooted the family and took them to Talna. He and his brother Hershl went to school with Reb Dovidl's children in the rabbinical court. Both boys were softly spoken and serious, but Velvl was the brighter of the two. By the time they came to study the Talmud, he could even outsmart the young Twerskys when it came to questions of logic. When they grew up each of the brothers had his own small house a few paces from the synagogue on one side and the court of the great rabbi himself on the other, along a narrow cobbled street that sloped down toward the river and the green meadows beyond, which stretched as far as the eye could see.

When Reb Dovidl died his eldest son became the next Rabbi Twersky of Talna and one by one the younger brothers moved away to other towns to establish satellite religious societies that remained linked to the Twersky dynasty. Often they were accompanied by a retinue of members of the original community and that was how my grandfather Velvl was uprooted for a second time, accompanying one of Reb Dovidl's sons to set up a new rabbinical court at Makarov, a day's journey to the northwest of Talna.

Makarov was a big, dusty town not far from Kiev with wide streets and few trees. It lacked the charm of Talna, but the new court would be able to attract disciples from the city and the many smaller towns and villages that circled Kiev to the south and west. Velvl was kept in the

3. Rabbi Dovidl Twersky (1808–1882) was the grandson of Rabbi Nochum Twersky of Chernobyl (1730–1798). Rabbi Nochum was a disciple of the Baal Shem Tov (c1700–c1760), also known as Besht, an acronym of the Hebrew letters of his title. He was a mystic from Mezheboz in southwest Ukraine who founded the Hassidic sect.

rabbi's inner circle, entrusted with the job of educating the rebbe's sons in the finer points of Talmudic learning and debate, equipping them to continue the work of their forefathers and become rebbes themselves. Even as a young man, it was clear that Velvl had inherited more than just his father's name. He was a distinguished scholar in his own right. He also had Velvele Tallner's high forehead and sunken cheeks and, when I knew him, the most enormous moustaches dangled over his bushy beard, which, had he not been such a serious man, would have made him seem quite comical.

Jewish life centered around the rebbes in the new communities they established. They became the focal point for all knowledge in the area. The *Beth Din*, or Rabbinical Court, combined the duties of a marriage broker, law court, synagogue, study house and even advice center – men solemnly approached the rabbi to discuss family matters: "How can I find husbands for my daughters when I can't afford to pay a dowry?" a poor villager would ask.

Or, in the case of Akiva: "I've built a big house for my three sons, but I don't know how to divide it up among them."

Or Berl: "My wife and I have lost another baby in childbirth. What can I do to stop my children from dying?"

*

In the 1870s, war was looming as Russia prepared for battle against Turkey in the Balkans. Times had changed since my great-grandfather Akiva had had all his teeth pulled out to avoid conscription. But like Akiva, my paternal grandfather Velvl Shapira was determined not to fight. No man could be less suited to army life than Velvl. He didn't live in a world of reality like other people; his was a life of sacred scrolls and texts. The changing of the seasons, the birds in the trees, the men who brushed past him on his way to synagogue, the food that he swallowed, none of these registered with him. As for politics and international affairs, he wasn't even aware of the existence of such things.

But as soon as the war and his likely role in it were brought to his attention, he became determined that he would not exchange his long, black gaberdine and skullcap for a soldier's uniform, nor give up his place at the Twersky court in Makarov for the long march to battle. The wily debating skills that served him so well in the synagogue he now put to use to devise a ruse that would enable him to dodge military service. Unlike in Akiva's time, single sons were now exempt from the draft and, with a litany of cleverly reasoned, convincing arguments, Velvl persuaded a childless Ukrainian family by the name of Unikow to adopt him, in legal terms at least. What benefit the Ukrainians gained from this arrangement was never clear, but the scam was successful in saving both himself and his brother Hershl – whom the adoption also made an only child – from conscription.

My father, Meyer Unikow, came into the world in 1873, the eldest of eight children born to Velvl and his wife Chaya Rachel. He and his siblings were brought up at the Twersky court in Makarov and the boys shared their lessons with the sons of the rabbi under the tutelage of their father Velvl. Meyer adored his studies and the peaceful, pious life of prayer and Talmudic scholarship, and he grew up dreaming of becoming a rabbi himself.

But his hopes were to be firmly dashed. Once the rabbi's sons had grown up Velvl had outgrown his use at the Twersky court. Being such a loyal servant, the rabbi didn't have the heart to dismiss Velvl and he was retained in the capacity of a collector of contributions from the rabbi's disciples and the Jews of the neighborhood. But he cared little for fundraising; his passions were study and worship. He grew sad and disheartened and spent long hours at the synagogue each day to overcome his despondency, often forgetting to go out on his rounds to deliver collection tickets and write out receipts.

Once the boys he had grown up with had departed to various towns across the region to set up courts of their own, there was no role for Meyer among the Twerskys either. His parents, Velvl and Chaya Rachel, became increasingly concerned about him once he reached adulthood. He couldn't stay with the Twerskys forever, living off their charity. His younger siblings showed no interest in Jewish law and dreamed of gaining a secular education, even going to university. But Meyer had inherited the genes of his grandfather, Velvele Tallner, and was a Talmudist through and through.

The only solution, his parents decided, was to marry him into a family wealthy enough to support him. The daughter of the successful grain merchant Berl Shnier of Pavolitch was the perfect candidate. Berl was a follower of the Twerskys of Makarov, regularly travelling from Pavolitch to ask the rabbi's advice as God took away his children one after another. One of only two who had survived just happened to be an attractive daughter of marriageable age.

As far as I was aware my father never talked about the disappointment he harbored at leaving the Twerskys and abandoning his hopes of becoming a rabbi. He wasn't the kind of man to dwell on his own feelings. And besides, marriage to Reb Berl's daughter would bring him some advantages. Although the Shnier family was fairly wealthy, Meyer wasn't interested in their money. Reb Berl could offer him something much more valuable: rather than paying a conventional dowry for Ettie Leah, her family agreed to board and feed Meyer for the first ten years of his marriage, thus enabling him to continue his Talmudic learning and spend his days at the synagogue and Hassidic study house.

The deal gave Velvl and Chaya Rachel reason to rejoice. Not only was Ettie Leah's family highly respected thanks to its distant link to the famous Hager rabbis, but this was backed up by property and business standing, and the bride was fair and capable. Meyer would have ten years ahead of him during which he need concern himself with little other than eating, sleeping and donning the new prayer shawl that marked his status as a married man.

Although he displayed no interest at all in seeing Ettie Leah ahead of the wedding, Meyer agreed to undertake the long, uncomfortable journey to Pavolitch to meet her parents. He also played the role of a dutiful fiancé admirably, composing moving letters to his betrothed, while secretly dreading the day he would have to move away from the Twersky court and leave the only life he had ever known.

*

Meyer initially felt like an outsider in the double-fronted house in Pavolitch while Ettie Leah and her family struggled to accustom themselves to his rigorous religious observance. His every word and action was steeped in the Torah and grounded in a fear of God. Berl and Pessy balked at his obsessive washing of hands and insistence on shielding his eyes whenever an unknown woman came to the door, as was the custom among ultra-religious Jews.

However, after a few months living under the same roof, Berl and Meyer started to find, to their and everybody else's surprise, that they got along rather well. However, Berl despaired of Meyer's lack of desire or ambition to work. Most of his day was spent at the synagogue or study house and, although Berl was himself a religious man, he didn't consider hours spent in prayer and Talmudic disputation a gainful form of employment.

Meyer was far from lazy, however. He rose before dawn every morning to begin his daily ritual. Sometimes, when I couldn't sleep, I tiptoed out of bed and into my parents' room to snuggle up with Mama and there, in the half-light, I watched my father carry out his early morning ablutions. He crept around the room as silently as a cat, careful not to move more than the prescribed eight paces from his bed. Next he donned his prayer shawl and pulled on his phylacteries – small, leather boxes containing parchments of the Hebrew texts – one over his arm and another over his head as is the custom for morning prayers. His movements were slow and thoughtful, in keeping with his peaceful nature. I loved to watch these strange morning rites, spying on Tata from my warm cocoon when he thought the whole world was still asleep.

Once my father had recited under his breath the early morning service, kissing his phylacteries and the fringes of his prayer shawl, he could head into the kitchen and light the samovar for tea. As well as an extraordinary passion for religious texts, Jewish scholars like my father seemed by their nature also to have an exceptional appetite for tea. Tata was a phenomenal tea drinker and, after gulping down at least ten glasses, he moved into his study to start work just as my grandmother was rising to begin her chores. While Baba[4] milked the cow, lit the fires and scrubbed the floor, Tata studied: a couple of pages each from his great sacking-bound volumes of the *Mishnah* and the *Gemara*, which between them make up the Talmud. In the margins of the books he scribbled commentaries and interpretations in his tiny, rounded script, full of obscure abbreviations. Nobody but he could read his work let alone understand it. Sometimes he was so engrossed that he would miss first *minyan* – the seven o'clock service at the synagogue.

On these occasions he was often roused from his studies by my grandfather. Berl never missed a morning prayer meeting. He used the synagogue as a meeting place, somewhere to check on the latest gossip and maybe glean news of new grain consignments or landowners who

4. Grandmother (Yiddish).

wanted help selling their wheat. On market days, he would walk home via the marketplace. Forever urging my father to participate in the family business, despite the dowry of ten years' free board that he had agreed to, my grandfather would call to his son-in-law on his return, "Hey, I've just seen Yosep and Shmuel at the market and signed myself up for a couple of *pood* of beans from them. I think they had more to sell – why don't you go and find out what's going on?"

"Yes, yes, in a minute," Meyer would reply. "I'm nearly done. Just half a page left then I'll go to the market for you."

But even if he made it to the market, my father never had the business sense to buy or sell any goods. More often than not he would use it as a tea stop before heading on to the synagogue.

Although she knew better than to interfere with her husband's relationship with God, my mother despaired of his lack of interest in any work that was not of a religious nature. If only he could harness his wealth of natural talent and intelligence in another direction, then he could become very successful, she thought. Eventually my father agreed, reluctantly, to accept a proper role in the family grain business. So day after day he followed his father-in-law to the klet, the warehouse at the side of the house, and used my grandfather's scales to weigh out sacks of wheat or pood of corn. Poor Tata was so bored and frustrated that his mind would wander and my grandfather would return from the train station to find him staring into space as he tried to fathom some tricky issue of Talmudic logic, the grain that he was supposed to have bagged up still scattered all around his feet. Meyer was so ill-suited to the work that after a few weeks Berl released him from it.

What my father enjoyed most were visits from Rabbi Twersky of Makarov and his sons who would stay at our house whenever they were in Pavolitch. Rabbinical families travelled frequently, visiting their followers and looking into new locations to set up court for their dynasty. Together again with the Makarover rabbis, Tata's face lit up like that of a little boy with a bag of sweets and he delighted in the hours they spent in animated discussion of sacred texts.

My father's many younger brothers and sisters visited regularly, too, and the double-fronted house became a focal point for our large, extended family. The conversation was always loud and animated and, although I couldn't follow the debate, I loved to sit cross-legged under the little coffee table in the lounge nibbling the sweets that my aunts and uncles had brought me. Casting my eyes from one animated face to another I watched as the impassioned grown-ups lost all sense of decorum and shouted at one another at the tops of their voices. My sister Sarah was more timid than me and always stayed well clear of these noisy discussions and even I sometimes got scared when fists were banged on tables – especially if someone forgot I was there and pounded on the wood above my head! Then I would dart out and cling tightly to Tata's knees, knowing that he would never lose his temper.

The difference of opinion between my father and my aunts and uncles always came down to the same issues: should Jews isolate themselves and rely only on the holy texts for their life's guidance, or should they assimilate, fight for equal rights with other citizens of Russia and take part in the affairs of the world outside the shtetl? My father, of course, was in the first camp. Strangely, though, for a family brought up in a rabbinical court, none of Tata's siblings upheld the Hassidic tradition, instead choosing progress, science and socialism over the Torah. They earnestly and vehemently voiced their views and criticized my father's way of life.

The two youngest, my Feter[5] Avrom and Mima[6] Maryam, even as teenagers were determined to become doctors and improve welfare in our country while their older sisters, Mima Yetta and Mima Bassy, were supporters of the revolutionary movement that had prompted the awful pogroms of 1905. Even those closest in age to my father, his brothers Berl and Moishe, showed little interest in religion. However heated the arguments, my father always remained calm, unwavering in his conviction that his chosen way of life was the correct one, and his brothers' and sisters' opinions seemed to bounce off him without penetrating the surface.

5. Uncle (Yiddish).
6. Aunt (Yiddish).

The Double-fronted House

MY ZAYDE Berl and Baba Pessy often told the story of how the big, double-fronted house where we lived had been divided up all those years ago by the drawing of lots. It was lucky for us that my grandfather had been awarded the larger part of the property, for our household was large and growing. As well as my siblings, parents and grandparents, my aunt Hana Tzirl – five years younger than my mother and not yet married – lived with us, too. And the last member of our family was our hairy, grey dog, Rabchik. He was a large beast, part guard-dog, part plaything and barked so frantically whenever anyone came to the door that he had to be kept tethered in the yard when activity at the warehouse was brisk. But his entire rumpus was just a front; in reality, he was harmless. He didn't mind his shaggy coat being pulled and plaited, or his tail being swung around like a hairy skipping rope, or the insides of his ears being poked. He put up with my stroking and prodding with a stoical placidity quite remarkable to anyone who had experienced the hullabaloo he made as they approached the door.

Rabchik was my main playmate. Sarah, two years older than me, was a shy little girl. Beautiful and doll-like with her long, fair hair and pale face, she had our father's disposition and belonged in a calmer world than our boisterous household. Rabchik scared her. Zayde positively terrified her. And I was too rowdy for her. She clung to Baba's apron strings or Mama's skirt tails in the hope of more tender affection. As for my brother Naftula, he was just a baby and too young to play with.

As well as our extended family, we always had at least one lodger living in the house, too: friends of Zayde's who had had arguments with their wives or had fallen on hard times, or refugees whose livelihood had been destroyed by pogroms. Jacob Kreinis had lived with us for as long as I could remember, earning his keep by doing odd jobs for my grandfather. For us children, more fun than Jacob himself was his son, Haskl, who seemed to spend most of the day sitting at our kitchen table drinking tea and was like a favorite uncle to me and my siblings. Haskl was a hunchback, a tiny, wiry man, bent almost double under his deformity, he would haul us onto his lap and talk with us for hours in his deep, gravelly voice as if our childish prattle were the most interesting topic on earth. He also had two little daughters of similar age to me. They didn't have many toys of their own because Haskl never had much money so I would let them share my dolls and building blocks. The girls, Yetta and Ruchel, and I grew up together and remained the best of friends into adulthood.

I had few cares as a young child. Just as my mother had been cosseted in her youth, Sarah and I were brought up like the daughters of a princess. Our mother shunned the local tailor and instead we travelled to Berdichev to visit the dressmaker who made us fashionable outfits fringed with velvet and lace. I loved these visits to the city. I was always enthralled by the clamor of the market traders and the horse-drawn streetcars that clattered along the cobblestones. And then there was the excitement of collecting our new clothes. We believed we would be the best dressed girls in all of Pavolitch.

Sometimes the purchase of new dresses made a good excuse to visit the local photographer and we gathered solemnly in his studio to pose for a portrait. The photographer stood in his dark suit, gesticulating and barking orders to move an inch to the left or the right, bend an arm or straighten a leg, or brush away a stray lock of hair while we wriggled nervously. Zayde had little patience for such trivia as photographs and refused to take part while, for fear of the Evil Eye, Baba wouldn't allow images of herself to be captured.

Like our mother before us, we girls were never taught to sew or darn or cook. Baba was responsible for looking after the needs of the entire household as well as helping Zayde by collecting the takings from the klet and keeping his books up to date. A tiny, energetic woman whose life's sorrow was reflected in her eyes, she was the linchpin of the family. Baba never let a single second go to waste. Every morning she would rise at daybreak to milk her cow, light the fires then set to work on the kitchen floor, scrubbing the flagstones until they sparkled. As her children and grandchildren washed and dressed she prepared the table for breakfast. The kitchen was Baba's domain and she ruled it as strictly and efficiently as Zayde ran his warehouse. In any quiet moments she was always to be found there, knitting needles clicking, a ball of wool trailing across the floor, as she engaged in the never-ending task of knitting and darning the family's socks and stockings.

Every afternoon was spent chopping, boiling, frying and, best of all, pastry-making. As befits the wife of a successful grain merchant, Baba, too, had a special relationship with wheat. The fine-milled flour it produced came alive as she caressed it in her gnarled hands. She could make a ball of pastry dance, stretching the dough over both knobby fists, pulling and turning it in the air like a magician with a wand, creating paper-thin sheets that were an even thickness from one side to the other without recourse to a rolling pin. For me, seeing Baba at work was as mesmerizing as watching conjuring tricks.

She cut the pastry into squares and filled them with vegetables or berries to make delicious blintzes. But her greatest specialty was her little round knishes. A ball of liver or peas formed the heart of the dish and it was wrapped in an almost translucent layer of pastry. Later in life, when I taught myself to cook, I found that the hours I had spent enthralled by Baba's tricks with pastry served me in good stead as I succeeded in recreating my grandmother's art.

Although Baba did most of the cooking herself, baking bread for the whole family was too big a job even for her to undertake alone. Every Thursday she would enlist the help of a local Jewish woman to prepare the dough for the week ahead. With so many mouths to feed, Baba needed a lot of bread. That meant an awful lot of kneading. Whereas it was acceptable for non-Jewish servants to help with washing and sewing, no goy could partake in food preparation for the resulting dishes wouldn't be kosher.

Hodl's prominent nose and black eyes attested to her Jewishness and she was more muscular than many men with arms like hefty joints of beef. She dragged huge sacks of flour across the floor from the klet into the kitchen and emptied them into a low, wooden trough. Then, rolling up her sleeves to reveal her stocky forearms, she poured water from a jug into the mound of flour. All day Hodl would stand at the kitchen table pushing and pulling rounds of dough until her whole body sagged from exhaustion.

On the rare occasions that Hodl was ill or unable to work, Baba called upon Sarah to help with the kneading. But she would soon flag and start complaining. Sarah wasn't used to physical activity. Even as a little girl she preferred to sit quietly watching Baba work, or to surround herself with books, than to run around outside. She learned her letters very early and would spend hours reading her books aloud to Mama.

"I can't do it, Baba, my wrists hurt," she moaned every time she was asked to help knead the dough, "How long do I have to keep doing this for?"

"Unless you speed up, you'll be at it till the cows come home," Baba told her. But Sarah couldn't work any faster and sometimes I would have a go, too, pummeling the dough for all I was worth. I lasted only a matter of minutes. Only then did I fully appreciate how valuable Hodl and her enormous arms really were.

A portion of the flour was kept aside to make challah, the Sabbath bread. Now Baba helped Hodl with the leavening and murmured words of prayer over the plaited loaves before placing them in the blazing oven on flat, floured paddles. It was well into the evening before Hodl could go home and Baba was left to serve our dinner and clean the kitchen in preparation for the next day.

On Fridays she rose even earlier than usual for much work needed to be done ahead of the Sabbath. The special *cholent*, or Sabbath stew, had to be prepared and set on the stove for the following day and all the rest of the food for the holiday needed to be made in advance for it was forbidden to cook once dusk had fallen. The whole house was cleaned from top to bottom. Tables and benches were taken outside and scrubbed and the silverware – candlesticks, cutlery and salt cellars – was polished until it gleamed. Shortly before sunset, the *shamus* came from the synagogue and walked all around the Jewish neighborhood banging on the shutters of each house with a mallet calling, "Men, women, time to light the candles!"

Baba would change her dress and swap her everyday cotton headscarf for a bonnet decorated with colored ribbons. Placing the silver candlesticks on the table, she recited prayers while she lit the wicks. As the light outside faded, the candles emitted a warm, shimmering glow over the room and cast their reflections in the cutlery and glasses that had been laid around the table. I always loved that moment of anticipation, after the candles had been lit, when we waited for my father and the rest of the men to return from the synagogue. Like us girls, they were specially dressed for the occasion in satin caftans trimmed with a vertical band of velvet. Broad satin belts hung around their waists. We all joyfully wished each other a *Gut Shabbas* and sat down for the Sabbath meal. Even Zayde was cheerful as he recited the kiddush over the loaves and cut slices for us children, then he passed around the beaker of wine.

Every Friday Baba prepared the traditional chunky balls of gefilte fish in sweet broth, which was my favorite meal. All week I looked forward to the Sabbath dinner, especially in winter when the lake was frozen and fish became a rare treat that had to be saved for the holiday. Throughout the winter we were lucky enough to eat meat every day, unlike most families, for kosher meat was taxed heavily. The *korobka* tax was levied on each animal slaughtered by Jews and on every pound of meat sold, which could make it as much as twice the price of the meat that gentiles ate. Poorer families could afford to eat meat only rarely.

For the really tiresome chores around the house, Baba enlisted the help of Ukrainian servants. Alexandra came every morning to help Baba with the routine washing and cleaning. Our underwear and stockings she washed in a big tub at home, but the bulkier items she carted down to the lake, in winter dipping them into a hole in the ice. Alexandra was about as old as Baba, but almost twice as tall. Her expression was always sour and she never paid the slightest attention to me or Sarah. For some reason, though, our dog Rabchik was fond of her and trotted beside her to the lake, often carrying in his mouth the long wooden hammer that she used to press out water from the laundry by running it against the scrubbing board.

We much preferred Katarina and Pritska who came once a week to tackle one of the biggest jobs – washing the linen. They must have both been in their thirties, but their hands were almost as coarse and wrinkled as Baba's from the rough work they did. First they scrubbed the bed sheets in the washtub and rinsed them in washing soda. Then they bundled all the linens into huge vats of boiling water and stirred them with sticks. Despite the heat and steam, and the heaviness of the wet laundry, Katarina and Pritska sang cheerful Ukrainian songs as they worked and always enjoyed teasing and petting us. And they simply adored Baba even though she could be a hard taskmaster. When we were a little older my sister and I were given a job to do, too, on washing days. We sat on stools in the kitchen peeling dozens of potatoes, which were boiled up to make the starch that was used to keep the linen crisp.

"Chop, chop girls! Let's get those spuds into water now!" Katarina would cajole us as we scraped away seemingly without end.

Sometimes we ran out of water on laundry day. Then Sarah and I would be sent to the public water pumps to fetch more. The rusty handle would often stick fast and, however much I tugged it, I could rarely get it to budge. The water pumps were controlled by Zhukov, our Ukrainian neighbor. He could take the pump handle in his colossal hands and force it down with such energy that a fountain of water spurted into the sky. If I didn't get out of the way in time, I would end up drenched. If we were lucky, Zhukov would even carry the slopping pails home for us. On our own we struggled to lift them and had to drag them back to Zayde's house. In winter the task was harder still as it was almost impossible to keep one's balance on the slippery road while pulling the heavy buckets and we rarely made it all the way home without tumbling over on the ice, spilling the water and having to go back to Zhukov for more.

Once the sheets were washed, Katarina and Pritska would heave the sopping loads to the lake where they rinsed and beat them – on the rocks in summer and on the ice in winter – before carting them back up the hill and hanging them outside to dry. In winter they turned as brittle as chalk and I helped thump the sheets with a pole to remove the ice that formed as they dried. Finally the bedding needed to be pressed with irons that were heated on coals until they were red hot. The kitchen filled up with so much smoke and soot that my eyes would sting and everything turned blurry while the smell of coal made me feel faint.

PART II

1906–1914

A Marriage

WHEN I was four years old, we began to prepare for the most exciting event so far of my short life. My aunt Hana Tzirl was to be married! The wedding would be a grand affair and Sarah and I were to be bridesmaids. I was so intoxicated by the hubbub all around me that I could barely be coaxed into my puffy, ivory-white dress. I ran about the room in my underwear while Mama tried her hardest to dress me. I was desperate to sneak into my Mima Hana's room for a peek at her sumptuous wedding dress. Eventually poor Mama gave up and Baba had to be summoned to give me a stern shake and make me stay still.

Sarah and I curtseyed demurely before the guests as they arrived, showing off the new frocks that we considered the prettiest things we had ever seen. Anyone who didn't know us wouldn't have realized that we were sisters. My eyes were almost black, my hair a tumble of dark curls, while Sarah had long, straight hair that was unusually fair for a Jew and pale features. Sarah, I was always given to believe, was the perfect little girl – calm and polite, she always did as she was told. I, on the other hand, was forever being scolded for being too fidgety or too headstrong. Even at the age of four I already resented her.

There were so many wedding guests that my legs hurt from all the curtseying. Invitations had been sent to all the relatives, both near and far, and the marriage announced at the main synagogue. All the Jews of Pavolitch were welcome to join the celebrations – not just the wealthy ones that my grandfather might have wanted to impress – and the party was to last the whole week.

I watched with my mouth agape as Hana Tzirl stepped beneath the wedding canopy. My usually plain aunt looked magnificent in her long, white gown and flowing veil. Her wiry, unruly hair had been tamed and she held herself with an unfamiliar assuredness. Could this fairy-tale princess really be my own Mima Hana, the wild, garrulous character who was always laughing and singing and – when Baba was out of earshot – telling rude jokes? Standing beside her, the groom Yossl Duchov looked like a handsome prince, the bridegroom of every little girl's dreams.

The young couple stumbled over their wedding vows, flushing before the assembled crowd, and each took a sip from the beaker of wine. My grandfather stood proudly beside his daughter, a rare smile on his face, while my grandmother held back her tears and spat to avert the Evil Eye. Everybody roared with delight when Yossl lifted his bride's veil to reveal Hana Tzirl, her face crimson from stifling her giggles, as a beaming grin lit up her face.

Baba had recruited a dozen women to help prepare the elaborate wedding feast. The reception was held in a huge barn laid out with rows of long tables where the guests feasted on turkey, roast chicken, goose and gefilte fish and, of course, the golden consommé that is traditionally served to newly wedded couples. Special cakes had been brought all the way from Berdichev.

A rope cordon stretched across the middle of the barn dividing the men from the women. In their separate enclosures, male and female guests spread into a ring, each singing and clapping in time with the music, jigging their feet and pulling into the circle all those too shy or too sober to join in. Once or twice a man even sneaked over to the women's side to invite a lady to dance. Some of the guests gasped in horror at the lack of decorum, but my grandfather didn't mind. He considered himself a modern thinker and recognized that the world around him was changing. Young people no longer followed unquestioningly the ways of their parents as they used to.

Despite the celebratory atmosphere and the happiness Berl felt for his younger daughter, an uneasy feeling was lurking in the pit of his stomach. As the evening continued the sensation that something was wrong grew stronger. Was he imagining it or was it really the case that some of his guests were avoiding him? My grandfather went through the motions of hand-shaking, back-slapping and accepting congratulations, but the food on his plate remained virtually untouched.

Time and time again his eye caught that of the businessman Josef Nath-

anson, but the tall, black-suited Jewish merchant repeatedly turned his
head away. His suspicions aroused, Berl then noticed that when Pessy approached Nathanson's glamorous wife, she scuttled off into the dancing
circle, clapping and singing a fraction more animatedly than is natural.
Something was definitely wrong. My grandfather and Nathanson were
competitors. Both were leading dealers in dry goods and both had vied
for the same contracts before. What had Nathanson been up to now, Berl
wondered, to make him so nervous to meet his host's eye?

The answer came soon enough. A stocky, red-headed man drew up to
him, put his arm around Berl's shoulder and led him to one side. It was his
old friend Verkula, the estate manager who worked for Poritz Baskakov,
the local landowner for whom my grandfather acted as agent.

"I'm sorry to have to tell you this, and today of all days, but that fellow
Nathanson's been doing deals behind both our backs," the estate manager told him. As the musicians played and the guests danced he went
on to explain that Nathanson had proposed to Baskakov that he conduct
all his sales and purchases through himself, Nathanson, rather than my
grandfather. The terms he offered Baskakov were too advantageous to
refuse.

"How dare he?" barked Berl, kneading his fist in the palm of his hand.
My grandfather was furious; furious to have lost so much business and
furious that a man who had humiliated him was still availing of his hospitality. The day that Hana Tzirl's life with Yossl Duchov began was the day
my grandfather's relationship with Baskakov ended. Berl never spoke to
Josef Nathanson again and remained suspicious of him to his dying day.

The loss of Baskakov marked the beginning of a decline for my grandfather's business. And it came at the worst time – just when he needed
some ready cash for the invoices from Hana Tzirl's extravagant wedding
were piling up in the drawer. He began to rue his decision to invite the
whole town to the celebration. He aged severely over the course of the
following year and became increasingly embittered. Always a stern and
forceful character, now his ire was sparked by the mildest incident and I
made sure to keep well out of his way whenever his eyes started to flash,
signaling a warning that an explosion was near.

After the wedding Yossl moved in with our family. Although, unlike
my father, he wasn't a quiet man by nature, I rarely heard him utter a
sound for Mima Hana was so talkative that she always spoke for both

of them. Yossl watched and listened and, every now and again when he seemed on the verge of saying something, Hana Tzirl would flutter her hands in front of her face excitedly and recount another anecdote.

Mima Hana was pregnant and, to her mother's horror, she spared the family no details about the changes her body was going through. Not long afterwards Mama was expecting, too. What excitement! Not only was I to have a new little cousin, but a brand new brother or sister, too! Baba flapped around her two daughters making them tea and cooking whatever cookies and sweetmeats they desired. I tried to join in, making Mama and Mima Hana round cakes out of mud from the street outside, and picking pretty spring flowers for them, but Baba would shoo me away.

"Leave your mother alone, Perele, she needs to get some rest," Baba entreated, using the diminutive of my name to indicate that she wasn't really angry with me. She kept me away for a reason: Baba was terrified of infecting her daughters with germs from outside. The winter snows had melted and the kaluzha – the puddle outside the front door – was at its biggest. Baba spat every time she went outside in an attempt to keep the Evil Eye away from her home. With the same intent she muttered incantations and tied salt and pepper in a corner of her daughters' pockets to ward off bad spirits.

At long last, the wait was over. Hana Tzirl gave birth to a vigorous baby girl with a shock of curly, black hair. My new cousin was called Baya. And shortly afterwards, my sister Rachel arrived, too. I was overjoyed with the new members of my family and have probably never been more contented than I was that year, when I was five years old. I spent hours with my sister and cousin, letting them curl their tiny hands around my fingers, dressing them or just watching them sleep and, when they cried, I helped pacify them by stuffing their mouths with muslin rags filled with bread and sugar.

A few years later Hana Tzirl had a second baby, a little boy. Baba wept with relief, finally allowing herself to believe that her dark curse had been lifted, each of her daughters now having given birth to a healthy son. Mendl was a delightful baby with an ever-present smile just like his mother's, and all us girls crowded around his cot and made a fuss of him. Mendl's arrival completed our household: there was Sarah and myself, my brother Naftula and my little sister Rachel. And my cousins Baya and, now, baby Mendl. My grandmother's eternal wish for a house filled with children had come true at last.

When Mendl was still a baby, his father Yossl joined the wave of Jews from the Pale heading to America to make their fortune. He had been saving money for years, putting a little aside from his laborer's earnings each month and had finally raised enough to pay his fare. The great westward migration had started after the first wave of pogroms in the 1880s and the more recent slaughter of 1905 had encouraged another generation to try their luck in the new world. America was a land that promised a safer future, a future with opportunities.

Like many other men, Yossl travelled alone with the dream of finding a job in America and making enough money to send back to Hana Tzirl so that she and their two young children, and even the whole family, would be able to join him. He left on the train from Kiev to Moscow from where he would make his way slowly across Russia to Riga on the Baltic and from there to London, then finally onto the ship that would take him to America.

Two months after his departure, Yossl's first letter arrived from Chicago and we all sat around the dining table and listened with bated breath while Mima Hana read it aloud. He described the gigantic buildings that soared into the sky, streets like narrow canyons, and the wind that tore through his bones. He wrote about his search for work at a vegetable market, a blacksmith's shop and a factory. His letters arrived regularly, every few weeks, and over the months that followed he wrote about the job he had finally landed in the construction industry, his colleagues who came from places I had barely even heard of like Italy and China, and his American boss who smoked cigarettes with filters. He told Mima Hana how he was saving money, how he longed to see her again, how he missed Baya and little baby Mendl.

Then all of a sudden the letters stopped. Hana Tzirl wrote again and again to the address he had sent until she was able to inscribe the unfamiliar English letters without having to copy them. Nothing. She never heard from him again and Mendl grew up knowing his father only from photographs. Poor Hana Tzirl; she had become an *agunah*, a deserted wife, one of the worst fates that could befall a woman.

Holidays and High Holy Days

EVERY SUMMER my grandmother would take her two daughters, my mother Ettie Leah and my aunt Hana Tzirl, away to the country for a holiday. Even though they were now grown up with children of their own, Baba still insisted on spoiling them. She would rent a couple of rooms in a *dacha* – a large house belonging to a local landowner – sometimes several versts from Pavolitch. To me it felt desperately unfair that we children were never allowed to join them and I was resentful that they should want to leave us behind.

"You'll never believe what happened!" Hana Tzirl gushed on their return from holiday one year. Before she had even removed her boots she began recounting how one evening, as Baba was carrying dinner from the shared kitchen to her daughters in their room, somebody had caught her eye. A handsome, middle-aged man was lying languidly, watching her from a hammock on the porch with a book in his hands. His face was thin, with a small, neatly trimmed beard, heavy waves of dark hair pushed back out of his eyes and little round glasses.

"That smells good!" he called out to Pessy as she walked past him with her tray.

"Thank you," my grandmother replied, slightly flustered, for she was not accustomed to being addressed by unfamiliar men. She hurried back to the room to recount the encounter to my mother and Hana Tzirl.

Ettie Leah, always curious where dashing gentlemen were concerned, darted out to the porch and let out a gasp when she spied the man in the hammock. She sped back to her room.

"I know who that man is," she told her mother, her words tumbling almost out of control, "You'd better be careful. He's a writer and if you don't watch out, he'll put you in his stories, along with anything you might tell him." Ettie Leah knew she wasn't mistaken. She recognized Sholem Aleichem's face when she saw it. He was the most famous Yiddish storyteller of all, the creator of *Fiddler on the Roof*.

Only a few months before, Ettie Leah and Hana Tzirl had attended one of Sholem Aleichem's boisterous readings in Skvira, the provincial capital. He was a folk hero to the Jews of the Pale and spent his days travelling around the Jewish lands of Russia, meeting people, writing up their stories and reciting them at crowded gatherings in towns and villages to rapturous applause. My mother and aunt had giggled like schoolgirls at the author's portrayals of shtetl life. But having spotted him at the dacha, they would make sure to give him a wide berth, terrified that they, too, might become fodder for his wit. My grandmother appeared to have no such qualms. She was clearly rather intrigued by the mysterious writer.

"He was lying down and didn't look at all well," she said. "If he's sick, maybe I should take him something to eat." Leaving her two daughters to finish their meal, Pessy set off with a bowl of soup to offer her fellow guest. She found him, still on the porch, and said, "I'm not going to give you any stories, but I've brought you some food. I thought you might be unwell and have nobody to look after you."

Sholem Aleichem laughed. "No, I'm not after your stories," he replied. "But the soup looks delicious. I must thank you." He began to eat, keeping one eye on Pessy as he sipped the broth slowly, taking care not to spill any onto his beard. He talked as he ate.

"Where do you hail from?" he asked Pessy, the customary Yiddish question on first meeting. Trusting Sholem Aleichem's word that he wouldn't take advantage of her, Pessy started to recount the story of her childhood. Before she married and moved to Pavolitch at the age of fourteen, she had lived above her family's kretchma in a little hamlet not far from Kiev.

As Pessy talked, Sholem Aleichem began to smile. "I know that hamlet," he told her. "I have an uncle who lives in the very same spot!"

"Forgive me for contradicting you, but you must be mistaken," Pessy replied. "Ours is the only Jewish family there."

"Well then, my dear, we must be related!" Sholem Aleichem announced with a triumphant grin. And so it was. Families in those days were so big that it was often difficult to keep track of all one's relatives, let alone figure out the relationships between them. My grandmother and

the great writer put their heads together and worked out the link. Pessy's
father, Menachem Mendl Rabinovitch had a brother, who had moved
away from the hamlet. That brother was the father of Sholem Aleichem,
whose real name was Sholem Rabinovitch.

"So there we are – Sholem Aleichem is our cousin! What do you think
of that?" Hana Tzirl concluded. Even though I was too young to have
read his stories, I was as excited as my aunt and mother to discover that I
was related to the most famous Yiddish storyteller of all time. I never did
find out, though, whether Sholem Aleichem ever wrote a story about his
meeting with my grandmother.

While Baba was at the dacha with my mother and aunt, my great-
grandfather Akiva moved into the double-fronted house with his family
to look after us. Akiva's first wife had died long before I was born and he
had remarried a woman many years his junior. Leah was even taller than
Akiva and stocky, with a square jaw and solid features that made her look
much fiercer than she really was. Beneath her formidable exterior she was
as warm-hearted and doting as any woman could be. Because they were
so tall, Akiva and Leah always seemed to me like two giants from a fairy
tale. All the food that Leah cooked looked as if it were made for giants,
too. Her korzhas – poppy seed cookies – were as big as a plate and the slices
of pumpkin that she roasted with sugar were so thick that I could barely
pick them up.

Leah was in her thirties when she married Akiva and many would
have thought her too old for child-bearing. Indeed she suffered so many
miscarriages that nobody believed she would ever give birth to a healthy
child. But at the ripe old age of forty-five, a miracle occurred, and a vigorous baby girl was finally delivered to her. Leah named her Chaya Rissl,
but, as was the custom when a mother feared losing a child, she changed
the baby's name to Babtsy to mislead the Evil Eye, lest she be taken like
her unborn siblings. Despite the fact that Babtsy was my great-aunt, she
was only eight years older than me.

Akiva and Leah were always with us in late summer, for the nine days
of mourning before the fast of Tisha B'Av, the ninth of Av. This solemn
holiday commemorates the destruction of the great Jewish temples in
Jerusalem and part of the mourning ritual is to abstain from eating meat.
Because Akiva owned a millet mill, Leah would replace all our meat
dishes with millet: millet soup, millet knishes, millet dumplings.

"What are you doing giving the children all this millet, Mima? Their stomachs are going to burst!" Zayde would shout at her. (He always called Leah "Mima", or aunt, even though she was really his step-mother.) Our stomachs never did burst, but by the end of the holiday our dresses were always just that little bit tighter.

My grandmother would return from the country with Mama and Hana Tzirl for *Rosh Hashanah*, the Jewish New Year at the very end of summer. New Year was a time for sweets and my sisters and I would help Baba to create enormous cakes and platters of cookies with honey, dried fruits and sugar, which we carried with care to my great-grandfather's home. As we bounded into the house, he would haul us toward him and give each of us a hug, encircling us in his wide arms and kissing us in turn, his long, white beard tickling our cheeks as we squealed the festive greeting, "*Mazel tov! Mazel tov!*"

Sitting down to eat, we threw ourselves at the places closest to where Akiva sat, squabbling as the chairs scraped across the floor, pushing one another out of the way, each of us desperate to sit closer to him than the others. We all loved spending time with our great-grandfather. Once we had tasted all the different sweets that were arranged on plates over the table, and the grown-ups had taken a few glasses of wine to accompany their meal, the fun would begin. Akiva sat each of us in turn on his bony knees to tell us stories of his youth, like how he had avoided joining the army by having all his teeth pulled out. The fact that he was toothless never seemed peculiar to me, for many people had lost all their teeth by the time they were his age.

As Akiva talked, he would pull out his red handkerchief to wave in the air at dramatic moments. He spoke more in Ukrainian than Yiddish, with his own peculiar way of mixing up words and sentences as he went along. As well as stories of his own past, Akiva would also narrate terrifying tales of dragons, savage dogs or snakes. Sometimes one story became so tangled with another that he couldn't find his way out. Those of us who were sitting on his lap or had managed to win the prime spots by his side would grab hold of Akiva's arms in fear at the scariest moments and he would console us with a quick hug or a reassuring smile before continuing.

"You shouldn't tell the children these tales. They won't get to sleep at night," Mama would complain to Akiva, for ours was a nervous mother who treated her four children rather like precious dolls. But I could have listened to my great-grandfather's stories for hours.

We next returned to Akiva's house for *Yom Kippur*, the Day of Atonement, when we weren't allowed to eat all day. On the eve of this, the most solemn of holidays, Akiva would pick a rooster from the yard and Leah a hen. All the men in turn would take hold of the rooster's legs and swing it around their heads three times while chanting the prayer of atonement, and the women would do the same with the hen. We were too young to hold the chicken ourselves, so Mama would circle it above our heads while the poor bird clucked and squawked at the indignity of the whole affair. Even though it was such a serious occasion, watching my grandfather swing a rooster around his head always struck me as funny.

Leah baked extra special bread that day, which she fashioned into the shape of a ladder. "Each step on the ladder is a step that every one of us must take to draw closer to heaven and find forgiveness," she told us seriously.

We all ate a step from the ladder and I pictured myself ascending slowly, getting closer to God with every mouthful. The bread was finished by sundown, which marked the start of Yom Kippur. All the grown-ups went to synagogue, except Mama, who stayed with us and read to us from the psalms. The next day it would be Mima Hana who stayed at home and Mama went to the synagogue. No games were allowed and even talking had to be kept to a minimum. I couldn't even look out of the window and watch our Ukrainian neighbors going about their business as the shutters were kept closed. It was a day for praying and repentance, nothing else.

I fidgeted constantly with the frustration of it all, desperate to get outside and enjoy the last of the sunny weather. Already there was a chill in the air and soon the first snow would come. My mind wandered to the chicken soup that we would have for supper when Yom Kippur was over. By lunchtime I would be aching with hunger. Never did the hours pass so slowly as they did on the Day of Atonement.

In another week it would be *Succoth*, one of my favorite festivals of the whole year. We celebrated at our own house and needed to get back to start the preparations. In the yard my father built a tabernacle out of fir branches and there was a great air of excitement as we watched the structure take shape. My sisters and I spent hours making decorations for our tabernacle out of colored paper and helping tie ribbons into the branches. We all dressed up in our best clothes and every mealtime we carried our food out into the yard to eat beneath the canopy of leaves and branches. By the evening, it was cool already and we draped shawls over our shoulders and blankets over our knees to keep out the autumn chill.

The festival ended with *Shimches Torah*, rejoicing in the law. The whole family gathered to sing songs and our living room was cleared, creating space to dance around it in a big circle. Zayde always drank too much and became overly boisterous, while even Tata became more talkative than usual and lost his air of seriousness. Long into the night we would lie awake and listen to the grown-ups talking and laughing, and, even after everybody had gone to bed, in the distance we could still hear muffled strains of music and the drunken cries of other Jews who had spent the evening with friends or relations and were having trouble making their way home.

My Mother's Death

M Y MOTHER died when I was just six years old. I hardly remember her as a person, but more as a presence. Even when I was very little, it was Baba I ran to when I cried, not Mama. She was reserved for those times when I wanted to play quietly indoors, or for visits to the city to buy dresses. I grew up believing that mothers were for special occasions, while grandmothers dealt with the day-to-day. Baba cooked for us, knitted our stockings and scolded us when we were naughty. Of course, I loved my mother, but perhaps it was an instinct, a sixth sense, that prevented me from getting too close to her. Baba treated her eldest daughter like fine china that could break at the slightest pressure and so that was how we children saw her, too. We were never naughty around Mama, perhaps fearful that, if forced to shout at us, her lungs might burst.

My mother's whole life had been overshadowed by a fear of death. She had watched eleven siblings appear and then die; she had witnessed her own mother's hopeless despair, often going hungry as a child when Pessy had been unable to pay attention to her living children, so overwhelmed was she by her anguish over those who were dying. The endless cosseting and blessings against the Evil Eye, the spitting before entering the house, the amulets tied around her neck, all instilled in her an innate aware-ness of her own mortality. When she took to her bed the end seemed inevitable. She became terrified of a large black raven that perched on the windowsill of her room calling out to her coarsely. An emblem of destruction in Russian folklore, Mama saw the raven as a forewarning that she would not recover.

"You're going to die! You're going to die!" she imagined the raven's caw shrieking at her. Baba spent hours by her bedside as she grew weaker and weaker, her breathing becoming more and more faint, her coughing fits increasingly frequent and painful. I didn't understand that my mother was dying, but knew instinctively to be good, not to disturb her and to try to make her happy. And when she died I didn't understand it either. How can somebody who has always been there suddenly not be around? I was only six, but I knew what death meant. After all I had watched chickens being slaughtered often enough. But in the days and weeks that followed, I tried desperately to picture Mama's face in my mind's eye, to hear her voice inside my head so that I wouldn't lose her altogether. I thought of the warmth of her skin, the reassuring milkiness of her smell. And all around me the whole world seemed to stop. I knew that my life would never be the same again.

My mother was just over thirty years old when consumption took her from us and her absence haunted the house like a ghost. Baba could barely move under the pain of her sorrow. Of the thirteen children she had brought into the world only one now remained. But she was a stronger woman than she had been in her youth and refused to let Mama's death crush her in the way that her other children's had. She also had grandchildren who depended on her now more than ever. The following day she stood up at the long, wooden dining table, her eyes ringed red from tears, and declared, "No more crying! We have a young family to bring up and we'll all pull together." She took me and my siblings to be blessed against the Evil Eye and tried to make life go on as normal.

But the time for normality was over. I don't think Baba ever recovered the vigor she had had before my mother died. Zayde, too, became quieter and more withdrawn. And what about my father? Not only was he mourning a wife whom he had come to love deeply despite his initial reservations about marriage, but he also had to face up to an awkward reality. He had lived for eight years under his father-in-law's roof and, before that, in the security of the rabbinical court. Although his dowry agreement had specified that he would live in Berl's house for ten years without having to work, no concessions were in place in case of the bride dying before those ten years were up. Meyer knew he should no longer rely on my grandfather for his livelihood, but he had no means of supporting himself – and four children to look after. The mere thought of finding a job left him floundering helplessly.

My grandfather took pity on him. The two men had grown close over the years and Berl now treated Meyer like a son. There was no question of throwing him out of the double-fronted house. But to ease my father's conscience, Berl devised a position for him that would employ his sharp mind and suit his sedentary disposition much better than the attempts at trading and grain-weighing that he had encouraged in the past. My father became his bookkeeper. Although Talmudic scholarship always remained his first priority, he set out to study this profession with a modicum of zeal. He never became particularly skilled in his new career, but it did provide him with employment.

Velvl and Chaya Rachel, my father's parents, had rushed from Makarov as soon as they received the news of their daughter-in-law's death. They, too, were concerned about Meyer's situation and that of his children and had come up with a proposal of their own.

"You can't continue to look after the whole family by yourselves," they argued with Berl and Pessy. "Even if Meyer stays in Pavolitch, let us take the little ones back to Makarov, at least for a while, so you can recover from your grief. Our own children are grown up now and it would be a pleasure for us to have youngsters running around again."

Meyer loved the idea of his brood growing up in the Twersky court where he had been so happy in his youth. But Berl and Pessy were upset at the thought of losing their grandchildren. Eventually the grown-ups reached a compromise. Sarah was already at heder and would stay in Pavolitch. Naftula, as the only boy and Berl's favorite, was also to remain while Rachel and I would go to Makarov to live with our Zayde Velvl and Baba Chaya Rachel.

When I was told of the decision I thought my whole world had fallen apart. Already I had had to cope with losing my mother. Now my father had rejected me and I would be torn away from Baba and Zayde, too, and from the rest of the family and even my dog Rabchik. I wasn't yet seven years old. How could this be happening to me?

I started to cry. "I'm not going!" I shrieked, thrashing my arms to underline my determination. "I'm not going! I'm not!" Tata raised his hands in helplessness until Baba came to his rescue. Once I had shouted myself hoarse, she pulled me up onto her lap, brushed away the tears from my scarlet cheeks and stroked my hair.

"I don't want you to go either, my little Perele. It's your father's decision and it won't be for too long. Soon you'll come back to us. Besides, it'll be fun in Makarov. Your Baba Chaya Rachel has dogs you can play with and you'll see all your aunts and uncles."

I swallowed my sobs and gulped, "But why me?"

I couldn't understand why my father wanted to send me away. My mother was gone now and Tata was the one person in my life that I idolized. Although he could sometimes be distant – when he was working on his holy scripts he hated to be disturbed – he had always been a good father. He wasn't jolly like Akiva, or fierce like Zayde, but he always listened to me and eased my cares. Perhaps it was because of, rather than in spite of, the fact that my grandparents and not Tata occupied themselves with the everyday routines of my life that my father took on another role for me. He was a beacon of stability and trust.

Rather than allowing that trust to be broken when he chose to banish me to the Twersky court, the situation served to reinforce my determination to prove my worth to my father in everything I did. That way, I thought, he would love and appreciate me more and never reject me again. This resolve was to stay with me throughout my youth, but the blow dealt to me by the decision my father made that day would continue to sting for my whole life.

When it was time for us to leave Baba didn't come out to see us off. It broke her heart to see little Rachel, who was not yet two years old, disappear from under her roof. She had tried her hardest to persuade my father to let us both stay, but to no avail. Hana Tzirl stayed away, too. Ever since Mama had been confined to bed, Rachel had started following her aunt around like a shadow, adopting her as a replacement mother, and Mima Hana was happy to have another little girl to dote on. She, too, was devastated to see Rachel leave. Nobody seemed too concerned about me. Although I was still very young, they seemed to think I was tough enough to cope.

And so Rachel and I moved from one set of grandparents to another. Rachel didn't stop crying the entire journey, her sobs undulating as our carriage jolted up and down along the dry, pitted roads. Tata, who was accompanying us to Makarov, put his arm around his youngest daughter, but the screaming continued.

Baba Chaya Rachel came out to greet us as soon as our carriage pulled up at the Twersky court. She was plump, with a soft face and a smile that revealed several gaps where her teeth had been. She held out her arms to me, but I clasped myself to my father and wouldn't let go. He had to unhook me from his body, finger by finger. I started to cry, too, and I could see that Tata looked sad. Baba Chaya Rachel comforted us as best she could. She took us indoors and gave us warm milk and freshly baked cookies. She called in her three dogs and encouraged us to pet them. Eventually my tears dried up, but still Rachel wept.

"Can't somebody make that baby stop crying?" moaned my Mima Yetta who, along with Mima Bassy, also lived with my grandparents at the Twersky court. But no matter how hard any of us tried, nothing would calm Rachel down. For days she wailed through most of her waking hours. Although I wasn't any happier than Rachel, I was too big to cry all day. My grandmother seemed to understand how Rachel and I felt and treated us gently, lovingly, attempting to soften our feelings of loss and rejection. And rather than trying to make us sit quietly as befits good Jewish girls, she encouraged us to run around and try to enjoy ourselves even though frivolous behavior is normally frowned upon – even by children – at a rabbi's court. Sometimes she even bent down on her creaking knees and played with us herself, her white scarf slipping loose on occasions to reveal the stubble of her closely shaven head.

Mima Yetta and Mima Bassy made a fuss of us, too. They made us little dolls out of stems of corn and read us books about bears and wolves. They even surreptitiously gave us cookies to eat when we weren't allowed because it was nearly teatime. Most evenings they would go out to what they called "important meetings", and sometimes I woke up when they returned and stuck my ear to the wall to listen to their excited conversations, which bubbled with words like Socialism, Workers' Rights, Revolution and Commune.

Zayde Velvl we saw less often as he spent most of his time at the synagogue or with the men of the court. A thin, stern-looking man, his expression always reflected deep thought over some scholarly debate that he had brought with him from a study meeting. His head was too full of the scriptures, his thoughts too much taken up by God, to be aware of much that went on outside his own inner being. Just like my father, he was naïve and innocent in the ways of the world and events beyond the boundaries of the Twersky court passed him by completely. Newspapers were irrelevant to him; all that was important could be found in the Torah and the Talmud – any other writing was superfluous. Nevertheless, he made a special effort to make me and Rachel feel at home. Just has he had with me when I was little, he now sat Rachel on his lap and sang to her the song about Reb Dovidl, the founder of the Twersky dynasty, who had moved away from Vasilkov with our great-grandfather, Velvele Tallner: *"Reb Dovidl, Reb Dovidl der Vasilkover, voynt shoyn yetst in Talne."*

Velvele Tallner's wife had been called Hana Pearl, just like me. "She was a wonderful woman, my mother," Zayde Velvl told me, his eyes becoming moist as he gazed up toward the ceiling. "She was strong, intelligent and caring. You should be very proud to be named after her." I put my arms around his neck and buried my face in his prickly beard. I wasn't sure that I could grow up to be strong, intelligent and caring, but I didn't want to let him down.

All my father's brothers and sisters came to visit Zayde Velvl and Baba Chaya Rachel frequently. Most exciting were the visits of Feter Avrom and Mima Maryam who had both recently left home to study medicine at the university in Kiev. Smart in his student's uniform, Avrom would cavort around with us like a little boy, twirling us around the room in his strong arms and letting us ride on his back like soldiers on horseback.

Mima Maryam was striking and headstrong. She had refused all her parents' attempts at matchmaking and fallen in love with a young man called Rosen whom she had met at the university. When she brought Rosen back to Makarov to meet her parents, I stood rooted to the spot, my mouth agape. He was quite the most handsome man I had ever set eyes on. Unlike all the other men I knew, he had no beard, just a tiny, neat moustache, and the clothes he wore were like none I had ever seen before. His western-style suits were neatly fitted and his spotless white shirts had frilly collars that flounced around his neck. I wished that I was old enough to marry him myself. I longed for Maryam's weekly visits just so that I could see Rosen again.

My grandparents insisted that their youngest daughter wait until she completed her studies before marrying. Custom dictated that she couldn't wed ahead of her older sisters. Perhaps her parents also hoped that the romance wouldn't last and that she would agree to settle down with a good Hassidic boy. A couple of years later, however, Rosen died before he and Maryam could be married. Of course Velvl and Chaya Rachel felt terribly guilty that they had denied their daughter the happiness she deserved. I wept for my poor aunt whose heart was broken and I wept for myself that in my whole life I might never see such a handsome man again.

Even more than the visits from Maryam and Rosen, I looked forward to the times, about once a month, when my father, grandparents and siblings came to see us in Makarov. Each time they left I counted the days, and sometimes the hours, until I would see them again. Of course I missed them all dreadfully, but I resented them, too, for abandoning me. Occasionally they would all stay with us for the Sabbath at the Twersky court, which made it even more special than usual. All the girls and women would spend Shabbat with the *rebbetzin*[1] in her quarters at the front of the court. She had a large dining room and the meal was always rowdy with dozens of children present. We were kept in some kind of order by the rebbetzin, resplendent in her special Sabbath tichl – a white cloth embedded with jewels that she placed over the wig she wore to cover her shaven head.

The men celebrated with their own Sabbath meal, which could be shared among a hundred people or more as disciples swarmed to the court every holiday to pray with their rabbi. A different chef prepared each dish: one baked the plaited loaves of sweet challah bread, another cooked the gefilte fish and a third prepared the soup. Each loaf would be blessed and tasted by Rabbi Twersky then cut into small pieces so that all the guests could eat a morsel that had been touched by the rabbi's hand. Because everything – even the wine and whisky – had to be blessed then shared among so many people, the meal lasted for hours. Between the various courses the rabbi extolled the joys of the pious and led the singing of prayers and chants. Some of the guests had fine, deep voices that we could hear thundering from the other side of the building.

The following evening, the hurricane lamps could be lit once again – it was forbidden to do so on the Sabbath – and prayers were recited as the plaited valedictory candle was lit to mark the end of the holiday. The scent of wax and spices intermingled to produce the unmistakable smell that, from then on, I would always associate with the start of a new week.

In the rabbi's complex it was now time for him to say grace over the wine. Rabbi Twersky's followers dabbed drops of the holy liquid over their stubby fingers and touched their eyelids in the hope of securing good health and happiness over the next seven days. Some of the men smeared traces of the wine over their pockets, too, making sure to brush their hands over the pockets of their trousers and waistcoats as well as their outer black robes, to encourage prosperity and financial gain.

---

1. The rabbi's wife.

"A good week!"

"A prosperous week!" the final salutations of the holiday rang out around the court before the men returned to their tea and texts.

The rabbi's complex consisted of his own, private synagogue and a large study where he would greet the visitors who came from miles around to seek his advice. This was the same room in which my Zayde Berl would have sat on so many occasions to talk about the succession of deaths in his family and ask for the rabbi's guidance. Rabbi Twersky must have known all sorts of secrets because everyone came to him to discuss their problems. There were no seats for women inside, so the men would sit and any women present would have to stand away to one side where they would not accidentally find themselves in anyone's line of vision, for looking at a woman who is not a family member is forbidden. Even my grandmother would cause Hassidic heads to turn away, as if an old lady like her could arouse sinful thoughts in such holy men.

As well as the rabbi's private rooms, the Twersky court consisted of many other buildings including a synagogue, prayer houses, a ritual bath, an assembly hall, a shed for slaughtering fowl and several houses for the rabbi's family and employees. Behind them stretched an orchard of fruit and nut trees where Rachel and I would run and play hide-and-seek.

The synagogue was an old building with rounded windows through which birds sometimes flew in and out. It served as a study center for the rabbi's disciples, as well as a place where prayers were led three times a day. From the upper balconies where the women prayed, I would look down on the men's section – a large hall with benches and tables. At any given hour a dozen or so black-coated Jews could be found there reading at the tables or studying from the Talmudic folios on the pulpits before them, swaying to the sound of their own rhythmic chants. Sometimes a group of worshippers would break from their studies and engage in an animated discussion of the minutiae of Jewish law. Their arguments bounced from the walls as their debate became more heated and the details more obscure. Many important Hebrew books were kept in the synagogue, which the scholars could turn to if they needed to check a reference or confirm a point. During services, the Torah was read from the raised section in the center, which was surrounded by a low, carved railing and by the tall, sacred Ark shielded by red velvet curtains.

Grandfather's Wrath

AT LAST, after two long years in Makarov, Rachel and I returned to Pavolitch when I was eight years old and it was time for me to start heder. Sarah had been a heder student for two years already and was one of the best in her class. Although Naftula was two years younger than me, we joined at the same time for, if he was to end up a scholar like his father, as everybody prayed he would, he would have to begin early. He was only six years old, but there were some little boys who started school even younger.

For hours on end we sat at long benches chanting the Hebrew alphabet from *aleph* to *tav*. The *melamed* Reb Abram circulated around the room, now sitting with us and testing us on our letters, now moving to the older children like Sarah who were reading the psalms out loud to a monotone tune. But most of his time he spent with the more advanced students. Some were translating portions of the Pentateuch into Yiddish, while the oldest of the group, all boys approaching their teens, had started to learn Talmudic argumentation and spent up to twelve hours a day at heder. The brightest and most devout of them would soon be leaving Pavolitch to continue their studies of Jewish law at *yeshiva*.

I wasn't particularly interested in my school work and couldn't understand Sarah's passion for heder. Naftula, on the other hand, was mesmerized by the older children in the class. When my mind wandered I would catch him staring at them, entranced by the basic disputations of the Talmud that they were discussing. But I didn't mind heder too much. Reb Abram was a good-natured teacher and hardly ever used the smooth, wooden cane that he kept in his cupboard and which filled me with dread whenever I caught sight of it. I could well imagine the pain that an instrument like that would inflict and I prayed that Zayde would never get his hands on such a device.

For our grandfather had hardened in the years that Rachel and I had been away. The last glimmers of happiness seemed to have drained out of him since our mother's death, added to which, his business was no longer flourishing. Having lost the custom of the local landowner, Poritz Baskakov, a few years earlier, my grandfather had struggled to replace this lucrative part of his trade and, although he had found other pritzim to work with, none of them could offer him as much work as Baskakov had.

Zayde had never been a man to show his affection, hiding behind a stern exterior, but now he had become harsher than ever. Looking back, it was as if he were afraid to become close to his grandchildren, fearful of loving us too much lest we should be picked off one by one like his own sons and daughters. At no time was the change in him more obvious than on the Sabbath. No longer did I spend the week eagerly awaiting the holiday feast. Rather, it was an ordeal to be endured. When the men returned from synagogue, we all sat around the table in strict order with Zayde at one end with the men of the family and the women and girls at the other.

Baba continued to keep the silver candlesticks shining so brightly that we could see our faces in them and the linen tablecloth crisp and spotless. And she still cooked the gefilte fish that I loved so much and covered the challah bread with a crocheted doily. On the surface it seemed as if little had changed. But the silence that descended while Zayde said kiddush over the wine and cut the challah was an uneasy one. Rather than ending in an excited babble once the sweet Sabbath loaf was distributed, we ate what should have been our most celebratory meal slowly, self-consciously, barely daring to talk lest we should upset Zayde.

As well as the Sabbath wine, Zayde would take half a glass of whisky with his dinner. Once the meal was completed and the table cleared, he would take off his belt and fold it in two.

"Sarah! Where's Sarah?" he shouted. "Oh I forgot, she's a grand lady now and she's called Sonia, not Sarah!" For Sarah would soon be starting shkole, the secular Russian school that many children attended when they left heder. Sarah wasn't a Russian name so she was to be called Sonia at school. As one of the brightest pupils, Sarah joined the shkole earlier than most children, but Zayde was skeptical of her success. For her part, Sarah longed to start her new school, the long hours behind a desk a welcome escape from her grandfather's wrath. Sarah struggled more than any of us to come to terms with our mother's death and missed the quiet hours of reading and contemplation that they had enjoyed together.

Sarah walked up to the head of the table where Zayde sat and he took a swipe at her with his doubled-up belt. She returned to her seat, narrowing her eyes to keep out the tears. Zayde was always harsher with Sarah than he was with the rest of us. Perhaps he felt that, as the eldest, she should accept more responsibility for her brother and sisters. But Sarah wasn't made that way. She liked to be alone with her books and kept what was in her heart locked up inside herself. Instead it was me, the second oldest, who ended up in the guardian's role. Rachel, five years younger than me, had become my ward. After our years in Makarov together, nobody seemed to question that my little sister would remain my responsibility. Nobody asked me what I wanted: I wasn't interested in her childish babble and found her a burden.

When it was my turn to be yelled at by my grandfather and suffer a blow from his belt, he often only pretended to hit me and made out that this ritual was a family joke. But if he was in a bad mood, or had drunk a little more than his customary half glass of whisky, he would beat me every bit as hard as the balagula hit his horse when he wanted it to speed up. Even little Rachel and cousin Baya would receive a quick swipe with the belt before Zayde left the table and lay down for his afternoon nap.

Naftula, of course, was spared. He was Zayde's favorite, his little prince. Everybody doted on Naftula, the precious boy of the family. He was a serious child who liked nothing more than to sit in his father's study looking at the holy books and parchments he kept there. He willingly trotted to synagogue in the mornings at the heels of his father and grandfather, and was fascinated by the rites and rituals of Jewishness. Perhaps it was because he was brought up among so many girls that Naftula was never boisterous or boyish. Aside from his insatiable curiosity about religion, his other passion was singing. He loved to stand before an audience in the living room and sing high-pitched melodies that showed off the sweetness of his voice, closing his eyes and tilting his head toward the heavens. My sisters and I worshipped him and competed among ourselves for his affection, while he, in turn, wallowed in our attention. Being so adored by everyone around him had an effect on Naftula and he increasingly appeared to see himself as especially blessed – someone who would always be protected, whether by his family or by God – and could never come to any harm.

As the years passed, Zayde became impossible to please, finding fault with everything we grandchildren did. One evening he returned from synagogue and immediately set about closing all the shutters.

"What is this?" he grumbled. "I'm supporting a houseful of people here and it's me who has to go round and shut the shutters."

So the next night, before Zayde came home, Baba turned to us and said, "Children, why don't you check all the rooms and close the shutters to keep your Zayde happy." But as soon our grandfather walked through the front door, he exploded.

"What is this? The house is like a tomb! Why are all the shutters closed?"

We tried so hard to please him, to prevent his outbursts. Baba would attempt to predict her husband's whims and set us chores that she thought would placate him. But the tantrums didn't cease.

One of the jobs Baba gave us was cleaning the mud off Zayde's boots and clothes. Our grandfather would wear three different jackets, one on top of the other, but never buttoned any of them up. Throughout the spring and autumn the roads were thick with mud, which flew up from the wheels of carts and wagons, spattering the clothing of passers-by with hundreds of little specks. Zayde would come home filthy. Not only would his outer coat be covered in mud, but because he let all his layers flap around him, his two inner jackets would be dirty, too. When he lay down for his afternoon snooze, we set at his coats and boots with stiff brushes.

"What is this?" he exclaimed when he woke from his slumber. "What am I – an intellectual or something that has to be clean all the time? What's wrong with a bit of mud?"

But woe betide if Zayde awoke to find his boots still dirty. Even if we had been out at school all day, he still shouted at us for not cleaning them! The scowl became my grandfather's most common expression, and his tone was naturally severe, but his mood wasn't always sour. I think his ferocity was more an image he chose to project, his way of dealing with his unhappiness. Sometimes I caught him trying not to laugh as he scolded us. He always had a handkerchief in his pocket, ready to be whipped out to cover his face if he felt he was going to smile, so that he could keep his occasional bouts of cheerfulness to himself.

In time, Rachel and Baya joined Naftula and me at heder, but the two cousins, although almost exactly the same age and living under the same roof, kept their distance from one another. Desperate for a mother-figure, Rachel had spent years trying to attach herself to her Mima Hana who, for her part, welcomed her niece, feeling sorry for the lonely child whose older siblings paid her scant attention. But Baya fended her off viciously. When Rachel and I were in Makarov, Baya had been the youngest of the girls and had enjoyed all the attention that the grown-ups and her older cousins Sarah and Naftula paid her. She was jealous of every kind word, every generous gesture that was afforded to Rachel or me on our return, as if we had usurped her rightful position.

As the years passed, Baya's unbridled competitive streak and her aloofness toward Rachel became stronger. Baba insisted that we all walk together to school in the mornings, but Baya always dropped back, lagging a few paces behind the rest of us. Once in heder, she reveled in reciting her responses quickly and accurately, while Rachel often stumbled, for Baya, like Sarah before her, was a diligent student. Poor Rachel, always eager to please and willing to be a peacemaker, tried again and again to engage Baya, not understanding why her cousin was forever snubbing her. But pretty, haughty Baya merely flicked her away.

Rachel wasn't clever like Sarah or headstrong like me, she was just a meek little girl who had lost her mother at the age of two and craved affection. She was very small for her age, but plump, unlike the rest of us, and always hungry. She spent hours in the kitchen with Baba, nibbling bread or cookies while she watched her grandmother knit or bake. If she wasn't with Baba, she was with me. I had been the one constant in her young life, staying with her in Makarov and accompanying her home again. Now the whole family simply accepted that the role of Rachel's guardian was mine. It was a role I resented; it was my father's attention I yearned for, not my little sister's, but Naftula was the only one of us allowed into the haven of his study.

At heder, Naftula quickly graduated to studying the Pentateuch, performing a ceremony in which he stood before the whole heder class plus assembled parents and, in a half-singing tone, offered responses to the melamed's questions on interpretations of Leviticus. Naftula was in his element. He was a dark, handsome boy with a voice like crystal and loved to show off his talents. Soon he would embark on the early stages of Talmudic disputation and his lessons would hold him in even greater thrall.

He was already showing signs that he could become a talented scholar like his father, grandfather and great-grandfather before him. In another three years he hoped to join the yeshiva, the school for Talmudic learning that accepted only the most promising of heder students.

Of course, girls couldn't go to yeshiva, and I wouldn't have been accepted anyway; I wasn't a good enough student. But when I was twelve it was time for me to leave heder and follow Sarah to shkole, Russian school, where I would embark on a daunting range of subjects: Russian, arithmetic, literature and history. My new school was a low building painted a dreary grey both inside and out. The small windows were so filthy that it was impossible to see out. There we sat on benches at long, wooden tables speckled with dark splotches of ink and learned to write with sharp-nibbed pens that we dipped into inkwells hollowed out of the table top. Over and over and over again we inscribed Russian letters into little squares marked out on the paper. They were so different from the Hebrew letters I was used to and I found it tricky to get the curls and hooks in the right places.

The teachers were much stricter than at heder and I was forever being rapped on the knuckles with a ruler. Although I knew most of the students at my new school already, as it was reserved for Jewish children, I still found the transition difficult. Perhaps it was because I had too much to live up to, with a sister at the school who was a star pupil. I found the atmosphere stifling and oppressive, the gloominess of the building depressing, and I was terrified of the teachers. I couldn't understand the classes and didn't think I would ever get to grips with the Russian language. Each morning I awoke with a feeling of dread in my stomach. I barely ate a morsel of breakfast and Sarah had to almost drag me down the road to the shkole.

"It'll get better, Perele, I promise you," my sister tried to reassure me. But I didn't want to give it the chance. I would lie in bed at night turning over in my mind how I might get out of going to school. Once I had resolved to leave shkole a weight lifted from me. All I had to do was persuade my family. I argued and shouted and quarreled and at last my father consented. Although he was thrilled that Sarah was so successful in her studies, a lay education for girls wasn't really considered important; I wasn't a boy and it wasn't yeshiva that I was dropping out of.

Sarah, on the other hand, continued to go from strength to strength.

She won prizes and was chosen to recite poems at school concerts. Often she stayed on after the other children had gone home, preferring to do her homework in the tranquility and silence of the empty school. For her, learning was a retreat, a place she could go that was far from the hurly-burly of home, far from Zayde's angry words, his cynicism and the stinging blows of his leather belt. Sarah took after our father; she was an acutely sensitive girl, only happy when she was in a world of her own with her books, and uncomfortable with the noise and fist-thumping of our busy household.

The Free World

MY GREAT-UNCLE Menachem Mendl was Zayde's older brother. He lived next door in the other, smaller, side of the double-fronted house. A very tall, long-necked man with steeply sloping shoulders, he had intense, deep-set eyes that belied his mild and gentle nature. Despite their dissimilarity of character, he and my grandfather were the best of friends and it was rare for an evening to go by without a visit from my Feter Mendl. At least once a week he would bring with him a letter from his daughter Faiga and all the grown-ups gathered around him excitedly, eager for news from a distant world.

I barely remember Faiga. I do, however, have a distant recollection of attending her wedding to a man called Dudi Rusen. Everybody had talked about how clever he was, what a good match Faiga had made. Dudi had always dreamed about emigrating to the West and, although he was a local boy, he was already very western in terms of his outlook and appearance, so much so that he hardly looked Jewish at all. Soon after the wedding they departed, taking with them Faiga's younger brother Moishe who had just turned twenty and was eager for adventure.

At that time everybody in Pavolitch was talking about emigrating to America. "In America, people eat white bread and meat every day!" people said. "It's easy to make money and everyone who goes there becomes rich!" And "Jews can become doctors, or lawyers, or farmers or whatever they want to be and nobody cares that they're Jewish! What is more, education is free in America; not only is it free – it's obligatory!"

It was hard to know what was true and what was merely rumor, but the dream of a life without discrimination was a great draw, with memories of pogroms still fresh. For several years the Yiddish newspapers had been publishing announcements from Jewish relief organizations abroad urging Russian Jews to emigrate to America.

Instead, Faiga, Dudi and Moishe travelled north to Canada. It was a vast, under-populated country whose authorities were inviting immigrants to snap up good farming land for next to nothing. Dudi jumped at the chance. But as a Jew, always denied the right to own land in Russia, farming wasn't for him. He settled in the city of Winnipeg where, with the help of some Jewish immigrants already established there, he set up his business. He started with a pushcart on a street corner selling fruit and vegetables to passersby. Soon he had enough money to buy a truck and within a few years he was running his own wholesale produce company and had bought a handsome house in the best part of town.

Faiga's letters arrived each week, from half way across the globe, as regularly as if she lived in the next town. She described how Dudi's business was going from strength to strength and how, after a few years, he had made enough money to pay for the whole of Faiga's family to come and join them in what she called the Land of the Free. But Menachem Mendl read her letters with distaste. "You won't get me to America," he growled, "I'm not setting foot in *Das Treyfe Land*."[1] Like many observant Jews, Feter Mendl believed that emigration would lead his people to neglect the Jewish customs and rituals and assimilate with the decadent world around them. He would play no part in such desecration.

I was so used to seeing my great-uncle at the kitchen table that I didn't think twice about it, but apparently his visits had once been the cause of much debate and anguish. Baba laughed as she told me how Feter Mendl's wife Bluma used to be jealous of her and tried to prevent her husband from visiting. I looked at Baba quizzically, finding it hard to believe that my gnarled old grandmother had ever been a beauty, and giggled as she recounted how Bluma used to screech at her husband when he came home. My grandparents could hear her curses resonating through the walls.

"You're in love with her, aren't you?" Bluma would wail. "I've seen how you look at Pessy – well it's sinful, the Bible says, to covet thy brother's wife. May the Evil Eye take you, you useless wretch!"

Menachem Mendl seemed able to simply brush off his wife's accusa-

---

1. The non-kosher country.

tions like so much dust and refused to retaliate. It wasn't that he really was in love with her, Baba said, rather that he found Bluma's claims so ridiculous that he couldn't be bothered to deny them. Eventually Bluma grew weary of her daily outbursts, but she never stopped resenting my grandparents. Even when I was growing up, a simmering resentment still existed between the two women, both of whose hair was now grey and their faces lined.

As well as envy of my grandmother's looks, Bluma was jealous of Berl and Pessy for having a larger and more comfortable home than she did. She blamed her father-in-law Akiva for favoring Berl over Menachem Mendl and blamed luck for awarding the larger part of the double-fronted house to my grandfather when lots were drawn to decide how it was to be divided. But most of all she blamed poor Menachem Mendl for giving up his God-given rights as the eldest son and allowing the rabbi to decide how the house should be divided up in the first place.

Now that Baba was no longer young and attractive, Bluma didn't mind Feter Mendl visiting my grandparents in the evenings although she still resented them for having a bigger house than she did. She also missed her daughter Faiga and son Moishe terribly and had always wanted to take up Dudi's offer to pay for her and the rest of the family to join them in Canada. But for almost ten years, Menachem Mendl had held out against her and Faiga's entreaties. By now Dudi owned a successful wholesale produce company in Winnipeg, while Moishe ran a grocery store in nearby Emerson. They could afford not only to bring the whole of Faiga's family to Canada, but to pay for housing for them, too. Menachem Mendl still feared for the continuity of Jewish traditions in the West, but having resisted for year after year, he wasn't so sure anymore. There was talk of war. Already battles were raging in the Balkans where Russia was backing the Serbian army. The tsar was building up his forces in preparation for an escalation of hostilities. The newspapers reported that Germany was militarizing, too. Menachem Mendl's two younger sons were in their twenties and it was only a matter of time before they would be conscripted.

My grandfather did all he could to persuade Feter Mendl that he should take up Faiga's offer and go to Canada. Once the young men received their draft papers, it would be too late. The only one in the family to read the newspapers assiduously, Zayde was convinced that full-scale war across

Europe was inevitable. Yet still Feter Mendl dithered. Even though he was aware of the dangers if he stayed, he found the idea of life in the god-less West unthinkable. It wasn't until my grandfather threatened to write to Faiga himself and set the process in motion that he finally relented and agreed for his daughter to fill out the immigration forms.

More and more young men in Pavolitch were being called up by the military authorities and it became a race against time for Feter Mendl's sons Yankl and Haskl. Which would arrive first – their draft papers or their Canadian visas? Week after week, month after month, they waited in fear and dread of what the mail would bring. What relief then, finally, when the immigration documents arrived, along with travel permits and instructions from the Jewish relief agency. Within a matter of days they were ready to go, along with their wives and children, their parents Menachem Mendl and Bluma and their sister Gittl. There wasn't time to organize a farewell party but my grandfather accompanied them to Kiev and waved them off on the Moscow train wondering whether any of us would ever see them again.

When at last they arrived in Winnipeg and settled into a comfort-able house paid for by Dudi, Bluma could finally look back on her life with some satisfaction. After decades living in the smaller section of the double-fronted house, playing second fiddle to pretty, capable Pessy in the spacious property next door, it was she, not Pessy, who had made it to the Free World to live out her days in a life of contentment and ease.

A Jail Sentence

M Y BABA Pessy was a calm and even-tempered woman, but one thing she resented was injustice. More than anything she hated the fact that Jews had to pay a special tax on their Sabbath candles. Nobody should have to pay to honor God. What was worse, tax collectors were notorious for bursting uninvited into private homes to count the number of candles even though those so poor that they couldn't afford candles still had to pay the tax. If they refused, their possessions could be confiscated. Thankfully the tax collector in Pavolitch was a friend of ours; he was the son of Zhukov, the Ukrainian neighbor who controlled the water pump. Zhukov's son would never barge into anyone's house unasked or take their possessions. On one occasion my grandmother had held him up for so long grumbling about the injustice of the tax that for months he had surreptitiously passed by our house without stopping to ask for payment.

One day there was a sharp knock at the door.

"Pessy Shnier?" a tall man with the overcoat of a civil servant demanded. "We don't appear to have any payment on record of your candle tax. Can you explain to me why that would be?" The authorities had clearly caught up with the fact that Zhukov's son never collected money from us and had sent a local government official to investigate.

My grandmother, like most Jews, was terrified of government officials. They seemed to delight in humiliating us, punishing Jews for any minor transgression. A civil servant could stop a man in the street and demand that he remove his black gaberdine or fur-brimmed hat. He could even pull a Jew back by his peyes and chop off the dangling locks on a whim. Most men had stopped wearing the traditional hats and side-curls out of fear. Trembling internally before the figure of authority, my grandmother managed to still her nerves and remain, on the exterior, cool and polite.

"*Podozhdite*[1] . . . Please wait until my husband arrives," she said in her faltering Russian. "He will be back shortly and will pay you straightaway." When the visitor interrupted her, Pessy had been making tea for Hana Tzirl, who was in bed with a fever. Out of politeness, she turned to the official and offered him a glass of tea while he waited for Berl to return.

"I know your sort!" he snapped back at her. "You've been bribing that tax collector Zhukov, haven't you? Now you're trying to win me over with your glasses of tea and your fancy manners. Well, I'm not having it. I'm confiscating your samovar – now pour that water away!"

Pessy exploded. "My husband is at the synagogue, but he will pay you whatever we owe as soon as he returns. I have just offered you my hospitality and this is how you treat me! You lot are all the same. *Nechelovechesky*[2] – inhuman, that's what you are – inhuman!" she cried. She slammed down the glass in its silver holder and turned to face the civil servant. "What are you – a man or a pig?"

"You'll soon see what I am!" he retorted as he snatched the hot samovar from the table and walked out, pouring what remained of the scalding water over the floor.

When Berl came home, Pessy recounted the whole sorry tale. She was still fuming about the man's terrible rudeness and the loss of her samovar.

"Inhuman, these people, simply inhuman," she continued to mumble, in Yiddish this time.

Berl laughed at her and set off straightaway for the local government office to pay the overdue tax. As a fluent Russian speaker and a man of high standing in the community, he had no fear of petty officialdom. The samovar was duly returned to him and we celebrated Baba's moral victory over the tsarist regime. She was delighted that she hadn't lost face to the taxman and that she had her precious samovar back. As far as we were all concerned, the matter was forgotten.

But two weeks later, an official-looking letter arrived for Baba in the mail. She opened it quickly then sat down in shock.

"They want to prosecute me!" she exclaimed. "As if it's not enough for

1. Wait (Russian).
2. Inhuman (Russian).

him, taking my samovar away like that." Baba spent all morning snorting at the indignity. But underneath she was terrified. She was accused of insulting a public official and was called to appear in court the following week.

"I won't go. They can't make me," Baba said. But when she showed my grandfather the letter he just roared, "That'll teach you, woman!" He refused his wife's entreaties to visit the public prosecutor and beg him to drop the case.

"I can't do that, Pessy Tochter. It'll serve no purpose. You shouldn't have sworn at the man."

"Oh, you rascal. I didn't swear at him as you well know! This whole thing is such a scandal!" But there was nothing for it; she had to go to court.

"Do you admit, Pessy Shnier, that you insulted this man when he came to your house to collect unpaid candle tax?" the public prosecutor asked, indicating the familiar official, now looking smug.

"No, Your Honor," my grandmother mumbled nervously. Then she lifted her head, like the proud woman she was, her voice strengthened and she began to tell her story. "I've had thirteen children, Your Honor, but they've all been taken by God, all except my one remaining daughter, Hana Tzirl. And she is sick. I have been cursed in my life already and now I have six grandchildren to take care of. This man came into my house and when I offered him a glass of tea, he emptied onto the floor the water I was boiling to make tea for my poor daughter as she lay in her bed and then he took my samovar away. That's not the action of a human being. It's the action of a beast. Now you understand why I insulted him. Wouldn't any normal person insult a creature like that?"

My grandmother's plea went some way toward appeasing the prosecutor. "Pessy Shnier, the punishment for insulting a public official is thirty days imprisonment in the prison in Skvira."

Pessy gasped.

"But in light of the circumstances you have outlined," he continued, "I sentence you to two days in jail here in Pavolitch." Even my grandmother realized that she had been lucky to get away with such a short sentence and no longer complained.

"Yes, Your Honor. Thank you."

"Your sentence will begin right away," said the prosecutor.

"Oh, but it can't!" exclaimed my grandmother. "What about the children? If I'm to leave them for two days I need to prepare food for them to eat while I'm away. And they'll need clean clothes. I need a few days to get everything in order."

"Hmm. Alright, I will grant you your request," said the prosecutor. "I will give you time to prepare what you need. But you must present yourself at the jail on Thursday. If you fail to do so, I will rescind the leniency I have shown to you thus far and you will be imprisoned for thirty days at Skvira."

My grandmother nodded sagely.

For Baba, the following days were a frantic whirl of shopping, cooking, cleaning and washing. She had never left us before, not without Akiva and Leah looking after us, not even for a night. Baba prepared so much food for the two days she would be gone that it would have taken an army to finish it all.

When Thursday finally came, all the family gathered to accompany Baba to jail. Zayde and Tata were almost invisible under the huge piles of mattresses, blankets and pillows that Baba wanted with her in her cell. After much discussion the family had decided that Sarah should accompany Baba so that she would not have to suffer her ordeal alone. Sarah wasn't overjoyed at being asked to spend two days in jail, but at fourteen she was the eldest of the grandchildren and understood that it was her duty. Everyone agreed that Baba couldn't possibly go alone.

We parted at the gates. Baba and Sarah walked slowly into the distance, weighed down by their piles of linen and bedding. A jail sentence was the most humiliating thing that had ever happened to our family. It was a disgrace, a dishonor. But nobody blamed Baba for what she had said. We all agreed that she was right to insult the official in the way she did, so we all shared her indignity. None of us could possibly imagine what conditions inside the jail were like and we watched with a feeling of fear and dread as the two women, one old, one young, became smaller and smaller in the distance until, finally, the tall wooden doors slammed shut behind two pale dots.

Inside the cell were two wooden benches and two buckets – one with a lid to use as a toilet and one full of water for washing. There was a small window that was too high up to look out of. It certainly wasn't comfortable, but at least it was relatively clean. Pessy and Sarah made their beds on the wooden benches with the bundles of bedding they had brought from home and settled down to pray. When nightfall came, the jail warden entered the cell. He carried a list with the names of all the inmates.

"Which of you is Pessy Shnier?" he barked.

"I am," said my grandmother, standing to attention.

"So who is this?" he asked, pointing to Sarah.

"She is my granddaughter, Sarah."

The warden laughed. "But what is she doing here? She's not on the list. She hasn't committed a crime as well, has she?"

"But I couldn't come here by myself – an old woman like me all alone. You never know what might happen. It's not safe for me to stay here on my own," my grandmother cried in fear.

"What are you talking about, you stupid woman? Of course it's safe. It's a jail – we lock people up!" he roared with laughter and chivvied Sarah out of the cell. She just had time to kiss Baba on the cheek and whisper to her that everything would be alright before she was led away.

"Don't let her walk home on her own!" Sarah and the warden heard my grandmother shout from her cell as they walked down the corridor.

One of the jail's staff accompanied Sarah back to our house. She had cried all the way home, mortified that she had been unable to look after her grandmother who had cared for us all our whole lives. She had been forced to abandon Baba in her hour of greatest need.

"It's not your fault, Sarale, there's nothing you could do," Tata told her with a smile and, to make her feel better, he took her into the sanctum of his study, a very rare privilege for any of us girls. Father and daughter spent the evening in silence, lost in their own thoughts and prayers.

Of course Zhukov and his son were mortified that their family had been responsible for tarnishing my grandparents' honor. They apologized repeatedly and brought gifts of fish, soap and vegetables. Meanwhile, Baba returned home none the worse for her ordeal.

Retirement

EVEN WHEN he was well into his seventies, my great-grandfather Akiva continued to work in his mill, grinding millet for the local peasants and villagers. His wife Leah was always nagging him to spend less time working. His back was bent now and constantly ached from lifting sacks of millet. Finally, he felt, the time might have come to sell the mill. In fact, it was my cousin Lonchik, Menachem Mendl's grandson, who had put the idea of selling the mill into Akiva's head.

"You're an old man now," Lonchik had said to him, shortly before he and his family departed for Canada. "Why do you need to keep working when you've got family who can support you?" Lonchik suggested that the money earned from selling Akiva's mill and the house that adjoined it could help pay back the debt his family would owe to Faiga's husband Dudi Rusen for their passage to Canada. And it would help compensate for Menachem Mendl having to settle for the smaller part of the double-fronted house Akiva had built for his sons all those years ago.

Akiva mulled over Lonchik's proposal. It was true that he was tired of working. He didn't have the energy he used to. And the timing seemed perfect, too. His daughter Babtsy was twenty-one and was about to be married. Her fiancé was a watchmaker named Moishe Margolis who owned a large shop in Khodarkov, thirty versts north of Pavolitch. He was also a cantor at the synagogue there, a position that had belonged to his father and grandfather before him. It was an excellent match and he supposed that Babtsy and her husband would help to support him in his old age.

But my grandfather pleaded with Akiva to ignore Lonchik's advice. "Don't sell," he implored. "It costs you very little to run your business, but you have your independence ... self-respect ... and it keeps you active. And if you sell, you'll lose the family name." For Berl, this would be the worst of it – Akiva's mill had maintained the revered name of Hager, the name that linked us to the distinguished Hager rabbis and guaranteed respect. My grandfather had another worry on his mind, too. After decades of prosperity, his business was foundering. With talk of war in Europe, his international contracts had all dried up. Local landowners were finding other means to sell their crops. The wagons of grain arriving at the klet were fewer in number, and their loads lighter, as peasants began hoarding their grain, fearful of food shortages. It wasn't much, but until now Berl still had income from trading his father's millet. Now this, too, would be taken from him.

Akiva didn't heed his son's counsel and Berl was so incensed that he vowed never to speak to his father again. He even refused to attend Babtsy's wedding. Akiva wept throughout the ceremony, choking back his sobs as he watched his only daughter standing so proudly beneath the four-posted wedding canopy. Babtsy was the miracle that had come to him in later life when his hair was grey and his sons from his first marriage already had children of their own. And now she was grown up, too. How quickly the years passed. Whether Akiva's tears also reflected a twinge of uncertainty about the future now that his house and mill were to be sold, or regret about the squabble with his son Berl, was hard to gauge.

Leah, too, was crying like a baby. Babtsy meant the world to her, the daughter she never thought she could have, who had appeared after nearly ten years of failed pregnancies. Unlike most mothers, who feel joy for their daughters on their wedding day, as well as sadness for themselves, Leah's tears were tears of loss alone. The prospect of losing her precious girl was more than she could bear. Once the wedding canopy was dismantled and the decorations taken down, Babtsy moved to Khodarkov to live above Moishe's watch shop. Leah was bereft. The thirty versts that separated her from Babtsy felt more like an ocean to her and, as she and Akiva packed their belongings to leave the home where she had spent the whole of her married life, she made up her mind. The mill and house would be sold in a matter of weeks. Rather than remain in Pavolitch, she would move in with Babtsy and her new husband. Akiva had family to look after him. In Khodarkov, Babtsy would have nobody. To her, the choice was obvious.

Akiva begged his wife to stay. They would find a cozy little house, he told her, where they could be together and enjoy his retirement. Besides, he argued, Babtsy needed to make her own way in the world. She wasn't a child anymore. But Leah was a powerful woman and very headstrong; there was nothing Akiva could say or do to change her mind. She packed her bags and left.

"I married you and you alone! I didn't marry your mother as well!" Moishe complained to his new wife when Leah turned up on his doorstep. But Babtsy was delighted. She had quickly discovered that it was hard work being a wife, especially when there is a shop to keep clean as well as a home. She found her mother's help and advice invaluable.

"If your mother doesn't leave this house, I'm going to demand a divorce," threatened Moishe.

But there was nothing Babtsy could do, even if she had wanted to. Leah was more determined than anyone else she knew. She had chosen her daughter over her husband and that was that. Within a matter of weeks Babtsy was pregnant and Moishe's will dissolved. He continued to moan about his mother-in-law, but Leah made herself so useful that he couldn't resent her too much. She bustled around the house and shop ensuring the floor was always spotless, the linen starched and the silver sparkling. And she won her son-in-law over with her gigantic poppy-seed cookies. Moishe came to accept that the old woman would never leave Babtsy, and that he himself wouldn't either.

With his wife and daughter gone, Akiva's life was turned on its head. From being a happily married old man enjoying the first idleness of retirement, he was all of a sudden both homeless and alone. My grandfather was still so livid with him for selling the mill that he refused to let him into our house. He began renting a small, narrow room in the house of an elderly widow on the other side of the Jewish quarter. Pessy repeatedly tried to persuade Berl to forget his argument with his father and let Akiva move in next door, where the other half of the double-fronted house lay empty since Menachem Mendl's departure for Canada.

"I'll do no such thing. I never want to see the old man again," growled Berl.

"But he'd be in Mendl's house – you don't need to have anything to do with him," my grandmother pleaded. She tried every argument she could think of, in particular pointing out that Akiva had built the house himself and should have the right to live in it. But to no avail. There wasn't a

man on this earth as stubborn as my grandfather. Months passed without
a single word being uttered between father and son, while the rest of us
visited Akiva in his damp, narrow room and took him food as often as we
could. We had to be careful for, if Zayde found out, he would have been
furious.

One day Akiva's landlady banged on our door. "The old man is sick.
I don't know what to do with him. He says he hasn't any money to call a
doctor and I can't look after him," she squawked. My grandmother almost
screamed with anger and frustration. If Berl hadn't had that stupid argument with his father about the mill, Akiva would be comfortable now in
the big house he himself had had built, not wheezing in some cold, damp
hovel.

"Don't you worry," she told the widow. "I'll call Moishe the doctor and
we can bring the old man back here." As soon as my grandfather returned
from afternoon prayers, she turned on him and described bluntly what
had happened to his father as a result of Berl's obstinacy.

"You have to put this argument behind you. Go to Akiva and tell him
you forgive him."

"I will not," Zayde grunted.

"You stubborn old goat! You can't let your father stay there like that.
How would you feel if he died?" Baba screeched at him. But she knew
she was wasting her breath. She would have to take the situation in hand
herself. She set off to visit Akiva, finding him bundled up in dirty sheets
in the tiny room with mould growing over the walls. He stared up at her
weakly, his milky eyes peeping over the bedclothes as he coughed and
spluttered.

My grandmother threw her arms up in despair. "How could this ever
have been allowed to happen?" she cried, then promptly made preparations for Akiva to be moved. She knew that left alone he would soon die
a miserable death alone in this damp room. How was it that her husband
gave money to charity and invited guests who found themselves in dif-
ficulties to live in his house, yet treated his own father this way?

She organized a porter to carry Akiva home while Berl was busy at
the railway station and installed him in one of the rooms left empty by
Menachem Mendl's departure. The doctor arrived and administered
medicines and compresses. When her husband returned, Pessy took her
courage in both hands and confronted him.

"I've brought Akiva home. I don't care what you say – he's family and he's going to stay here whether you like it or not," she asserted as powerfully as she could. For once, my grandfather didn't argue. He, too, must have finally realized the folly of his stubbornness and at long last the dispute over the sale of the mill was forgotten. Berl even agreed that they should send a message to his stepmother Leah and invite her back from Khodarkov to live in the double-fronted house, too.

As soon as she received the news from Pavolitch of her husband's illness, Leah summoned a coach and driver and sped to his bedside as fast as she could. She fell to her knees and kissed his pale face as he dozed fitfully, noticing how thinly his skin was stretched over his hollow cheeks, then she turned and cast a critical eye about the room.

"It's not good enough for my Akiva!" she declared, her hands resting on her ample hips. Out went Akiva and in came brooms and scrubbing brushes, detergent and pails of lime. Leah swept and scrubbed, washed down windows and limed the walls. She worked solidly for two whole days before moving Akiva back into the bright, spotless room. Then she kissed him again and prepared to depart.

"Don't go, my dove. Don't leave me again," Akiva whimpered as Leah left the room. But his wife couldn't bear to spend another night away from her beloved Babtsy who was now large with child. Despite Akiva's frail health, she knew that, with Pessy caring for him, he was in the best possible hands and she felt that Babtsy's need was greater. For the second time, faced with the choice of abandoning either her husband or her daughter, she chose in favor of her daughter.

"I'll come back soon with Babtsy and the little one, God willing," Leah promised with a smile as she departed. Akiva nodded gratefully, his eyes moist with tears. But Leah wasn't able to keep her vow. Once Babtsy's baby was born, neither mother nor child was strong enough to manage the journey to Pavolitch and Leah felt unable to leave them, not even for a day. She sent a message to let her husband know that his grandson had been named after him, but poor Akiva never set eyes on the child who bore his name, nor did he ever see his wife or daughter again.

Akiva recovered from his sickness and settled comfortably into a routine in the double-fronted house with regular visits from the doctor who came once a week to drain the water from his knees. Even though he was almost eighty and suffered pains in his legs and terrible bedsores, he never grumbled or scolded us. He still told us stories and encircled us with his long, bony arms. In return, we, his six great-grandchildren, danced around him continually, bringing him hot milk and pastries, reading to him and making him comfortable. There was nobody we would rather be with than our great-grandfather.

But on the very day that war was declared, Akiva fell ill again. Having spent his entire youth trying to avoid war, it was the advent of another conflict that threatened his demise. The summer of 1914 was stifling and Akiva found the heat unbearable. We kept all the doors and windows open and took it in turns to cool him down by waving paper fans over his bed. When the weather finally turned, it was worse still. Winter came quickly and already fuel for the fire was becoming harder to find as supplies were requisitioned by the army. However much we wrapped him up in blankets and down quilts, it seemed impossible to stop our great-grandfather from shivering. Normally so stoical in his suffering, he winced and groaned each time the pains shot through his legs and up his body. All we could do was try to make him as comfortable as possible. We took turns at sitting by his bedside to talk or read to him, but sometimes I wondered whether he wouldn't be happier if we all left him alone and stopped bothering him.

We prepared for Hanukkah that year in much lower spirits than usual. Akiva insisted that he wanted to watch us all enjoying the festival of lights, normally one of the most cheerful Jewish holidays, to see the lighting of the *menorah* one more time. The special nine-branched candlestick was brought down from the loft and polished until it gleamed. Little jugs were filled with oil and the wicks of the menorah were threaded carefully and lit one day at a time. Akiva handed out Hanukkah *gelt* to the children, as he had done every year since we were born, and we took the coins from his yellowed hands. His skin had turned translucent, like parchment. We all played cards, wagering our new-found riches until one of us, usually Baya, ended up with the whole lot.

Our great-grandfather watched our games and tried to encourage the losers with a gummy smile, but for the first time in his life he was unable to laugh. It hurt his chest too much. He couldn't swallow the special fried potato *latkes* that Baba prepared, as she did every year, and nibbled delicately at the edges of the little pancakes, just pretending to eat them. His already thin body shrunk day by day until almost no flesh remained. I couldn't bear to see him this way, yet an unconscious will kept me flitting continually to the door of his room to watch his shallow breathing lest it should suddenly stop. My great-grandfather had been such a warm presence throughout my life that it was hard to imagine how things would be without him. He provided so much of the love that his great-grandchildren needed, counterbalancing the harshness of Zayde and the remoteness of our father.

On the third day of Hanukkah Doctor Moishe arrived for his usual weekly visit. He examined the old man meticulously, but declared he could find nothing out of the ordinary. Akiva was simply suffering from old age.

"There's no medicine I can give you if I can't find out what's wrong with you," he told Akiva. "So all I can do is wish you a Happy Hanukkah, and hope to see you on the third day of Hanukkah next year."

Akiva raised a feeble arm and pulled the doctor close. "Straight from your mouth to God's ear," he whispered to him with a wan attempt at a smile. Moishe took the old man's hand in both of his for a moment then left the room. Once outside, he took my grandmother aside.

"It's very close now. He could die tomorrow, or even today," he told her.

Zayde sat by his father's bedside for at least an hour when he came home from the synagogue that evening and his hushed tone could be heard through the door as a gentle drone. Our great-grandfather's voice was inaudible, but we could tell from the manner of the silences that father and son were having a conversation – the first time they had exchanged more than a few cursory words together since their ridiculous argument over selling the mill. Eventually the noise ceased. Zayde left his father's room slowly and thoughtfully, but said not a word to anybody. When I looked in on Akiva just minutes later, his head had rolled to the side and his eyes were closed. For long moments it appeared that the gentle rise and fall of his chest had stopped, then I discerned his breathing once again. I blinked back my tears and walked away. Later that night, Akiva's soul finally left him. My grandfather revealed neither what they had talked about in his final conversation, nor what his last words were. "It's between me and him," Zayde said firmly, but there was a certain unfamiliar serenity about my grandfather, which might, I liked to think, have indicated that old grievances had been laid to rest and forgiveness granted.

Akiva's body was laid out on a bed of straw on the living room floor and covered with a black shroud. Rachel sat cross-legged beside him for hour after hour, her tears glistening in the light of the candles that had been placed on either side of his head. On the windowsill was a bowl of water and a linen cloth so that my great-grandfather's soul could perform its ritual ablutions and I imagined him reawakening in the early hours of the morning to wash while the rest of the house still slept. Baba had covered all the mirrors in the house with black cloth, which remained in place for the entire week of ritual mourning. Before the burial, she wrapped Akiva's body in a prayer shawl. Zayde tenderly placed shards over his father's eyes and a piece of wood in his gnarled old hands so that his soul would be able to tunnel its way to the Holy Land when the Messiah came.

Ettie Leah, Sarah, Naftula and Pearl circa 1905

Makarov circa 1909.
*Back row: Bassy, Avrom, **Maryam, Sarah**, Isaac (grandson **of Hershl**)*
*Front row: Berl (brother of Meyer), Chaya Rachel, **Rachel**, Velvl, Meyer, **Hershl** (brother of Velvl)*

Leah, Babtsy, Akiva and Sarah circa 1910

Pavolitch circa 1914.
Back row: Maryam, Rosen, Bassy
Middle row: Meyer, Pearl, Sarah
Front row: Rachel, Naftula

Hana Tzirl and Babtsy circa 1915

Pearl, Sarah and Rachel circa 1922

Pearl and Nathan in Winnipeg circa 1926

Pearl & Itzhik's wedding 1926

Baba Pessy surrounded by her grandchildren circa 1928
Nathan (Naftula) & Bessie, Pearl & Itzhik, Rachel, Morris (Mendl), Sarah & Shaya

Baba Pessy circa 1928   *Pearl circa 1930*

Pearl 1950s

Pearl in California in the 1970s
as the author remembers her

PART III

1914–1919

❀

War

AFTER GERMANY declared war in 1914, the train station at Popilna changed from a stock exchange to an army embarkation point. Goods trains no longer brought news of grain prices from Kiev and Odessa, but transported military apparel to the distant front, and passenger services were replaced by troop carriers. Instead of throbbing with merchants and speculators, the train stations were drenched in the tears of mothers, wives and children waving their beloved goodbye as they ran along the platform until it ended and they could run no further. Instead of talk of prices, bushels, poods and exchanges, all conversation was of mobilization, detachments, regiments and ultimatums.

My grandfather's routine was disrupted without his trips to the station. Although the scope of his business no longer required him to visit Popilna every day, he still undertook the journey with the balagula once or twice a week. Now even this was denied him and he began to pace around the house restlessly. He missed his outings and the social contact they provided, and he despaired of the murkiness that was settling over grain prices. The daily dealings at the train station had kept pricing transparent: dealers knew how much was being paid for each product at every location. Now it was impossible to keep track. To make matters worse, inflation had started to increase, making it more important than ever to keep a close eye on the market. But exchange rates, tariffs and prices were all becoming harder and harder to gauge. They rose, gradually at first, then faster and faster, until they were running out of control like a downhill sled on an icy track.

Thankfully my father wasn't called up to fight in the first months of the war. As the men folk of Pavolitch marched off to the station to fill the never-ending line of trains heading for the front, I prayed every night and every day that Tata wouldn't one day join them. He wasn't meant for fighting, this gentle, studious man, who still dressed every day in his long, black coat and skullcap.

The first wave of recruits were green-ticketers. My father hoped to be granted a blue ticket, which would mean he was allowed to study rather than go to war. Only the feeble-minded and the infirm were lucky enough to be granted a white ticket, which exempted them altogether, while those who failed the medical exam were red-ticketers. Pavolitch was full of young men trying to make themselves ill by fasting, drinking salty water or over-indulging in salted herring to gain a red ticket. The rich took a different tack by bribing doctors or officials to reject their sons. Meanwhile the mothers of one or two young men we knew ran themselves ragged going from one office to another through the warren of Russian officialdom trying to prove that their last remaining boy should get the automatic exemption that applied to only sons. The official registers were notoriously inaccurate and many hadn't been updated properly when people died or emigrated, but the process of verifying that a son was unavailable for service could cause weeks of frustration and distress.

When the newspapers began publishing lists of those killed in battle and widows and mothers were first seen around Pavolitch shrouded in black mourning dresses, I thanked God every day that Tata had so far been spared. Life became harder as food and equipment continued to be sent down the railway tracks to the armies fighting thousands of miles away. It was a blessing for us that Zayde ran a grain business so we still had enough bread to eat. But elsewhere, especially in the cities, people were going hungry as war sapped the country dry. The war was deeply unpopular, and not only with those who had lost sons, husbands, fathers or lovers. With food supplies scarce and rooms left unheated for lack of fuel, people shivered and grew sick. In Kiev, crowds of demonstrators gathered, demanding an end to the fighting, the return of the troops, more bread to eat.

Still I waited for Tata's conscription, dreading the day that he would leave us. But in the end we were lucky. He was awarded his blue ticket and, to help the war effort, he was assigned as bookkeeper to a government-owned mill not far from home. Now that he would no longer be earning his keep by helping Berl with his paperwork, he decided it was finally time for him to move out of his father-in-law's house. The ten years of lodging that his dowry agreement allowed him had long since expired, and six years had passed since my mother's death. In spite of their protests, he felt he could no longer burden Berl and Pessy, especially with provisions becoming harder to find. For the first time in his life he would have money in the pockets of his black gaberdine and, working for the government, he would be entitled to a certain amount of basic supplies. His salary should suffice to pay rent and buy food for himself and his children. But without a wife, who would look after the cooking, cleaning and washing for him?

Sarah was fifteen, but she spent all her time reading and studying. Still top of the class at the shkole, Sarah by now spoke Russian fluently and was devouring the thick novels of the great Russian writers Gogol, Turgenev, Dostoevsky and Tolstoy. My father held learning in such high esteem that even though Sarah was a girl, there was no question of taking her out of school to look after the house. And besides, Sarah herself would never have agreed. Although placid by nature, my older sister could be forceful when she needed to be, and she was determined to continue her schooling then carry on all the way to Kiev – to the university.

I was thirteen years old; I had come of age, so I believed it was my duty to keep house for my father. In fact, I would have given anything to look after him, to learn how to cook and clean and sew for him. I still worshipped Tata and would have offered him my soul if only he had asked me. But that was something he never did.

"You're too young, Perele," he repeated, in answer to my entreaties. "You can look after Rachel, but it's too much to take on a whole household. And in war time, too. It could be dangerous."

Dangerous! The danger was at the front hundreds of miles away. It certainly wasn't in Pavolitch. Shortages yes, but fighting – not anywhere that I could see.

Instead my father had come up with another solution: he would take a wife. He called upon the matchmaker to find a suitable bride for him. It was not easy. My father was a middle-aged widower with four children. He didn't have much money and insisted on an educated wife from a respectable family. In less uncertain times, marriage to a Talmudic scholar was considered an honor, but since the war had started, the most important attribute for a new husband was that he should have sufficient means to buy food and fuel. The matchmaker found my father's request a struggle; this was one of the most difficult challenges she had been set in all her years of business. She called upon all the reputable marriage brokers in the area to try to find a suitable bride.

"Tsch, it won't be easy," they all grumbled, shaking their heads.

At last a girl was found who seemed to have the necessary qualities. Her name was Chava and she was only a few years older than Sarah. She certainly could not be described as beautiful, but neither was she stupid. Her parents were willing to sacrifice her to a good family and a scholarly husband, recognizing that although we weren't rich, we were hardly starving either. My father only met her once before the wedding and seemed satisfied with what he saw; we children never set eyes on her at all. Even if I had been asked to meet her, I would have turned my back and walked away. How could a young upstart like her come and take our father away from us? How dare she usurp the love that rightfully belonged to us – his flesh and blood?

My father remained immune to the anguish his betrothal was causing me and continued to go about his routine in the customary placid manner: praying, working, eating, studying, as if nothing had changed. I was barely able to even broach the subject of his marriage with him, let alone dissuade him from going ahead with it. The dreaded day duly arrived. But these were somber times. The wedding was small, taking place in Rabbi Twersky's study in Makarov with none of the gaiety and dancing that we were accustomed to at family celebrations. Only immediate family was invited and once the marriage was sealed the assembled guests called out "*Mazel tov!*" with as much enthusiasm as they could muster (I refused to open my mouth – I wasn't congratulating anybody). Then my father lifted Chava's veil to reveal her face. Only it wasn't Chava at all.

Tata was standing beside a complete stranger; a much older version of Chava, her hair already coarse and graying, her face beginning to crumple under the lines of age. In Jewish families, it was customary for daughters to marry in order of age and Chava's accursed parents had despaired of finding a match for Rivka, their old maid of an elder daughter. No wonder they were content to have a small wedding!

I was furious. The fact that Tata had remarried at all was hard enough for me to come to terms with, but knowing the duplicity of the family we were now a part of made it unbearable. To me, Rivka was an ogre. I refused to let her near me and barely spoke a word to her. I had earned my father's love in the long years I had lived apart from him during my time in Makarov as a little girl and by all my thoughts and deeds since. She, on the other hand, had made him look a fool. How could she deserve his love?

But Tata didn't even complain that Rivka wasn't the woman he had been betrothed to. In fact, he seemed quite satisfied with the match. I begged him to go to Rabbi Twersky and get the marriage annulled. Surely, under the circumstances, the rabbi would agree to such a thing. If not, my father could get a divorce. But Tata remained as calm and unconcerned as he always did.

"If God had wished me to marry Chava, he would have willed it so. He must have his reasons for giving Rivka to me," he answered. And that was the end of the matter.

A week or two after my father remarried, Rachel and I were summoned to his lodgings, which were to become our new home. He had rented a small, wooden cottage. Yellow paint flaked off the outside walls and the wind seeped into the narrow rooms. There wasn't sufficient space for all four of us, so Sarah and Naftula stayed with our grandparents. Both spent most of their spare time studying and there they could each find a quiet place in which to work. Besides, in another couple of years, Sarah would, she hoped, be off to the university in Kiev. And soon it would be time for Naftula to start his Talmudic scholarship at the yeshiva in Skvira.

I had very mixed feelings about moving into the cottage with Tata. Although I longed to be close to my father and to spend more time with him, I would also have Rivka to contend with. If Tata had married in order to gain a housekeeper, he had clearly made a big mistake. It wasn't that Rivka was lazy. In fact, she kept the house spick and span. Just setting a foot across the threshold in our felt *valenki* in winter was enough to send her marching to the kitchen for a cloth to wipe the entrance porch clean.

"Don't you dare walk in here with those boots on!" she shrieked.

"What do you want me to do? Walk up the path in my stockings?" I retorted, unfastening the boots.

"Always answering back. Always insolent. I'll be having words with your father, see if I won't"

I stormed up the stairs to the bedroom I shared with Rachel, my step-mother's angry complaints following me as if she were a dog snarling at my heels, until I slammed the bedroom door closed. Still worse than Rivka's obsessive cleanliness was her meanness. It was over a year since the war had begun. Food had become scarcer, but most goods were still available for a price, and Tata didn't earn so little that we couldn't afford to eat. Yet the portions Rivka served at mealtimes would barely feed a bird. I didn't care so much for myself, but Tata was a grown man who worked all day. He needed to keep up his strength. One day I confronted my father.

"She doesn't give you enough to eat," I insisted. "Potatoes aren't that expensive at the market; you must make her buy more."

"Shhh, Perele, I'm fine. I sit down in my job. It's not as if I'm outside shoveling coal all day. You shouldn't worry."

"But Tata, she's stingy. I bet Baba wouldn't ever cook so little, however much potatoes cost."

"Now, now, Perele, that's enough." But I refused to drop the matter.

"But we're all going hungry! Rachel's starving all the time! You know, I bet she steals the money to buy things for herself."

That was it. "Enough, Pearl! I won't hear another word!" Tata didn't often get angry, but I knew when I had overstepped the mark. For one thing, he no longer called me by the affectionate diminutive Perele, instead using the proper version of my name.

I never had much of an appetite, but it was true that Rachel always seemed to be famished. Now eight years old, she was still small for her age, but as plump as ever. She was too scared to complain to our father that she wasn't getting enough to eat, but most evenings after she finished heder I accompanied her to Levi's shop where we would buy something to keep her going until dinner. Our family had always been on good terms with Levi and ever since we were small children we had dropped in now and again to pick up a slice of halva or some smoked herring. Levi put our little purchases on a tab that my grandfather used to settle up once a month. Since moving out of our grandparents' house, Levi had been happy to continue accepting our custom, only now Tata paid our account. Levi greeted us each evening with a cheery smile. One day Rachel and I approached the counter to find Levi wringing his hands and twitching the corners of his mouth as if he was embarrassed by something. I asked him for a couple of bread rolls. Levi fidgeted some more.

"I'm sorry, Pearl," he mumbled.

"Why? What's wrong?"

"It's just that ... ," more twitching, "... your stepmother, you know ..."

"Oh, no, what has she done?" I snapped. Poor Levi stuttered and stammered and eventually managed to explain that Rivka had paid him a visit and demanded that he refuse to serve us. She was in command of the purse strings now and she would no longer settle our bill. I managed to stifle my scream of fury as Rachel and I marched out of the shop. Rachel wanted to run straight to Baba to tell her of the injustice and to ask for something to eat from her kitchen, but I held her back. I refused to let her complain to anyone that she was going hungry, lest it should reflect badly on Tata.

Instead, Rachel and I tried to spend as much time as we could at the big, double-fronted house whenever my father wasn't at home. Despite the war shortages, Baba always had cookies or pastries in the kitchen and Rachel would help herself without a fuss. Even though the atmosphere was often infused with Zayde's bitterness, our grandparents' house still felt like home, and both Rachel and I hated to leave for the wooden cottage with its peeling yellow walls and the poisonous mood that Rivka created.

But to our disgust, Baba always insisted that we return before darkness fell, even if our father wouldn't be back yet. When we made a fuss, Haskl, the hunchback, would take us. Haskl was my grandfather's most loyal friend, the son of his old lodger Jacob Kreinis, and he was as close as family. He spent most evenings at my grandparents' house, but he lived next door to Tata in a couple of rooms that he shared with his wife Batya and their two daughters. He would lift me up onto his humped shoulders, take Rachel under his arm like a book, and carry us home as if we were no heavier than rag dolls. Looking at his tiny stature and his physical deformity, it was hard to believe he could be so strong. Despite our outraged squeals, Haskl refused to put us down until we had arrived at his lodgings. Then we would peer through the windows of the yellow cottage to see if Tata was home yet. If our stepmother was alone, I climbed the tree outside the house, offering a supporting hand down to Rachel who was always afraid of falling, and we both squeezed in through our bedroom window so that we didn't have to go through the front door and face Rivka.

✺

Revolution

THE WAR lingered on. Months of shivering and chilblains passed interminably slowly. Fuel was dear and my stepmother Rivka too mean to light the fires until Tata came home from work. When at last spring arrived, I greeted the melting snow with relief despite the slush and mud that seeped through my boots and turned the kaluzha outside my grandparents' house into a pond. The buttercups in the meadows turned slowly to the dusty ochre of summer, rustling expanses of grain and wilting heat. Another new year celebrated, another Hanukkah. Prices continued to rise by the month, even by the week, until even bread became a luxury. How grateful we were for my grandfather's grain supplies. But with the incoming cartloads from the peasants dwindling, he was forced to raise his prices. The townsfolk were so desperate that they had no choice but to pay – or else go hungry. The bakers ground my grandfather' wheat with chestnuts and potato peelings and baked bread that was so glutinous it stuck to the gums and was almost impossible to swallow.

Zayde's trips to Kiev became rare, but he recounted stories of the increasing unrest he had witnessed each time he returned. People talked openly, fearlessly, in the streets about the end of the tsar's reign, he said. They talked about Russia withdrawing from the war and abandoning her allies; power to the workers; people's soviets. Students handed out leaflets and waved red banners. What did it all mean? Would the war soon be over? Could the tsar just resign? How can the workers take power? And what were the soviets? To a fifteen year old girl in small country town, the reports from the city were all very mysterious.

But far away to the north, in Petrograd – as the Russian capital was now called – the demonstrations were coming to a head and at last they culminated in the tsar's abdication. It was as if a black cloud had lifted from above our heads. Alexander Kerensky and the Provisional Government filled the power void left by Tsar Nicholas and represented everything we had ever hoped for. Sarah came home from shkole early, rejoicing that she would no longer have to sing the national anthem: the hated *God Save the Tsar* was now banned. The Pale of Settlement was dissolved at a single blow; censorship was abolished, and my grandfather began devouring newspapers and any other source of information he could find, hungry for news that had not previously been considered fit for public consumption. The hated candle tax that had landed Baba in jail was eradicated, as was the box tax, which kept the price of kosher meat unjustly high.

"Kerensky has come, and it's like a blessing!" Zayde repeated again and again to anyone who would listen. The dream of freedom that had sent so many of our friends and relatives far away across the ocean to Canada and America was actually coming to Russia! No more tsar! No more restrictions on Jewish jobs and residence permits! Now we had the same rights as everybody else in the country. I didn't understand the politics of it all, but I could feel the difference in my daily life. The mood of oppression that had settled over Pavolitch since the beginning of the war was suddenly lifted. People smiled, chatted, laughed; they talked about their hopes and dreams, voiced aspirations that they had never dared to speak about before; some even danced in the street. Zayde was more cheerful than he had been in years and Baba's eyes sparkled in a way that I had hardly ever seen.

"We're free, my children! We're free!" she laughed when she first heard the news, scurrying around the room hugging each of her grandchildren in turn, then finishing in a long, fierce embrace with her daughter, Hana Tzirl. Even Rivka's sour expression lifted for a while and only my father seemed immune to the excitement. Even though he no longer spent his days immersed in the Talmud, he remained fastidiously unaware of the outside world.

In our capital, Kiev, our relatives in the city later reported, the mood in the streets changed overnight with the tsar's abdication. Decades – even centuries – of fear were lifted and the population brimmed with excitement and optimism. Not just Jews, but Ukrainian factory workers, railway men and laborers all rejoiced in the new sense of hope. Jubilant processions were swiftly organized, concerts planned, and enthusiastic bands of actors performed hastily rehearsed plays that had previously been banned.

Under the tsars, the Jews had been stifled. We had experienced nothing but suffering at the hands of the authorities ever since our land had become part of the Russian empire. In Pavolitch we were lucky that our relationship with the local Poles and Ukrainians was healthy. My grandfather counted his Ukrainian neighbor Zhukov and his family as friends. Likewise, my grandmother was immensely fond of Katarina and Pritska who continued to help her with the laundry, and they were devoted to her, too. But we knew how things stood elsewhere. We knew that in many towns and villages Christians avoided shopping at what they called the "Jew stores". They refused to conduct business with us, called us swindlers or cheats and thought us haughty and scornful. They only spoke to us to mock, to jeer, to laugh at our dress and our sacred customs. Their newspapers portrayed us as leeches who sucked the blood of the peasants. To them our shtetl folk were backward, while in the city, Jewish doctors and lawyers were troublesome competition to their own practices.

None of my family in Pavolitch, Makarov or Khodarkov had witnessed riots first hand, but the pogroms of 1905 were still fresh in the memory of every Jew in the land. Even now, twelve years later, my grandfather still occasionally provided shelter for distant relatives, or even complete strangers, who had been burnt out of their homes, or lost a husband or a father as a result of the violence. And each Passover the same vicious rumors about Christian blood in ritual sacrifice emerged. In fact, a few years earlier, in Kiev, a Jewish factory worker by the name of Mendl Beilis had been accused of abducting and murdering a Christian boy so that he could use his blood to make Passover matzos. My grandfather followed the trial in the newspapers and even Tata, who was usually completely immune to worldly affairs, was gripped by the story. Of course Beilis was found innocent of the charges, but the rumors and fears of a renewed outbreak of pogroms had persisted.

The tsar may not have organized the pogroms or circulated the rumors himself, but his government would surely have been found guilty of incitement in any court of law. It had sponsored the Black Hundreds to pillage and burn, rape, kill and destroy. It had ordered the police and army not to intercede. It had turned its back when newspapers printed lies about us, when rumors were spreading. For as long as the Jews had been in Russia, the government had been our enemy.

Now, at last, we felt we could breathe. Kerenksy would change everything. He was a socialist, a democrat and an amazing orator. He was an almost god-like figure and my family worshipped him. He roused the inhabitants of the Pale with his powerful speeches proclaiming that from now on, nobody in Russia would face discrimination on the grounds of religion or race. For the first time, Jews would be able to travel freely; to study and work in regions and professions from which we were previously barred; to settle wherever we wished, buy land of our own. There was a great feeling of hope, a new dawn.

Amid the excitement of the 1917 revolution, my sister Sarah, already accustomed to winning plaudits and school prizes, received the highest accolade of all: she was accepted into the university in Kiev to study literature. Everybody was terrifically proud of Sarah's achievement – even Zayde, who had snubbed her throughout her childhood, now clapped her on the back so hard that she almost fell over, and boasted to his friends of his granddaughter's triumph. Gaining a place at university had been almost impossible before because the tsar had set strict quotas for the number of Jews that could be accepted and the mass of applicants always vastly exceeded the allocation of places available. But now institutions could choose their students on merit, rather than by race, and Sarah was one of the first to benefit.

But my father and grandparents anguished over the wisdom of letting Sarah go to the city where she could get mixed up in violent demonstrations or dangerous student radicalism, and she might not find enough to eat. Sarah, meanwhile, agonized over the thought of going against her father's will. She knew she was his favorite. As well as being serious and studious, she was fair and beautiful with gentle, faraway eyes. She wasn't stubborn like me or frightened like Rachel. Usually Sarah was quiet and reserved and the mere thought of arguing with her family would upset her. But she was determined that this opportunity should not pass her by. She had a great thirst for knowledge and a desire to know more of the world outside the shtetl. She had learned Russian and now spoke it like her mother tongue. Studying had, for her, long been a means of escape. She had been an unhappy child, too sensitive to withstand Zayde's aggressive nature and, by working hard, she had finally achieved a means to break away.

"I'm going anyway, whatever they decide," she confided. "I'm not a child anymore – I'm seventeen. Baba left home much younger than that to get married. I don't want to hurt her, or Tata, but I have to go."

I looked up to Sarah and admired her, but I also rather resented her. Sometimes her intelligence spilled over into arrogance and there was an air of disdain about how she treated me and Rachel. I don't think she was really that much cleverer than me. Already I was regretting the fact that I had never applied myself to my school work and my refusal to attend shkole, which now left me unable to read or write properly in Russian, let alone in the Latin alphabet that Sarah would soon be learning.

At last Zayde and Tata relented and agreed that Sarah should not squander her opportunity. My grandfather consulted with his relatives in the city who assured him that Sarah would be safe with them. She was to lodge in their apartment, which was well away from the Khreshchatik, the main boulevard that was the focal point for all the flag-waving and gun-firing. My sister was elated. Rarely had I seen her show so much emotion as she did in the days that followed. She packed her books, her clothes and photographs with such great excitement that I thought she would burst.

"No need to be so happy that you're leaving us, Sarale," Zayde joked. And Sarah smiled at him with more warmth than she had shown toward her grandfather for many years.

That same year it was time for Naftula to leave home, too. He was thirteen years old and had celebrated his *bar mitzvah*, and now he was ripe to join the yeshiva in Skvira to receive instruction in the Talmud and other Jewish scripts so that he could hone the scholarship and debating skills that had served his paternal grandfather and great-grandfather so well. Now there were no arguments. Although the family was proud that Sarah had been accepted into the university, it paled beside the importance of Naftula's enrollment at the yeshiva. For a young man, a yeshiva education was everything. It symbolized Godliness, honor, tradition and the highest form of learning.

I dreaded his departure, for I idolized Naftula almost as much as I revered my father. Ever since my return from Makarov, when Naftula was six, I had doted on him like a mother. He had been such a sweet, docile child that it almost pained me to watch him grow up. As the years passed, Naftula had become ever more handsome, with dark, wavy hair and a thoughtful air. Even in the middle of winter, his skin had a lovely brown tint to it and, on more than one occasion, I had seen young girls staring at him in the street. He pretended not to notice, but I could tell that he enjoyed their attention. Even though Naftula was already spending more and more time away from home, taking extra lessons at heder in preparation for starting yeshiva, and accompanying our grandfather to synagogue in the early morning and evening, I would miss him dreadfully.

And so my sister and brother departed. I continued to avoid my stepmother whenever possible, spending as much time as I could at the double-fronted house with my grandparents, Hana Tzirl and my cousins Baya and little Mendl, now five years old. Despite the dawn of a new political era in the outside world, our daily life became subdued and I longed for the letters that arrived unfailingly each week. Sarah wrote of the city: the tall buildings with their ornate facades, wrought iron balconies and stucco curlicues; cobbled avenues and the clatter of horses' hooves; smoke that billowed into the air from the factories; the lamplighters who illuminated iron gas lamps along the streets at dusk so that people could go out at night without a lantern. She wrote about books and plays and writers: Russian ones that I had heard of like Tolstoy and Turgenev, and foreign ones that I hadn't: Shakespeare and Balzac, Ibsen and Goethe. I lay in bed at night trying to imagine what her life was like, but I couldn't.

Naftula wrote about the routine at yeshiva and his fellow students. He seemed to thrive on the brutal early starts, rising at five o'clock for a two-hour lecture before breakfast. These were followed by morning and afternoon services, evening prayers and study sessions that could last until ten o'clock at night. For my part, I could think of nothing worse. He described how the scholars sat in pairs poring over a different passage of the Talmud each day, questioning each other about its meanings and messages, delving into the text in a hair-splitting search for any paradox or relevance that could reveal a greater truth not already outlined in the existing commentaries and rabbinical responses. Meals at the yeshiva were poor. Naftula was surviving on little more than a breakfast of bread and water then liquid *kasha* for lunch and supper. Many of the boys came from impoverished families and their maintenance was paid by contributions collected from members of their shtetl. But the better off received food parcels from home and, once she realized, Baba set herself to work preparing packages of bread, *kolbasa* and cookies to send to Skvira so that Naftula wouldn't have to suffer a diet of gruel.

While the rest of the family devoured letters from Sarah in Kiev and Naftula in Skvira, Zayde avidly consumed the news from Petrograd in the Russian press. Things weren't looking good. Kerensky's position seemed to be weakening. One day it seemed the tsar might return, the next that the socialists would form a democratic government. My family prayed that it would be the latter, with Kerensky at its head. But there were too many initials and so very many groups – SRs and SDs, Lefts and Rights, Mensheviks and Bolsheviks, Cadets and Monarchists – that I found it all impossible to follow. I couldn't read Russian properly and picked up only scraps of information when I was with Zayde. My father, of course, paid no attention to the upheavals going on in the distant northern capital, a city he was only dimly aware of.

Just as the first snows of the winter began to fall and fears of finding sufficient fuel to last until spring were taking precedence over the political squabbling in Petrograd, we heard news of an event that shocked everyone. There had been a coup. Some radical called Lenin had seized power. Nobody, not even the newspaper men, seemed to know what would happen next. How long could Lenin and his Bolsheviks keep power? And what would they do with it? We soon learned that many of the leading Bolsheviks were Jewish – Trotsky, Lenin's right hand man, the most prominent among them – so we were reassured that, if they remained in control, the country would not return to the bad old days of the tsars. But at the same time, we gradually became aware that attitudes toward Jews were hardening among the Ukrainians and Poles. They were saying that the October Revolution, as the coup had been dubbed, was a plot hatched by the Jews to grab power. It didn't make much sense. Lenin wasn't a Jew after all, or we didn't think so anyway. And besides, the Bolsheviks appeared to be threatening dealers and merchants like my grandfather. In the Pale, most traders were Jewish, so how could the putsch be a Jewish plot?

Lenin's men took control of Russia promising to end the war. Everybody was weary of the fighting, which appeared to be achieving nothing. And at first it seemed that the Bolsheviks were as good as their word: they begged the European powers for peace and managed to extricate thousands of Russian troops. Over the weeks that followed, the railways became a teeming mass of humanity. Not even Zayde would dare go to the train station in Popilna now; his once daily haunt was heaving with unwashed bodies, many racked with disease and crawling with lice as soldiers dribbled back home from distant lands, weak, thin and bedraggled like stray cats after a storm. From the windows of the double-fronted house I watched the slow, trudging progress through town of these grey bundles of bones, men who had once represented the tsar's brave army. Baba was terrified lest these pitiful creatures, who looked too exhausted to lay a hand on anyone, rape her daughter and granddaughters and insisted that we stay indoors.

But other townsfolk took pity on the returning troops and went out of their way to offer them soup and give them any old clothes or shoes they could spare. Even after three and a half years of wartime hardships, it was clear that the privation we had all suffered was nothing compared with the needs of the soldiers. But week after week the ragged creatures kept on coming, more and more of them, until people began to worry that if they kept giving their food and clothing away, they would have nothing left. And as the months passed, the reality dawned that the pale, unshaven men criss-crossing the countryside with guns couldn't all be soldiers returning to their homes after all. So who were these men? It eventually became clear that bands of armed thugs were roaming the land. It was impossible to tell who was who. But gradually all those generous souls in Pavolitch who had been welcoming the soldiers home with hot soup instead began hiding away their potatoes and their winter boots, lest the men take them all.

Although the Bolsheviks were pulling Russia out of the Great War, they had failed to deliver peace. The October Revolution had given way to anarchy. Just as one war was ending, another was beginning, as if the wives, mothers, sisters and grandmothers of Russia hadn't suffered enough in the last four years. And this time it was much closer to home. While the Great War was fought on distant battlefields with unfamiliar names written in unknown alphabets, the Civil War tore right through the former lands of the Pale, ripping out the hearts of villages and scattering their limbs in the snow. Crawling out of the woodwork came rebels and hoodlums, peasants and ex-army officers representing every kind of faction, every ideology imaginable. Some fought for Communism, others for Nationalism, Anarchism, Freedom or Holy Russia. Each recruited fighters to his cause, often luring the impoverished and the illiterate with the promise of food and action, arming them with guns brought back from the war – the other war – and hidden in hayricks or underground hideouts.

Having previously dismissed my grandmother's fears about the return-ing troops violating her family as Baba's paranoid imagination, now I, too, was scared. The newly created *banda* of soldiers were everywhere. All over Pavolitch, stories of their atrocities were rife. One woman had a rifle pointed at her as she collected her laundry from the line outside her house and all her husband's newly washed clothes were stolen. Another had cigarettes stubbed out on her face and arms when she refused to let soldiers into her house. Most terrifying of all, I heard gossip that one of my friends had been raped, although the family tried to keep it quiet.

From our own experience and the accounts my grandfather read in the paper, it seemed that each banda was competing to be more blood-thirsty than the last. They appeared to take pride in acts of rape and pillage, mutilation and murder. Their armies were each represented by a color, like pieces in a giant board game. Every banda was competing against all the others, occasionally forging an alliance to gang up on one enemy, only to break the pact a few months later and start fighting again. There were Reds, Whites, Greens and sometimes even Red-Greens and White-Greens[1] and names that instilled fear: Petlyura, Makhno, Zeleny, Denikin. The Greens took their name from their little flat caps and those of Zeleny's men were yellow. Makhno's anarchist fighters wore black hats and carried black flags crudely painted with the words "Liberty or Death". The Cossack fighters had scarlet caps, while the Bolsheviks deco-rated their arms with thick, blood-red bands. As well as those sporting what could pass for a uniform, there were other banda made up of rag-tag bunches of ruffians.

Banda of all colors passed through Pavolitch at one time or another in the years that followed the Bolshevik revolution. Some marched swiftly on in search of the latest enemy, others stayed for days or even weeks. One banda would be bedraggled and hungry, another brisk and ruthless. Sometimes my family escaped their atrocities, other times not. But all the rampaging parties had to live off the land they captured, with no estab-

1. Defectors who lived in the forests were knows as Greens. Both Reds and Whites attempted to recruit them to their cause, creating the Red-Greens and White-Greens.

lished government, no regime to feed and pay them. Typically it was the Jews that owned the stores, granaries and drinking dens, so naturally our communities were first in their firing line. But the violence and pogroms they reveled in weren't just a result of finding supplies. The banda harbored a deep hatred and resentment toward our studious, peace-loving people.

Germans and Nationalists

MY STEPMOTHER died suddenly in the spring of 1918, without the two of us ever making our peace. Her marriage to Tata had lasted just three years. On her deathbed she asked my forgiveness for taking our father away from us, but I couldn't give it. I felt guilty for feeling the way I did, but I was glad she would soon be gone. Many years later, however, I finally began to regret my stubbornness toward Rivka. She wasn't really an ogre and who could blame her for trying to stop me from walking into the living room in muddy boots or for making provisions last as long as possible in wartime? I was an obstinate stepdaughter who did all I could to make her life impossible. Eventually I came to realize, as my father had repeatedly tried to persuade me at the time, that Rivka was a good woman who cared about our family and always tried to do her best for us.

Once my stepmother died, I had Tata to myself at long last. My life took on a new routine. Rachel was at heder all day and finally my father consented for me to take over the running of the household. I learned to cook and keep house, sew and clean and, with plenty of assistance from Baba, bake. I rose early to prepare breakfast as best I could. By now many basic foodstuffs were very scarce. Ration cards had been issued and I queued for hours before being assigned my small quota of bread and sunflower oil. Thankfully we still had our own supply of wheat, too, but I cut the bread thinly to make it last longer. If tea was hard to come by, I would economize by mixing it with dried lime flowers plucked from the trees. Tata never mentioned the tea, but I did notice at these times that he drank less than the prodigious quantities he was accustomed to.

Tata continued to work at the mill he was assigned to during the war and, while he was out, he insisted that I return to my grandparents' house for it wasn't safe for a sixteen year old girl to be at home alone. It had become common for soldiers to show up at the door, proffering a slip of paper, which allegedly gave them the right to take food or furniture, or even to station themselves in the house. It was never entirely clear on whose authority these documents were signed (each bore the illegible signature of some supposed major or lieutenant), nor sometimes even which army the soldiers were fighting for, but there seemed to be a piece of paper to suit every purpose. They always carried a blue rubber stamp to make them official and it was best to take them seriously.

The way the soldiers knocked at the door usually gave a good indication of what they would be like. If they started pounding it with a stick and trying to kick it down, they clearly meant trouble. A bunch of hefty men in heavy boots was likely to barge in, push the occupants aside and tear the house apart searching for hidden supplies of food, money or arms. Anyone in the house would be lucky to get away unharmed. But a regular, rhythmic tap at the door meant that they would probably be courteous. Some peasant soldiers were so overawed by the sight of the books weighing down Zayde's shelves and Baba's china tableware that their jaws fell open and they dropped to one knee blessing my grandfather for the husks of dry bread he gave them.

Occasionally soldiers were apologetic about their demands. One night a gaggle of tired-looking Ukrainian nationalists turned up at the double-fronted house asking whether we could spare any chickens or eggs.

"The peasants are no longer bringing us any," Baba told them, but a single glance at their dejected faces, still pimpled with youth, and their thin, wretched bodies, was enough to melt her heart. They had no boots and the baggy peasant trousers hanging beneath their army greatcoats were covered in mud right up to the knees.

"We have some bread and cabbage, though," said Baba. "Why don't you sit down and I'll heat up the samovar to make you some tea." And while everybody else went to bed, Baba sat up drinking tea made from tree bark with the solders – she wasn't soft enough to give them proper tea, of course. The next morning she was bleary-eyed from lack of sleep, for the soldiers hadn't left until past one in the morning.

"Poor mites," Baba said, "they were so hungry and so young, just boys really. I don't know how they can call themselves independence fighters. They didn't look as if they could free a mouse from a trap, let alone a whole nation."

Those weak and hungry Ukrainian nationalists that Baba had taken pity on were, in early 1918, supposedly, representing our government. It was terribly difficult to keep track of who was in charge because it could change from week to week, but Ukraine seemed somehow to have become an independent state; its leadership, the Rada, was controlling more and more of the country as those pitiful, spotty youths wrested land from the Bolsheviks. But as the winter's snow finally melted away, the scrawny nationalists started disappearing from Pavolitch, too.

In their place came handsome, solid German soldiers with dignified faces and huge red moustaches. Their uniforms weren't tatty and thread-bare, but thick, warm and elegant. They wore gunmetal grey tunics, long woolen coats and kidney-colored tin pudding bowls on their heads, which they fastened under their fleshy chins with sparkling brass straps. They paraded around the town on glossy horses that they allowed the children to pet. Zayde explained to me that the Bolsheviks had finally signed a deal with the Germans that meant we were no longer officially at war with them. Now the Germans were occupying our land and I wondered why Russia had been fighting them at all. They were by far the nicest soldiers to have set foot in Pavolitch. While the Germans were with us, we felt safe. They were civilized men who brought with them law and order. They paid proper prices for the grain they purchased and their money kept the Jewish shops and tradesmen in towns like ours afloat. My grandfather's income increased thanks to the soldiers' custom and, with the extra cash, he could once again stock up on tea, salt, sugar, eggs and butter: goods that had been luxuries for many months.

But with prices rising often by the day, it was difficult to know how much the produce should cost. The peasant woman that my grandmother bought milk from charged forty-five kopeks for a pail one day, fifty the next. Soon it would cost a whole ruble. The price of bread doubled, trebled, despite the fact that wheat made up less than half the loaf. Even paper money was changing hands: tsarist notes in exchange for Kerensky rubles, and the long, oblong Ukrainian state bank certificates that looked like toy money, with a picture of a mustached peasant and his wife printed in green ink on one side, circulated at the same value as credit notes.

We Jews could talk to the Germans in Yiddish and they would nod and reply in their own tongue, laughing at what they considered our bastardized form of their language, and offering sweets to the children. Sometimes my cousin Mendl, now a charming boy of seven with big, dark eyes and a cheeky grin, together with his little friends, would go out to play with the soldiers who joked with them and hauled them up to sit on their great, solid knees just as they would their own children.

But when I or any of my friends walked past them, the youngsters were quickly pushed aside.

"*Hübsch, sehr hübsch!*"[1] they called out, the boldest even daring to wolf-whistle, pinch our cheeks or take hold of a girl's arm, while his friends guffawed from the sidelines. We could understand their language perfectly and knew they were trying their best to flatter us. In fact, some girls I knew rather enjoyed the attention; no Jewish boy would ever dare approach us like that. But woe betide any young lady who let her God-fearing mother or grandmother catch a glimpse of such antics. She would be banned from leaving the house for days while ferocious Yiddish curses were hurled in the soldiers' direction from behind closed doors.

That summer Pavolitch enjoyed a greater sense of peace and security than it had for years. More food was available, and besides, there were berries to pick in the woods and mushrooms in the fields. It was a joy to be outside after the long months trapped fearfully indoors and I moved between my father's cottage and the double-fronted house at will. My grandmother taught me how to make jam, and to pickle the mushrooms so they would last until winter, and I carried my jars of preserves proudly back to Tata.

But by the time the summer was drawing to a close, our German protectors were departing as best they could, back to their own girls and their own children. They had lost the war and their leaders wanted them to play no further part in it. Many had trouble leaving, for explosions along the railway line could be heard even in Pavolitch. A rogue by the name of Petlyura had been released from prison and was regrouping the Ukrainian nationalists. One of his first actions was to order railway stations to be attacked so that he could grab the weapons of the evacuating German soldiers, which were more sophisticated and in better condition than the guns and grenades that his own men had stowed away in chicken sheds and stables across the land. He and his banda didn't only steal weaponry, they took clothes, money, munitions, trucks, carts and horses, anything

1. Very pretty.

that would help them to seize Kiev and the government of the land for themselves.

Thieving was a way of life to them and in the towns and villages Petlyura's men passed through, they stole first and foremost from the Jews. All across the land, the experience was the same. They didn't knock at the door, but hammered and kicked, giving an indication of what to expect. Once I was alone in my father's cottage when the Petlyurists came. I hid in the wardrobe upstairs rather than answer the door, my heart pounding. First they tried kicking it down, then they shot bullets at the hinges so that the door collapsed. They walked in and dropped cigarettes on the floor, grinding the stubs with the heel of their boots, crushing shreds of paper and tobacco into the earth floor that I spent hours sweeping and watering so that it looked like polished tiles. Seeing that there was nothing for them, they soon walked out, and I could hear them hammering on the neighbors' doors, shooting other people's door hinges, and shouting, "You filthy yids!" as they pushed occupants aside and took all they could find: food, clothing, silver and especially money.

Looking at the mess the soldiers had made, I myself felt trampled, violated. I wanted to scream, but was too terrified to utter a sound. I knew I was lucky not to have been discovered. I surely would have been raped or tortured. But I had tried so hard to make a home for my father, to keep the little cottage clean and tidy, to provide a proper meal each morning and evening. Now the door was hanging off its hinges, the floor consisted of mounds of churned up earth and the contents of cupboards and drawers were strewn across the table. I sat down with my head in my hands and wept.

Our family was luckier than most. My grandmother was much loved by everyone who knew her and the Ukrainians who used to come to help her with the household chores would do anything for her. At the first sign of trouble, if it was safe to go outside, we were all under orders to head straight for the house of Katarina or Pritska, the now middle-aged ladies who for years had helped my grandmother with the laundry. Baba had a little routine she would follow. First she hid away her precious Sabbath candlesticks in the loft, along with the silver cutlery and spice boxes, then she bundled together all the money in the front pocket of her apron, filled a string bag with bread and any other food she could lay her hands on, then herded the family out of the house and into the Ukrainian quarter.

We were enormously grateful to our Ukrainian friends. Both Katarina and Pritska were born of solid Ukrainian stock; their wide faces and flaxen hair bore testament to the fact. Petlyura's men wouldn't come near them. Another safe haven was my grandparents' neighbor Zhukov's. He and his four sons welcomed us at all hours of the day or night. Of course his tax collector son still felt guilty for his part in the candle tax incident that had landed Baba in jail, but we could all laugh about it now. That whole episode belonged to another world. He and his family more than compensated by allowing us to shelter in their back room, sometimes for days on end.

Ever since the Petlyurists had broken into my father's cottage, I had returned to my grandparents' house while Tata was at work. But daily routines became increasingly disrupted. Sometimes I lost track of how long I had spent with Katarina or Zhukov. Days and nights passed with the dull thump of distant gunfire an almost constant backdrop to our lives. It became difficult to ensure that all the meals we ate were kosher when our Ukrainian hosts prepared food for us. Katarina baked bread and cookies, which she brought out to us with fresh butter, milk and sour pickles. Dairy goods were a rare treat, even if the hands that milked the cow were not Jewish hands. I told myself that sometimes it was better not to think too much about it and that God would surely understand.

We did try our best, however, to keep the Sabbath holiday sacred. My father worked from early morning until nightfall at the government mill, but dashed back across the bridge into town like a huge, flapping raven on Fridays to get home in time for the lighting of the candles. Sometimes Tata, Rachel and I ate our Sabbath meal alone, and I had the honor of lighting the candles, chanting the sacred incantations as I did so. More often, we shared the holiday meal at my grandparents'. Especially with winter on its way, it was too difficult to light two stoves, to keep two houses warm and, ever since the Germans departed, to find sufficient food for two Sabbath meals. Besides, it didn't feel like a real Sabbath when we were on our own. Together with my grandparents, Hana Tzirl, Baya and Mendl, we could sing the traditional holiday songs and, for a few hours at least, forget about the terror raging on our doorstep. Often our beloved Haskl, the hunchback, was there, too, and numerous other guests who, for one reason or another, were unable to spend the Sabbath with their own families.

Bolsheviks

By 1919 it was no longer safe to take cover in Katarina's or Pritska's home, so they would hide us in their barns and cellars where we burrowed under hay or among sacks of grain and potatoes to try to keep warm. One freezing January night our whole family slept in Katarina's barn, huddling together in our blankets and covering ourselves in straw in a bid to keep the frost at bay. My sleep was fitful, jolted by a fresh burst of gunfire every few hours. By morning the shots sounded like they were coming from the very next street and I lay motionless, not daring to move or utter a sound. Were we still safe? How long would we have to stay here?

Finally I heard the creaking of packed snow outside the barn. Could this be the end? I shut my eyes in dread and felt Baba and Rachel, who were lying on either side of me, stiffen in fear, too. But it was only Katarina. Her plump face appeared in the doorway, washed with tears, and we all pulled ourselves awkwardly upright, shaking limbs and pulling straw out of our stockings.

"In God's name, Katarina, what's happened?" whispered Baba, seeing the petrified look in her pale Ukrainian eyes.

"Pani Pessy, I'm so sorry. You will have to go. Petlyura's banda has put notices up all over town. They say that anyone found hiding a Jew will be killed. I'm scared for my son, Pani Pessy. If they take him, I'll have nobody. I can't let you stay here. Please don't think badly of me."

Baba nodded. "Of course not, Katarina, we understand," she said, brushing herself down.

"Let me ask Pritska. She might have a safer place where you can hide," said Katarina, and she ran off. A few minutes later, we heard Pritska's voice in the yard. She stepped into the barn looking worried.

"What can I do for you, Pani Pessy? You have always been so good to us. I'll do whatever I can to help you," she babbled, crossing herself repeatedly. "You know I can't risk letting you stay in the house, but the cellar is still safe. If we take some of the potatoes up to the kitchen there will be enough room for all of you, and you can hide under the sacks if anyone comes. You'll be quite safe, I'm sure of it," she clucked, patting down our unkempt hair, and led us, trailing after her like young chicks, back to her house. We walked in convoy, carefully and in silence, ducking behind fences and jumping over garden walls to avoid being seen lest we should offer neighbors reason to gossip, to denounce both ourselves and Pritska and deliver certain death to us all.

I lost track of the amount of time we sheltered in the musty cellar, wallowing in a sea of muddy, damp-smelling potatoes. It was dark day and night, and airless, and there was nowhere to pee. We had a candle, but Baba kept blowing it out every time she heard a noise up above for fear that we would be discovered. I tried to sleep. I attempted to guess what time it was. I spent long hours planning meals I would cook for Tata when finally we got out – if we got out. But thinking about food too much made me hungry so I tried to sleep again. Every once in a while, Pritska opened the trap door above our heads and told us that it was safe to come out and use the privy in the yard if we needed to. Then she sent us back down the ladder with bowls of warm cabbage and sour pickles. And finally, after an interminable period that Pritska insisted was a mere two days, the cracks of rifle fire came to a halt. The battle was over. The nationalists had retreated, ceding Pavolitch to the Bolsheviks.

When we finally left the cellar and crossed the Jewish quarter to make our way home, we were met by a sea of carnage. Wooden doors hung open, their paintwork sprayed with blood, lifeless limbs just visible beyond. The sound of babies wailing rent the air crying for their mothers who had been run through with bayonets. Weeping relatives were loading their loved ones onto carts for burial or dragging them indoors to be washed so they could say the *Kaddish* over them and complete the required seven days of mourning. The thick snow was criss-crossed with red-streaked channels indicating where bodies had been moved.

I walked as if in a dream. Nothing seemed real, as if we had entered a different universe, one in which we didn't belong. All those hours in the cellar that had felt at the time like a form of suffering had saved us from this: suffering on a scale that I could not imagine. It seemed incredible that these were the very same streets that I walked down almost every day of my life, the very same townsfolk that I had grown up among. None of them looked at us – a group of ordinary people, a little bedraggled, but unbloodied – as we passed. I found myself gagging and it was all I could do to prevent my insides from coming up.

Tata hustled Rachel and me ahead of him, shielding his own eyes with his hand and urging us to do the same. Behind me I could hear Baba's voice, higher than usual and cracking with the fear she was trying not to show.

"Mendl, stay with me. Come closer!"

Then Mendl's voice, "But I don't understand. Why are they lying there in the cold? Can't we do anything to help them?"

Now Baya, bossy, twelve years old: "Idiot, Mendl, they're dead."

Hana Tzirl chivvied her two children along and we left them as they turned off to the double-fronted house at the edge of the Jewish quarter and we continued to my father's lodgings. Tata immediately turned to his prayer books and started to chant fervently, swaying his body so vigorously that he almost knocked his head against the wall. Never had I seen him pray so passionately, so violently. Rachel and I held each other tight, tears pouring down our cheeks.

We weren't the only Jews in Pavolitch to owe our survival to Ukrainian neighbors. But as time progressed it became harder for our fellow Pavolitchers to protect us. Loyal families like the Zhukovs would never turn their backs on their friends, but the punishment for anyone found to be aiding or hiding Jews was so severe that everybody became cautious and fearful. One man was shot just for offering food to a Jewish family that had lost everything in the Petlyurist pogrom. Anyone who had sheltered Jews was tortured mercilessly first. We felt guilty for inflicting such terrible danger on our friends, while they felt guilty for our suffering.

Now that the Bolsheviks were occupying our town, though, the guilt and fear could lessen a little. There were some unpleasant individuals sporting the red bands of the Communists, but generally they were more educated and less thuggish than the Petlyurist peasant rabble. And their revered leader, Lenin, preached equality for Jews and other minorities, so we expected to see no more pogroms for now. In fact, some of the new soviet officials in Pavolitch were Jewish. Jews had been barred from public office under the tsars and, for the first time in our lives, we no longer had to cower fearfully before authority.

Although attacks on Jewish homes diminished, it didn't mean an end to our worries. The Bolsheviks viewed merchants like my grandfather as class enemies. They also needed grain to feed their supporters in the cities, which were running out of food. Zayde knew that a knock at the door was inevitable, but when it came, he was still caught by surprise.

My grandparents knew young Vanya well. He was Sasha the Baker's son and lived down the road. They had watched him grow up, from a wailing baby in his mother's arms to a smart young schoolboy and later a recruit in the tsar's army. When he came to the house, Baba almost shrieked as she pulled open the door. She barely recognized him in the black leather coat that reached down to his calves and heavy black boots. In his hand was a wooden truncheon. He was surrounded by a group of youths all in identical black garb, talking loudly to one another, but Vanya was clearly their leader. My grandfather hurried to the door, alerted by the commotion and the rush of cold air.

"Vanya!" Zayde exclaimed, "What are you doing here, young man?" Vanya looked a little sheepish, perhaps embarrassed that his fellow Bolsheviks should see that he had associated with class enemies like my grandfather in the past. One of his Red Guards brushed Baba aside and headed toward the warehouse.

"The Bolsheviks are in charge now and we need to take your grain to feed the workers in the towns," the youth dictated as he stamped through the house.

"But what about us? Who will feed us if you take away our grain?" Baba countered.

"You bourgeois! You're all the same! The workers and peasants need bread if they are going to build socialism. Bread, Land and Freedom!"

Zayde just sat in his chair and watched as Vanya and his friends shoveled away his already diminished pyramids of grain until all that was left was a few thin scatterings of yellow spread across the grey, stone floor like dirt that had come in from the street and needed sweeping up. He knew he couldn't argue with them. He'd heard the news on the grapevine. Grain merchants all over Ukraine were having their stores ransacked. It took the youths half an hour to empty the warehouse. When the last shovel-load was piled onto their wagon outside, one of the young men returned, swept all of my grandfather's papers off his desk, picked up his set of heavy, brass scales and rested them across his leather-clad shoulder.

"You don't need those," Baba told him, quietly but firmly.

"What did you say?" the youth scowled and turned quickly to face her.

"Leave the scales, son. You don't need them. No need to weigh it."

"I guess you're right, old woman," he said as he tipped his body sideways and let the scales drop to the ground with an almighty clatter that made the whole warehouse shake. Then he turned and walked back out through the open door.

Zayde picked up two of his brass weights and held them tenderly to his face. He fell back onto a chair and began to shake uncontrollably as Baba placed her arm across his shoulder.

"Vanya, of all people," he muttered. "Young Vanya, who would have thought it?"

It was clear that from this day on our lives would never be the same again. Zayde appeared to age overnight. He became bitter and even fiercer than he was before, but he also became more determined: determined to overcome adversity, to keep his business going at all costs and against all odds, determined that his family would be one of those that survive. My grandmother had saved his precious scales, and that was a great blessing. Gradually, much more slowly than before, the mounds of wheat and rye and corn began to accumulate again. They grew nervously, lest they be so ruthlessly hacked away again, as if they were small animals poking their way gently out of a burrow, uncertain about the light and noise outside.

The peasants that came to sell their produce were more timid, too. They had also suffered the forced requisitions and some of the wealthier ones – those that the Bolsheviks called *kulaks* – had been robbed of everything by the youths in black leather. My grandfather's major contractors stayed away. Landowners whom Zayde had worked with for decades disappeared overnight. We never discovered what had happened to them. No doubt their estates were confiscated; maybe worse, they may have been imprisoned or shot. Poritz Baskakov, whose custom my grandfather had lost the day Hana Tzirl got married, was stripped of all he owned.

All over Russia Bolshevik authorities were taking over towns and cities replacing local leaders or the tsar's loyal servants. And it wasn't just in Pavolitch that many of the men now sitting in the town hall were Jewish.

For the last twenty years a large number of Jews had been attracted to the revolutionary movement, their zeal for the Torah and the synagogue outstripped by their determination to create a new regime, a life in which everyone was equal and where nobody could be persecuted for the way they dressed or where they prayed. The same opportunities would be open to all. Now, they hoped, that utopia was on its way. The Jewish revolutionaries were bright, educated and vigorous, unlike the factory workers from the cities on whom their comrade Lenin also counted for support. The smart, young Jews made ideal civil servants, leaders of local soviets and state officials; they were assigned to civic posts across the country.

The anti-Semites in the lands that had belonged to the Pale didn't like this situation one bit. Many of them supported Petlyura and were resentful that the Bolsheviks and their Jewish followers had forced their man to retreat. They remembered how Jewish merchants had grown wealthier during the German occupation by selling goods to the foreign soldiers at prices the local peasants couldn't afford to pay. And now Jews were in the town hall ruling over land that the Ukrainians considered their own. Anger and resentment were brewing.

Just as they had in Pavolitch, Petlyura's rabble attempted to clear towns and villages of Jews before ceding them to the larger and better organized Red Army. Angry shouts of, "How long are you going to rule over us, Jewish wretches?", were soon followed by Petlyura's rallying cry: "Kill the Jews and the Jewish children!" Petlyura roused his followers into a drunken frenzy of killing and looting. The scenes that my family and I had witnessed in Pavolitch were repeated not only in the towns and cities that had suffered pogroms in the past, but in the countryside, too. Petlyura's men spared barely a single village or hamlet in the whole region. Entire streets were washed with rivers of blood and everywhere mounds of snow were tainted red.

Although my family had been saved from the carnage by the kindness of our Ukrainian friends, the images we had seen as we walked through the Jewish quarter once the banda had left continued to haunt my dreams. Almost every night I woke up in a sweat just as a burly peasant was about to cut me down with his scythe. I would lie in the dark too scared to move for a long time. In the next bed, Rachel tossed and turned, and occasionally screamed, in her sleep. She was clearly having nightmares, too.

When the Petlyurists reached Berdichev they began calling themselves
the Clans of Death as they swept through the city's Jewish quarter. Baba
heard about them from our childhood dressmaker, whom she had known
for years, having taken my mother and Hana Tzirl to him for their fittings,
and later me and my sisters. Now an old man, he had also lost part of his
arm in the massacre. He had given up his shop years before, as nobody
could afford to have new dresses made anymore, but he had continued to
mend clothes and make alterations. With only one arm, he would have
to give this up, too. Compared with others, though, he was lucky. Most
families in the city had lost at least one member of their family.

*

In February 1919, refugees began to reach Pavolitch from the nearby
towns of Brusilev, Vaselkov and Skvira. They travelled by train, piling
into wagons filled with soldiers who taunted and abused them, or onto
carriage roofs where they clung on like monkeys or perched like frozen
birds. Sometimes the railcars were so full that people had to smash windows to get out. Opposing armies stopped the trains, pulled men off and
shot them, seemingly for no reason at all, before the eyes of the other
travelers. A journey of only a few dozen miles could take days. Nobody
would use the railway in those days unless their life depended on it, but
the migrants were desperate.

The tales they recounted were dreadful. The banda had arrived carrying huge flaming torches. They marched from street to street throwing
bales of hay that had been set alight into all the houses, one after another
after another, until the whole Jewish quarter was burning. There was
no warning and those who managed to escape fled with nothing but the
clothes on their back. Many were trapped in their houses, especially the
old and the sick. Young mothers realized only once it was already too late
that a son or daughter must still be inside, burning to death.

Although my grandfather was harsh with his family and showed us
little sympathy, like all observant Jews, he took charity very seriously.
And deep down, buried far inside himself, was a warm heart. He took
pity on one young woman: a tall, willowy, but almost silent, creature
named Chaya who had lost everyone but her last remaining child, a baby
boy, and the as yet unborn child she was carrying. He invited the mother
and son to live in the double-fronted house, and there they remained for

several months. I tried not to think about what Chaya and her family had been through lest her experiences increase the ferocity of my nightmares. But I noticed how she flinched at the sight of fire. She shielded her eyes when Baba lit the stoves and, although it was winter and terribly cold, she would sit as far from the heat as she could.

My grandfather continued to garner information from the synagogue and the newspapers, but mostly he kept it to himself. The news was too shocking, too horrible, to share. But keeping up with events enabled him to predict which banda might be upon us next. He knew that the Bolsheviks' grip on power was weaker in our area than it was elsewhere in Russia and that the Petlyurists hadn't given up. In the city of Zhitomir, they had recently carried out a massacre at the railway station. Seventeen Jews were killed, many of them old men on their way home from synagogue.

Just as Zayde had warned, as the snow receded, Petlyura's men were marching back toward Pavolitch. My father was particularly shaken by the news from Zhitomir. The synagogue had always been his haven, a place where he could still immerse himself in sacred texts and block out the outside world that even he was now, reluctantly, a part of. Like Zayde, he, too, began listening to the gossip reverberating around the synagogue and the mill where he worked. News travels fast when people are desperate and fleeing for their lives, and we heard about the latest events from Zhitomir well before any newspaper could report, print and circulate stories of them.

Refugees were everywhere and all recounted an identical tale. Not satisfied with the bloodbath at the railway station, Ukrainian peasants had started a rumor that spread around the whole of Zhitomir in a matter of hours. They said that during the brief period that the Red Army had occupied the city, the Jews who had taken charge of the local government had put to death nearly two thousand Christians. Who were these condemned men? Why and where were they killed? Nobody knew the answer to these questions – because there had been no mass execution. The rumors were pure fantasy aimed at inciting hatred against the Jews. Thankfully the stories of Christian carnage provided a warning and, when the pogrom began, all those who were able had already scattered to the wind or sought refuge with Ukrainian friends or neighbors. The only Jews left were the elderly or infirm, pregnant women and nursing mothers.

But the slaughter went ahead regardless. Snatches of stories circulated among those who had escaped.

"Did you hear about the old man on his way to synagogue with his prayer shawl over his arm? He was the first to die."

"Was he the one the banda stood against a tree and shot?"

"I saw it with my own eyes. He was a stocky soldier, filthy looking, with hunched shoulders and a beak-like nose. He fired at the old man with a rusty rifle. I nearly jumped out of my skin. That was when I ran."

"But the bullet didn't kill him, you know."

"It didn't?"

"No, the old man dragged himself toward the synagogue on his hands and knees. I suppose he wanted to die in God's own house. But he didn't make it. Collapsed in the street just yards from the door."

"Oh, that poor man. What a humiliation!"

"That's right, and you want to know the worst of it? The banda stood and watched him, great big grins on their ugly faces."

Others spoke of seeing people having their eyes gouged out, their clothes torn off and the skin of their shoulders engraved by knife-blade with the badge of rank of their killer. I found myself gagging when I heard the stories and tried not to listen. But many people in Pavolitch were fascinated by details of the pogrom and the atrocities seemed to be all anyone could talk about for days. The pogrom had lasted five days. Over three hundred Jews had been killed.

A Hanging

By THE spring, all the talk in Pavolitch was of the White Army under General Denikin. With the Don Cossacks who fought for him, Denikin was marching from the east. People said Denikin's soldiers were professional warriors, hand-picked for their cruelty, and all over six feet tall. I imagined an army of giants, marching side by side, making the ground shake as their gargantuan feet all hit the ground in unison. They carried the best weapons, supplied by Western powers that were afraid of the Communists ruling Russia. But we were more scared of the Whites than the Communists. They carried before them the most terrifying reputation for slaughtering Jews.

The first I heard of Denikin was after he razed the whole town of Brusilev to the ground. Brusilev was to the north of Pavolitch and we knew it well as it lay on the road to Makarov. My grandfather had often stopped at a tavern there for a glass of whisky while his balagula fed and watered the horses. Who knew what had become of the tavern-keeper now? The Whites had barged their way into Jewish homes, drawn their great swords and cut the inhabitants down regardless of age or sex. It was clear from the stories of those who had survived that the soldiers' orders were not to rob and plunder, but simply to kill as many Jews as possible. Equally clear was that they had carried out their orders with relish. People were cowering in fear in attics and basements, but Denikin's men dragged them from their hiding places and slashed them across the chest. Anyone who tried to escape by running into the street was shot in the back.

Baba tried to keep Hana Tzirl and her grandchildren indoors to shelter us from the talk of what else had happened in Brusilev, but terrible news has a way of permeating, like smoke, whether we wanted to listen or not.

Somehow we knew without being told that scores of women had been raped before they were killed. We knew of the grenades that were thrown into cellars, blowing up entire families. We knew petrol had been poured over the synagogue and the houses of the wealthy and that they had burned to the ground until all that remained was a spiral of black smoke and charred remains, like a pie that had been left in the oven too long.

When news reached Pavolitch of a pogrom in Khodarkov, we were petrified. Our great-grandmother Leah still lived in the town, with her daughter Babtsy and her family. There were no survivors, some people said. Others believed one or two families might have escaped. The Cossacks had rounded up all the Jews and accompanied them to the sugar beet factory that stood beside the lake. Then they herded them past the plant to the water's edge. To terrified screams and cries for mercy, the soldiers forced the Jews to continue walking into the lake until the icy water entered their bones and froze them to death or pulled them down into its depths. Bloated bodies could be seen bobbing on the lake's surface or washed up on the shore for days.

At last a letter arrived from Kiev to tell us that our relatives had survived. Leah, Babtsy, her husband Moishe and the children had hidden in the cellar beneath Moishe's watch shop. Babtsy had stuffed her young children's mouths with rags to stop them from uttering a sound when they heard the Cossacks destroying the shop upstairs. Moishe winced at the noise of his precious display cabinets being beaten to splinters, panes of glass being smashed into tiny shards and his valuable clocks hitting the wooden floor above their heads.

At last the heavy thump of hob-nailed boots above them receded and they dared to breathe again. But they weren't yet ready to risk emerging from their shelter. They listened carefully and heard the sounds of distant screams. They sensed the sweetness of the lilac that drenched the town in springtime being overpowered by the smell of fear and the stench of burning houses. They remained in the cellar all night and the next day rose to witness the devastation. Their town lay in ruins. Houses were smoldering all around them and the lakeside was littered with pale corpses. Barely stopping for a moment to grab a handful of belongings, Moishe and Babtsy fled to the railway station, a young child in each of their arms and a third running by their side, while Leah, over seventy years old now and much less vigorous than she used to be, stumbled along behind them holding onto the belt of Babtsy's coat. They took the first train to Kiev and remained there with Moishe's parents and sisters who harbored them through the years that followed.

Now that it was spring and the ground was no longer frozen solid, Denikin's murderers found new ways of torturing and killing. Although nobody we knew had seen it with their own eyes, it was said that the Whites dug big pits in Jewish cemeteries and, when their pogrom was over, they carted all the Jews away in trucks – the dead and the wounded piled in together – and tipped them into the mass grave. When all the bodies were unloaded, the soldiers threw in buckets of lime as a disinfectant then filled in the pit. Anyone still alive when they landed in the pit would have been burnt horrifically by the lime, then suffocate as the earth was piled on top of them. It was said that later, when it was safe for the townsfolk to emerge from their hiding places, they dug up the mass graves. But the faces and bodies were so disfigured by lime that not a single person could be recognized. Their jewelry had been stolen and the only way people could identify their loved ones was by their buttons.

Sometimes Jewish men and women themselves were forced to dig the communal burial pits, haunted by the bullying laughs and taunts of the soldiers nearby. Women were threatened if they started to cry as they shoveled earth for their children's graves. Elsewhere, the rumors went, Jews were rounded up by the banks of a river and ordered to strip down to their underwear. Then the Cossacks lined them up, facing the water, and fired three volleys of bullets at their backs.

I didn't know whether to believe what the people around me were saying or not. It sounded so inhuman that I found it unimaginable. How could these men hate Jews so much that it brought them to murder in such a routine and systematic way? Looking back, I probably chose to be skeptical about what I heard of Denikin's methods – which turned out, after all, to be true – rather than have my faith in humanity completely destroyed.

Despite all I had heard about Denikin and the White Army, when his Cossack warriors approached Pavolitch, some sensation deep within me made me believe that we might be lucky. It was said that merchants like my grandfather, who had suffered under the Bolsheviks, would be allowed to flourish again under the Whites. And some maintained that, despite his cruelties, Denikin was well disposed toward Jews that had shown no loyalty to the Communists. What was more, herring, a favorite delicacy that we hadn't tasted since the war began, had started arriving in the region from the Don Basin, the Cossack homeland. Maybe it was a good omen.

They arrived just after Passover. Each year, in the days before the holiday, my grandmother had all the furniture taken out of the house to be cleaned. The tables and benches had to be scrubbed thoroughly to remove even the tiniest trace of leaven, which was forbidden during Passover, and the whole house was swept, mopped and polished – even the corners where nobody looked. The exterior was always whitewashed before Passover so that it was as clean and bright as the interior. When we were younger, Rachel and I had joined in slaking the lime, taking care not to spill a drop on our skin, because it burned like hot coals. Now we were busy making sure our father's lodgings were spick and span. Baya refused to dirty her hands with any kind of labor, so Baba summoned Katarina and Pritska, who came to help her rub down the walls with damp sand to fill in the cracks before setting at it with huge brushes and rags.

But many goods were in short supply that spring. Yoshe the Storekeeper had run out of lime and didn't know when his next supply wagon would arrive. There was nothing we could do; the house would have to remain as it was – only half painted and covered with sand – until after the holiday. Katarina and Pritska laundered the curtains and Baba brought down the special Passover plates and dishes from the loft. My father, assisted by my little cousin Mendl, fetched the matzo water in large wooden pails that Tata carried on a pole over his shoulders. It was the one time in the year when the men fetched water rather than the women. Baba cooked the matzos for both our households, while all of us grandchildren joined in. Making matzos was a sacred job and even boys could participate.

The whole family celebrated Passover at the double-fronted house as usual. Sarah was home from Kiev for the holiday and Naftula had returned from the yeshiva in Skvira. Mendl, as the youngest child, asked the Four Questions about the unleavened bread and the bitter herbs, and the whole family sang the responses that tell the story of the Exodus of the Israelites from ancient Egypt. The *seder* lasted well into the evening, but when it was over I bombarded my brother and sister with questions. Had they seen pogroms like we had? Were their lessons difficult? What new friends had they made?

Naftula was unwilling to say very much at all. He had always been softly-spoken, but the yeshiva seemed to have made him positively silent. I longed to hear about his new life, to listen to him sing, and to embrace him like I did when he was a boy. But every time he came home he was too exhausted and just wanted to sleep. Skvira had recently suffered a terrible pogrom and I wanted to know whether he had witnessed scenes like those we had passed in Pavolitch when the Petlyurists left, to find out if his dreams were haunted by death as mine were. But my brother refused to talk about it. All he seemed interested in was sleeping and washing his hands every few minutes, a religious observance he had picked up at the yeshiva, and one that I recognized from time spent watching the rabbi when I lived in Makarov as a little girl.

"But you just washed them!" Rachel would yell at her brother with a smirk, as he headed to the water pitcher in the kitchen yet again. Naftula mumbled something to himself and Rachel and I burst out laughing.

Sarah was happy to talk to us about Kiev. She described her friends, Mirl and Adele, who lived in the city, and a boy called Shaya who was in her class. She told us about the refugees who had flooded into the city from Moscow, where there was nothing to eat. Every house was filled to its bursting point with too many people. She brought news of Zayde's cousins who traded in geese at the market. Their house had been raided, and all their Kerensky rubles stolen, leaving them with only worthless Ukrainian *karbovantsy*. She recounted how the city authorities kept changing hands. One week they were Bolshevist, the next Petlyurist and then Denikinist. It was impossible to keep track.

In such terrible times, we were happy to all be together again for Passover. But we knew Denikin's army of giants would soon be upon us. I thought we would hear them coming, for I imagined that the ground would shudder beneath their feet like an earthquake. But they weren't really giants and they arrived without warning. We had no time to flee to Pritska's barn so we pelted up the stepladder to the attic and waited. All around I could hear doors being thrown open and screams rent the air. Hana Tzirl held her hands over Mendl's ears and pulled her young son to her chest. Babies wailed then all of a sudden stopped and I tried not to think why. I could hear mothers pleading with the soldiers to spare their children. I heard the sounds of a struggle, furniture crashing to the floor, glass breaking. Again came the noise of women screaming. Still we waited, holding hands, our breath fast and shallow. We could hear the shouts of the soldiers as clearly as if they were in the next room.

"Here is your commune for you! Here's your Jewish empire!"

"Open, you communist Jews, or we'll slit your bellies and drown you!"

We listened to the heavy sucking sound of many boots marching through the mud, then heard a knock at our door and a badly aimed kick that failed to dislodge it. I stopped breathing altogether for what felt like minutes on end.

"Nah, forget it," we heard a voice calling nearby. "Nobody in there, that'll be a bath-house – look at it." Some more squelching and a splash. Somebody had put his foot in the kaluzha outside the door, which was covered with slush.

"Damn your filth!" a harsh, Russian voice shouted. Then, at last, they were gone. We squeezed each other's hands with relief. Thank God for the shortage of lime that had made our grandparents' house look like a public bath!

*

Denikin's men stayed in the area for several months throughout the whole long, hot summer of 1919. They papered the walls with proclamations demanding the attention of our townsfolk in thick, black letters, calling them "Underlings of the Red Guard" and urging them to make their own pogroms against the Jews. Christians pasted crosses on their walls and hung crucifixes and icons in their windows to ensure their houses would not be targeted next time the Whites went on a rampage.

When that time came, again, the Cossacks arrived quietly for such big men. I was alone with my father in the wooden cottage when we heard the soldiers outside. There was no time to escape to Katarina's barn, so we cowered in the wardrobe upstairs, listening to the shouts and the screams.

After an hour or so, all seemed quiet outside. It appeared that our street had been spared. We tiptoed back down the wooden stairs and almost immediately I heard a gentle tapping like a little bird at the front door. That was our code. It must be one of the family. Sure enough, Baba was at the door bent almost double and clutching her stomach. Her hands were covered in blood and I could see it seeping through the dark fabric of her dress.

"It's Berl. Get the doctor! Quick!" she said to my father, then turned on her heels and started shuffling back to the double-fronted house.

"But Baba, you're bleeding! You need to sit down!" I cried after her.

"It's not me you need to worry about, it's your grandfather."

While Tata ran off to find Moishe the Doctor, I followed my grandmother home. Despite the fact that she was old and clearly in great pain, Baba moved quickly. She didn't want to waste her breath talking. When we arrived, I opened the door to see Zayde lying face up on the kitchen floor. I gasped, but I could see that he was still alive. Hana Tzirl, Baya and Rachel soon emerged from Zhukov's house next door where they had been hiding, and we all crowded around Zayde trying to find out what had happened to him.

An hour before, five huge men had burst in through the front door. Baba said she really thought they might be giants after all. They were clad in tatty greatcoats that reached almost to the floor. Grease pencil marks indicated their rank, outlining stars that had once been sewn onto their shoulder straps. Long, shining swords were tucked into their belts and they carried rifles fixed with rusty bayonets, which they used to poke Mendl who hadn't managed to escape. With their huge frames, they seemed to fill up the whole house. The tops of their heads almost touched the ceiling and, with each great stride, they squeezed my grandparents into the corners of the room where they cowered, shaking.

The Whites weren't like the anarchists who burst in and began smashing the furniture to pieces. They had brains and intuition that they used to figure out just where their victims might be hiding money or jewelry or hoarding food. The soldiers sniffed around like dogs, tapping at walls and floor boards, listening for a hollow echo that might indicate a hiding place. They found nothing. Months before, my grandfather had taken everything of value and buried it in a big wooden chest in the field behind the house.

"Money. Give us your money, old man!" the first giant had demanded in Russian, prodding Zayde with his bayonet.

Zayde's carefully learned Russian seemed to desert him and he mumbled something incomprehensible, his eyes fixed on the scuffed leather boots of his interrogator.

While his companions continued to search the house, kicking down the door to the warehouse, which by now stood empty again, the leader of the group dealt my grandfather a swift blow with his rifle butt and watched poor Zayde crumple to the floor like a rag doll. Then he kicked him in the stomach with his huge leather boots until Zayde curled into a ball on the hard kitchen floor as pitiful as a tiny child. Again and again he beat him with his gun and kicked him.

By that time the other four soldiers had returned. Zayde wasn't a big man so it didn't take them long to hustle him onto the table, pull his scuffed leather belt from around his waist and force his head into the noose they made with it. Then they hanged him from the hook on the kitchen ceiling that we used for drying meat before the very eyes of Baba and Mendl. They were powerless to help him. When my grandmother screamed and tried to throw herself at the soldiers, they beat her back with the butts of their rifles, smashing her in the chest and breaking her ribs. Another of the men – the dirtiest one – shoved her out of the kitchen and shut her in a bedroom to stop her from getting under their feet before hitting Mendl over the head with his gun and hurling him in after her.

Chaya, the refugee whose home in Brusilev had been destroyed, was in the house, too. Now seven months pregnant, her stomach ballooned under her ragged dress. But that didn't bother the Cossacks. One after another, they raped her on the kitchen floor directly below the spot where Zayde was swinging like a pendulum, slowly suffocating. When they had finished, they grabbed what possessions of ours they had found and marched out, on to the next house.

Poor Chaya; she had never told us who the father of her unborn child was, but my grandmother had her suspicions and guessed that it wasn't the first time this silent woman had been violated. She said it would help account for Chaya's reluctance to talk and her misty eyes. We did know that Chaya had been beaten, her family murdered and her home burnt to the ground; she and her baby son had arrived in Pavolitch with nothing but the clothes on their backs, praying that they would find safety. But, like the smoke of burning Brusilev blown toward us by the wind, the Cossacks had followed her south as if trailing her to her new refuge.

Crack!

Zayde's frayed, old belt snapped in two, weakened, no doubt, by all the floggings he had administered to his grandchildren with it over the years. He landed with an almighty thump on the hard stone floor, missing Chaya by inches, as she pulled herself slowly along the ground and away from the scene of her humiliation. Baba crawled out of the bedroom on all fours to find her husband lying supine beside the table, the broken belt still attached to his neck. His face was crimson, his eyes bulging and he was gulping for air. When she unfastened the noose, she found that a welt had formed around his neck and his skin was chafed and bleeding.

Bent in two with the pain of her broken ribs, that was when Baba had half-run, half-hobbled to my father's house and urged him to fetch the doctor. The two men arrived at last and the doctor sewed stitches into my grandfather's wounds. There was no lasting damage, not in a physical sense at least. Zayde was unable to speak above a whisper for a day or two, but before long his voice returned and was as loud as ever. He had always had a tendency toward violence and now it was even more difficult to find the heart that lay hidden deep within him.

The Banda

DENIKIN SPARED Pavolitch the fate of Brusilev and Khodarkov, the towns to the north of us, and rather than burning it to a cinder, he chose instead to station some of his men with us. We were terrified to have these monstrous soldiers living among us after all we had been through. Jews rarely left their houses during daylight hours and women especially kept themselves indoors, hidden away. Even to cover the short distance between our grandparents' house and our own, Rachel and I were no longer allowed to walk unaccompanied. We had to wait for Zayde, Tata or our family friend Haskl to come with us.

How cruel it felt to be locked up inside. The double window panes that were usually removed when spring arrived remained firmly secured as an extra precaution; the doors, normally left wide open in summer so the house could be cooled by the breeze, stayed locked and bolted. After the long months of winter I always longed for spring, for the sight of white acacia blossoms on the trees, the sweet smell of lilac that suffused the town, the graceful purple lupins dotting the grassy verges and the poplar-seed fluff that floated around like summer snow. This year they went unnoticed.

And we were desperate for news of friends and family elsewhere. There were all manner of rumors, one often contradicting another, and so many different banda, that it was impossible to know who or what to believe. Everybody bombarded with questions the numerous refugees that pitched up in Pavolitch, most of them Jews who had escaped certain death at the hands of one or another of the banda.

In July we heard about a pogrom in Makarov, but it was many weeks before we could be sure that all my father's siblings and their children were safe. It wasn't the Whites that had attacked the Jews in Makarov, but one of the banda led by a local *batko*, or leader. These were groups of peasant hoodlums who followed a village strongman and seemed to be joining in the war for the sake of it. They didn't support Denikin and most of them didn't back Petlyura and the nationalists either. But they hated the Communists and, most of all, they detested the Jews. They blamed us for making money from the German occupation while they went hungry, accused us of stealing from the peasants and workers; most of all they accused us of being Communists and trying to rule over them.

Holed up again in our neighbor Zhukov's back room one stifling summer day, we heard the shouts of Batko Zeleny and his men:

"Kill the Jews and save the Ukraine!"

"Jewish rabble! Will you keep ruling over us?"

We could hear them dragging furniture out of people's homes and smashing it up for firewood. We listened to the sounds of floors being torn up, sheds pulled apart, doors, shutters, window panes, all were removed and stolen or crunched underfoot as if they were no thicker than eggshells. Even nails were pulled out of walls and secreted in pockets. They swooped like vultures after a kill, picking houses clean of all that their owners possessed: food, clothing and furniture were ransacked, while pictures and books were burned at night on their huge bonfires. To Jews, who held learning in such high esteem, the book-burning was a clear sign that Zeleny's band were not men, but animals. As they robbed and plundered, they struck their victims down with their rifle butts, even cutting off women's fingers if they were wearing rings. Again and again they turned over the soil in yards and cellars searching for valuables that might have been buried.

It wasn't a random and voracious killing spree like those carried out by the Whites. Zeleny's men preferred humiliation and torture. Their favored victims were Jewish shop-keepers whom they blamed for the rising prices that were slowly leading to starvation in the countryside. Zhukov stole into our hiding place and recounted how they had forced grown men upon pain of death to kiss each other or to cross themselves like *goyim*. Even though he was a Christian, Zhukov knew all the Jews in Pavolitch and was a great friend to many. It pained him to see his friends and neighbors treated this way. Chaim, our local tobacco seller, was stripped naked, scourged with whips and branches, and made to dance with his mouth stuffed full of tobacco. They threatened to shoot him if he stopped dancing. The bald tailor, an old man who was unsteady on his feet, was forced to re-stitch clothes looted from other Jews, turning them into uniforms, coats and warm underwear for the banda, working solidly without a morsel of food from eight o'clock in the morning until midnight.

Like the Cossacks, Zeleny's bandits urged the local populace to turn upon the Jews. They dragged old men out of their houses and strung them up by their belts from the branches of trees. The local Ukrainian children were encouraged to throw stones at them. When a group of young boys started picking up pebbles from the ground and lobbing them toward the trees, their parents looked on helplessly. They were horrified, but didn't dare tell their sons to stop. Placards had been affixed to the trees: ""Whoever takes this man down has not more than two minutes to live". The poor men were left there for hours or, occasionally, even days. Zayde said he would rather be hanged than tormented like that.

Any Jewish woman unwise enough to leave her house when Zeleny's banda was around risked being violently raped. It mostly happened to widows, those forced to go outside in search of food because they had no man to get supplies for them. One day a woman crawled to my grandparents' door on her hands and knees. She had a face like raw meat, one eye closed and several teeth missing. Her dress was torn and blood was gushing down her legs.

"I can't go home. They know where I live!" she wailed, and collapsed on the kitchen floor. It was only when I heard her voice that I realized it was Hodl, the muscular-armed lady who used to help Baba with the baking. I tried to recognize her features through the pink mush that her face had become, but the sight of all that blood made me feel sick. Baba stoically heated up water, cleaned her wounds and attempted to put her face back together again. How I admired my grandmother at times like this. Nothing fazed her and she could withstand all kinds of horrors herself as long as her daughter and grandchildren were spared.

Hodl stayed at the double-fronted house until Zeleny's bandits departed. Her face gradually started to heal, but soon Moishe the Doctor had to be called out for another reason. It transpired that she had caught an infection from her rapists. Moishe assured her that she wasn't the only one – a veritable epidemic of venereal disease had spread across Pavolitch since Zeleny arrived. Poor Hodl seemed to cry all day and all night. She was so humiliated; she felt dirty, she said, and terribly sinful. But in one respect she was lucky. Numerous other women who had been raped, many of them widows who had lost their husbands in the war, soon found they were pregnant. Some tried throwing themselves down the stairs or drinking tea made with a concoction of herbs to try to flush the fetus out. But nine months later, dozens of unwanted babies were born.

In those humid, stuffy summer days of 1919, it was as if the crack of gunfire had become the normal backdrop to our lives. Denikin's men were still close by and the Reds were regrouping. It seemed that our town was criss-crossed by the banda week by week; if it wasn't one it was another. The sprint to Zhukov's house or Pritska's cellar became a routine commute, the smell of fear our constant companion. The sight of blood became so common that it no longer shocked us. Dead bodies in the street were such an everyday occurrence that we no longer shrunk away from them and shielded our eyes. The flow of blood made our fertile soil even darker and redder than it was already.

At last the stifling heat of summer dispersed and, while the cool winds and rains of autumn brought relief, the Cossacks also scattered. Zeleny's raids on Pavolitch grew less frequent and, regaining some of the confidence that had been sapped by the terror the banda instilled, the Jewish families that remained called a meeting at the synagogue to organize a protection system. It would be a self-defense brigade to provide warnings of any banda approaching the town based on intelligence passed on from the surrounding area. All able-bodied men were to play their part and even my father, who before the pogroms had been so utterly oblivious to the outside world, was eager to carry out his role of beating on the wall of each Jewish house in our street with a stick when a warning came.

We all felt a little reassured by the self-defense league, but we knew that ultimately there was little we Jews could do against the might of the banda. Some of the younger Jewish men dismissed the protection brigade altogether and decided the only way they could attempt to save the lives of those they loved, to protect the honor of their wives and daughters, was to join the Red Army, even if they weren't sympathetic to the Bolshevik cause.

My grandfather was still recovering from his hanging and was exempt from defense duties. He spent his days sitting in an armchair chewing his beard and growling at anyone who tried to approach him.

"I'm finished," he grumbled despondently to himself, "Look at me, I've got no strength left." For the first time, he looked much older than his years. This energetic, intelligent man, who had always thrived on hard work, had become lifeless, introspective and miserable, as if the Cossacks had beaten all the energy out of him when they kicked him to the ground and strung him up by his belt buckle. Even the newspaper no longer interested him. He had become skeptical of all the parties fighting for control of the country. The euphoria that had greeted the tsar's demise and the rise of Kerensky now seemed like a distant dream.

My grandmother tried to encourage her husband to go out and buy food for the family, to see if he could procure some grain and start trading again. But there was a limit even to her energy. She was sleeping badly, waking up at the slightest sound, imagining the house filling up with soldiers all wanting to take Hana Tzirl and her grandchildren away from her. And there were other members of the family to worry about, too. Mendl had been having nightmares ever since he witnessed Zayde hanging by his belt from the meat hook in the kitchen. He was only eight, four years younger than his sister Baya, and was a sensitive boy. He had no memory of the time before the war and pogroms began. Apart from the brief, safe period during the German occupation, all he knew was fear and bloodshed. It was too much for a young child to take. Hana Tzirl sat up at night with her son trying to reassure him. The war would be over soon, she said. But Mendl was an intelligent child and he knew his mother was only saying that to make him feel better. How could she know? Mendl retreated into himself, becoming shy and silent. Baya became even more irritable than usual with him and began to distance herself not just from Mendl but from her entire family.

*

That October there was a pogrom in Kiev that everybody said was the most brutal yet. People were talking of little else and the newspapers were full of reports of atrocities. The killing had continued for days and still there was no word from Sarah to tell us she was safe. And what about my grandfather's numerous cousins, friends and business associates in the city? Denikin's army of giants was back and the methods they used in Kiev showed a methodical ruthlessness beyond anything that had been seen before.

They marched from one house to the next systematically robbing, raping and murdering the Jewish inhabitants. Floor by floor, apartment by apartment, they left no Jew alive before moving on to the next house, the next street. From their windows, onlookers could see bodies flying through the air as anyone weak or elderly enough not to put up a struggle was thrown out into the street below. Kiev's tenement blocks were five or six stories high so few would survive the fall. Young women were raped into submission then discarded from the windows, too.

Lofts and cellars were packed with frightened families holding onto one another and hoping against hope. Some raced down to a cellar only to find it already full to bursting with anxious neighbors. Over and over, people were caught by the banda in the act of running from loft to cellar or cellar to loft in search of somewhere to hide. Stairwells were littered with the body parts of those who had been hacked to pieces in mid flight, children with their heads split open, young babies left all alone on the steps to die of hunger.

Anyone who still had money or valuables hidden away rescued their precious notes or jewelry from hiding places beneath floorboards or behind loose tiles to offer to the soldiers as ransom. It served no purpose. The men took what was offered then killed them anyway.

The roads were littered with corpses. Those hurled from the windows landed one on top of another, crushing the bones of those underneath, and squeezing out any last gasps of life that might remain. The paved streets, glistening from the rain, oozed with the blood and guts of the dead. Despite the filth, and the terrible stench of death, the streets were soon filled with scavengers picking at the bodies for their clothes and shoes until nothing was left but mounds of pale, bloody flesh.

Some people tried to flee into the woodland that rose steeply from the banks of the mighty Dniepr River and hurled themselves into the icy flow. Few could have survived the cold and the strong currents. Witnesses said the river was filled with bodies and, although I tried hard not to, I couldn't help seeing a vision in my mind's eye of my sister Sarah, her fair hair fanned around her head, floating downriver surrounded by translucent corpses.

For several days after news of the pogrom reached us we lived like shadows, barely speaking, barely eating, fearing the worst and hardly daring to believe that Sarah might be safe. Since the Civil War began, mail had become increasingly unreliable and a letter from Kiev could take over a week to arrive.

At last, one morning came a heavy knock on the door of my father's cottage. Rachel and I raced to the door as Tata opened it to reveal a well dressed stranger. A visitor newly arrived from Kiev. We all held our breath.

"Is this the house of Meyer Unikow?"

"Yes, yes," Tata stuttered. "Have you got news?"

"Your daughter Sarah is alive!"

Tata raised his eyes to God and whispered a prayer, while Rachel and I hugged one another with relief. Together with my grandfather's cousins, Sarah had hidden in a coal cellar for the entire duration of the pogrom. After five days with nothing to eat but a little bread and water, she and her companions were black from the soot and parched with thirst, but they had survived.

Typhus

THE BLUSTERY autumn weeks passed quickly and by early November the first snows had arrived. At last the banda seemed to have left us in peace. But with the piercing northerly winds came another equally vicious invader. Typhus seeped its way into houses all over Pavolitch through gaps in the windows and cracks in the woodwork, or camped itself outside like the drifts of snow, waiting against walls for its victims to come out of their homes to strike them down with its rashes and fever. No house was safe; no crosses or icons in the window could offer protection now.

First Baba fell ill and Zayde banned me and Rachel from visiting lest we catch the disease from her. Hana Tzirl took over the running of the household and was shocked to discover what heavy, exhausting work her mother carried out every single day. Shortly afterwards, Sarah was sent home from Kiev with a fever. Her skin was so hot to the touch that it burned. Sarah moved into my father's cottage where she lay motionless in the bed that Tata had shared with Rivka. Tata and I brought her tea, changed the sheets, which were drenched with sweat again almost as soon as we had remade the bed, and took it in turns to traipse down to the lake to cut ice, which we placed on her forehead to try to keep her cool.

At the lake we met many others like ourselves, collecting ice for their relatives and praying that they wouldn't fall victim themselves. Soon Rachel was sick, too. The itchy red rash started around her tummy and quickly spread over her legs and arms. We closed the shutters because the sunlight hurt her eyes, and she and Sarah lay in the dark emitting sharp, hacking coughs from deep in the chest. It pained me just to listen to them. Tata and I continued to trek daily to the lake and brought back double the amount of ice that we did before, with two fevers to calm.

Despite her tiny frame and fragile appearance, Baba was soon fighting fit again. She darted around her kitchen as energetically as before, thawing old chicken bones she had packed in ice to make chicken soup for the family and preparing vats of carbolic acid to spray around the house to keep the germs at bay. She visited her special "doctor" for incantations and charms to expel the Evil Eye, and made amulets to protect us all, which she hung around our necks with lengths of the coarse, brown yarn that she used to darn our stockings. Some mothers went further and gave their sick children additional names to deceive the Evil Eye. For boys, they added Alter, meaning old, or Chaim, which signifies life. For girls it was Alte or Chaya.

In Pavolitch, as in other towns and villages where typhus was raging, women started to make regular visits to the synagogue to beseech the religious scholars to pray for their sick relatives. Covering their faces with their shawls, as Jewish custom demands in the presence of unfamiliar men, they begged and cajoled anyone who would listen. But the synagogues and prayer houses were much emptier than before. Besides those who had been killed in the war and pogroms, men were now too concerned with searching for food for their families to spend long hours in prayer and religious debate. Only a few hungry scholars were left, dozing over their Talmud volumes.

After a couple of weeks, Rachel's condition began to improve, but Sarah continued to lie motionless. Even the slightest movement was too much for her weakened body to bear and she began to rave and moan incomprehensibly as the fever went to her head. She whistled as she breathed as if a rock had lodged itself on her lungs and a blue shadow appeared around her nose and mouth. Tata spent hours sitting by her bedside, preparing his farewells to his eldest daughter, his golden girl, the tranquil-eyed student with the long, fair hair that now clung damply around her red face. It seemed that Sarah had survived the most vicious pogrom Russia had ever known just to be taken by typhus a few weeks later.

But the hours my father spent at Sarah's bedside served him badly. He himself started to scratch around his chest and belly and soon he sat by his daughter's bed with his forehead pressed against the cold stone wall to cool his brow. Still he refused to leave his precious girl. It was as much as I could do to move him into my bedroom and make him lie down. Soon he was raving, too, and producing that terrible hacking cough that made me shiver. I sat beside him and stroked his dark hair. It was shot through with grey now, and stiffer than it had been when I was a child in the days when I used to watch him prepare for his morning prayers from my snug position on my mother's side of the marital bed. With a shock, I suddenly realized that I no longer remembered what Mama looked like, nor could I hear her voice in my head as I had continued to do for so long after she died.

As Rachel regained her strength, she helped me trek down to the lake to collect ice for both Sarah and Tata. But soon I was sick, too. The fever took me away into a dark world where the days and nights passed in one long continuum of wake and sleep, fever and chill. I was vaguely aware of the presence of my grandfather, who came every day to sit at my bedside, taking my pulse and placing ice on my forehead. I lost track of how long I lay there, but eventually, after what felt like weeks or even months, my fever began to subside and I started to ask about the rest of the family. I suddenly remembered how ill Sarah had been, and feared that she might have died without my knowing.

"It's not Sarah you need to worry about, it's Tata," Rachel told me. Sarah had pulled through and had now almost fully recovered. But my father was still desperately ill. Tata's periods of raving grew longer and often he didn't recognize his own children, mistaking us for his sisters or even for one of the banda. My grandfather sat by his son-in-law's bedside, just as he had sat at mine, measuring his pulse and putting ice on his head to cool the burning inside. Tata, who had worn the black skullcap and gaberdine of his faith every day until the sickness struck him, had survived all the anti-Jewish pogroms without a scratch, only to be taken by a much more egalitarian killer. He finally left us in December, and many miles away in Makarov, Tata's younger brothers, Berl and Moishe, were also taken by typhus within two weeks of his death.

And so, at the age of seventeen, I was orphaned. My father was the person I loved more than any other in the entire world. I had idolized him ever since I was tiny and when he had sent me away to live with his parents at the Twersky court in Makarov I had vowed that I would prove my worth to him. I wasn't sure that I had managed to do so. True, I had kept house for him as best I could in the year and a half since Rivka died. I had learned how to make pickles and preserves for him, as well as tea from roots. But more often than not, I had brought back to the cottage ready-cooked dishes that Baba had prepared for us all. I had dropped out of school and abandoned my studies. I had looked after Rachel, but only very reluctantly. And then in my father's own hour of need, when he was sick and dying, I was too ill myself to be able to help him. I determined to be a better person from now on, to do more for my family and to become the kind of daughter that would have made my father proud.

Scores of Pavolitchers perished in the typhus epidemic of 1919 and the streets were full of sleds and carts carrying the dead to the cemetery. Rather than holding a wake for the deceased, families would bury their relatives straightaway for fear of infection. The cantors and body-washers worked around the clock, as did the gravediggers hacking at the frozen earth with pickaxes so that even if someone died at midnight, his body would be in the ground by morning. In those days, many people who had struggled before to gain work now found it easy to get positions as gravediggers and body-washers as their numbers increased to keep up with demand. Haskl, our hunchbacked neighbor, was one of them. Night and day he worked washing the bodies of the dead.

With a dozen or more people dying every day, demand for coffins far outstripped supply, and there weren't even any planks to be found for a makeshift one. Instead, we laid Tata's body out on a wooden pallet from the warehouse. We dressed him in a white robe that Baba had stitched together from some old sheets and shrouded him in a black blanket. It felt terribly undignified for such a scholarly man as my father and, once again, I worried that I was not doing all I could to give him a proper send off, but there was really no other choice.

Rather than let my father suffer the further dishonor of being towed away on a sled, Zayde called in some men who used to help him with grain transportation to carry Tata to the cemetery. Four of them hoisted the pallet onto their shoulders. Rabbi Twersky had come all the way from Makarov to conduct the funeral and walked solemnly behind the coffin bearers. The rest of us followed a few paces back. Cousin Mendl carried a metal box, which he hit with a stick to ask passersby for charitable contributions to help the poor after the family breadwinner had died. Minyan was held at the graveside and the mournful chant, *El maley rakhamin* – God is filled with mercy, was carried away by the wind.

Except for his brothers Berl and Moishe who were sick with typhus themselves, all Tata's siblings attended the funeral. It was the last time I was to see some of them for many years. His sisters Yetta and Bassy had long been involved in a left-wing movement and would shortly be departing for America. There Yetta would later join a nascent socialist group in the state of Utah and help found an, ultimately unsuccessful, utopian commune. Feter Avrom and Mima Maryam had completed their medical studies and both had been working intently since the start of the war in 1914 when they were recruited to help tend those wounded in battle.

Once she had regained her strength after her own bout of typhus, Sarah returned to Kiev. She was happier there than she was in Pavolitch, but, more than that, we discovered that she had an extra reason to hurry back to the city. Our sister had a boyfriend, a fellow-student at the university called Shaya Rabinovitch, the young man she had told us about the previous Passover. In a small town like Pavolitch it was almost unheard of for a Jewish girl to have a boyfriend. Older generations were scornful of love matches and feared that such a relationship would bring shame on the family. A bride or groom should be found by a reputable marriage broker and if the betrothed set eyes upon one another once or twice before the wedding, they were lucky. But times were changing and the thought of an arranged marriage was abhorrent to Sarah. As she revealed the secrets of young love to Rachel and me in whispers in our room at night, she made us vow not to mention a word of it to Baba, and especially not to Zayde.

Sarah and Naftula returned to Pavolitch a few weeks after my father's funeral to help erect a memorial to Tata in the cemetery just out of town. Once again Zayde recited the traditional mourning prayer while the tombstone was positioned at the head of the snow-covered mound. As I bowed my head in prayer, I tried to think back to how my father had looked before his body was shrunken and his skin mottled by fever. It was difficult to remember what Tata had been like before – before his illness, before war and pogroms had forced him out of his tranquil life of study and prayer. Lost in my thoughts, I suddenly became aware of a dark shape flitting around nearby. I raised my eyes to see a massive black dog about to jump up at me. Before I knew it, heavy paws were clawing at my coat and its bared teeth were on a level with my eyes. I turned and ran. Zayde

broke off from his chanting at the commotion and snapped an overhang-
ing branch from a tree to try to beat the dog away.

Although I was used to dogs, having grown up with Rabchik – now
long dead – as my beloved companion, this hairy beast frightened me.
I ran around the graveyard as fast as I could, the dog barking and snapping at my heels. Just outside the cemetery gates was a steep-sided hillock
covered in trees and I leaped to the top, aiming to clamber into one of the
trees where I would be safe. But as I turned to look over my shoulder, I
tripped over a tree root protruding invisibly beneath its coating of snow. I
fell to the ground, wincing in pain, as the dog galloped up to me. I closed
my eyes, trying to block out the throbbing in my leg and the fear in my
heart. When I opened them again, the dog was gone.

I looked down at my family, all padded in their winter coats and lined up
beside my father's grave, each still saying his own private prayers to Tata.
Apparently unaware of my plight, Zayde had resumed the minyan once
the dog ran away. Now he and Naftula were nodding fervently; Sarah's
and Rachel's heads were bowed. I was mortified that I had shown such
disrespect and that I had not completed my own farewell to my father. Yet
again, I had failed in my vow to be an honorable daughter.

My mortification deepened when Haskl picked me up, threw me over
his humped shoulder like a sack of oats and marched me back to the
double-fronted house. I flushed and pummeled Haskl's back with my
fists; I was almost eighteen years old and wanted to be treated like a lady,
not thrown about as if I were still a little girl. Moishe the Doctor came
that afternoon and set a cast on my fractured ankle. The pain was intense
and didn't ease for days. It would be several weeks before I could walk
again, Moishe said. I sat alone in my bedroom, the same room that Rachel
and I had shared for most of our childhood and that was ours again after
my father's death forced our return to the double-fronted house.

But the rest of the family paid scant attention to my pain and distress.
Something far graver was happening elsewhere in the house. Hana Tzirl
had come down with typhus, too, and Baba, Baya and Mendl were glued
to her bedside day and night. My aunt, ravaged by fever, flitted in and out
of consciousness. Everyone seemed aware, by some strange, subconscious
knowledge, that Hana Tzirl would not recover. Baba had been fighting
against the cruelty of her fate ever since my mother's death twelve years
before, but now destiny had got the better of her once again. The kaluzha

was frozen over, but my grandmother knew it was to blame. Baba steeled herself for the death of her last remaining child. Hour after hour she knelt on the bedroom floor praying until her legs were numb and her palms seemed permanently joined in the act of supplication.

"Look after Baya for me, Mama," Hana Tzirl moaned, pulling herself briefly out of the dark world that was trying to lure her away from her mother. "My beautiful girl, the apple of my eye, soon she will be grown up without a mother to guide her. And take care of Mendl – he's still just a boy. Oh Mama, I can't bear to leave them."

"Don't be silly," my grandmother scolded, "You'll get better and look after your own children." But both of them knew it wasn't true.

"I know what I want, Mama. I want to get better, but God knows what He wants, too. And I think He's going to take me," Mima Hana replied, and she slipped away again.

The next day Hana Tzirl called for Haskl. A couple of years earlier he had buried a trunk for her containing silver, fine clothes and linens that she had wanted to hide. Now Hana Tzirl insisted it be dug up so that she could distribute her possessions among her family. The ground was frozen and poor Haskl spent hours thrusting the point of a pickaxe at it to retrieve the buried treasures. It wasn't wise to be seen wearing the precious silks and satins that the trunk contained; times were hard and anyone, especially a Jew, could be stopped in the street and attacked for a good woolen coat. But Mima Hana gave away whatever she had that we could use: a shawl here, a linen tablecloth there, and the silver she entrusted to Baba.

She was particularly anxious to give away her shoes. It was next to impossible to buy proper footwear at that time – all that was available in the shops were ugly clogs made out of wood. But after a person has died, their shoes must be cut into pieces as they would bring bad luck to anyone who wore them. Sarah's feet turned out to be exactly the same size as her aunt's and she inherited a pair of stylish court shoes and black leather boots that Hana Tzirl had bought from the best cobbler in Berdichev before the war. Once she had assigned some of her belongings to each of us, she sent Haskl away again with the trunk and in the dark of night he took it back to its hiding place and buried it deep in the ground. The very next day, Hana Tzirl died.

After the death of their last remaining daughter, Berl and Pessy were left with six orphaned grandchildren to care for. Baba had buried all thirteen of the children she had brought into the world and, just as they had when she was younger, images of coffins piled one on top of another began to haunt her dreams once again. The life appeared to drain out of her from one day to the next. Always so vigorous and energetic in the past, she finally started to look like an old woman. Her brow became furrowed, her back hunched. She ate next to nothing and seemed almost to be fading away. She would sit at the table, pale and wan, her knitting abandoned on her lap, and stare into our eyes as if trying to foresee our fate.

My cousin Baya, who had always been aloof, now kept to herself entirely. All her life her mother had doted on her, but now she was one of six children, no more or less special than all the others. From the day her mother died, she became silent and distant, living in the shadows of the house and barely talking to her family at all. Her brother Mendl cried in his sleep all the more, but actively sought out company during the day as if he were afraid to be alone. Rachel and I took pity on the boy and indulged him all we could.

PART IV

1920–1925

A Gunshot

MAKHNO AND his men moved quickly. They travelled in peasant carts called *tachankas* driven by two scabby horses and loaded with weaponry stolen from other banda. Although the Jewish self-defense brigade now gave us more warning when a banda was heading in our direction, Makhno was upon us before we knew it. His men carried axes and hammers, dressed in peasant smocks and black hats, and waved banners that threatened "Liberty or Death" or "Land for the peasants. Factories for the workers". The Makhnoists were militant, anarchist communists, an impoverished lawless rabble who targeted railway junctions in order to hijack trains, shoot passengers and loot goods. We had heard about the ferocious attacks they had carried out in nearby Popilna. But a foray into a town away from the railway line like Pavolitch was less common.

"Quick! Go to Zhukov's and hide!" shouted Zayde when we heard the cries and banging that warned us Makhno was on his way. Baba scurried off with Rachel, Baya and Mendl. My leg was still in plaster after my fall in the cemetery and I couldn't keep up. I could still only hop or hobble with a stick.

"I'll have to stay here, Zayde, I can't even walk," I told him.

"Don't be stupid, Pearl, you can't stay here!" Zayde took a knife and tried to hack away at the cast on my leg, but the plaster was thick and hard and he couldn't break it. But he wouldn't give up. He put his arms around my middle and attempted to hoist me over his shoulder. A few years before he would have managed it without a struggle, but he was an old man now and I was an adult.

"You'll do yourself an injury, Zayde. Leave me here and go to Zhukov's," I insisted.

"I don't need to run and hide. I don't care if I die now – I'm already old. There's nothing more for me to live for," Zayde responded.

So the two of us made our way to the attic. I pulled myself slowly up the wooden stepladder, dragging my plastered leg after me. There we sat in silence for a while, listening to the shouts and gunshots getting louder. Then Zayde had an idea. He couldn't ask Zhukov to come and fetch me lest he put the rest of the family at risk. But he could go and ask his other neighbor, Hertzl. Although he was no friend of my grandfather's – in fact Zayde hadn't spoken to Hertzl for years – in an hour of need, even Zayde could put past arguments behind him and ask a favor of an old adversary. Hertzl was a colossus of a man and would be able to pick me up and carry me as if I were a child. I sat alone in the attic and waited. Who would reach me first – Hertzl or Makhno?

The noise of shouting, of men banging at doors, kicking them down, became sharper and clearer. I shut my eyes and tried to think of something else, anything, to take my mind off waiting, waiting for the banging to begin at our front door, for the door to fly off its hinges and for the banda to find me. Makhno had a terrifying reputation and I was more scared of him than I had been even of Denikin. Besides, my broken leg made me feel helpless, vulnerable. I tried desperately to focus on anything other than what the men would do to me when they arrived. I hummed the songs that Mama used to sing to me when I was a child. I repeated them over and over as if, as long as I could keep the music playing in my head, reach the end of one tune and start another, then I would survive. I wouldn't be harmed as long the song didn't finish.

Above the general din from outside I heard the sudden, sharp crack of a gunshot. It couldn't have been more than a few paces from our door. My heart started racing and I shut my eyes tight. I could feel the sweat rising on my brow. There was more shooting, but further away now, thanks to God. I recovered my composure and still I waited. At long last I heard a key turning in the lock and the sound of my grandfather's boots ringing on the stone floor. I clambered downstairs and the sight of his ashen face told me at once that something was wrong.

"What happened?" I asked him. "Is everyone alright?"

"The children are fine, your grandmother too." I let out a deep sigh of relief. Then Zayde continued: "But Herzl . . . Didn't you hear a shot? He was just coming to fetch you. The bullet went straight through his heart. Then another banda started shooting from across the lake. I think it was the Whites. They all fled." He spoke quickly, in short bursts like gunfire, a tremor in his voice.

I was dumbstruck. I wanted to scream, but no sound came out. The shot I had heard was a bullet striking Hertzl in the heart as he was approaching our house to carry me to safety. He had died instantly. And as for me, it was only the Whites shooting that had distracted Makhno and saved me from . . . from I didn't want to think what. Hertzl and my grandfather had hated one another thanks to an ancient family dispute, but he had always been pleasant enough with me. And now he had died coming to rescue me. A feeling of nausea rose up in my throat. My first sensation was enormous relief that I had survived. If the Whites hadn't launched an attack just when they did, Makhno's men would surely have found me. But my relief was soon tempered by guilt. Hertzl had died because of me. I felt stunned that I could be the reason for a man's death. By rights I should have been the one killed and Hertzl should be back with his family. How could I ever repay the debt?

My leg slowly healed as the great piles of snow melted gradually away to leave the streets covered in a thick, red slush and by the spring I was able to walk again. The tragedy of Hertzl's death and my part in it continued to haunt my waking hours, while the sound of the gunshot that killed him and a rising sense of panic woke me from sleep every night without fail.

*

One day a well-dressed officer sporting a general's insignia came to the door. He proffered my grandmother a slip of paper covered in official-looking stamps that she could make neither head nor tail of. The writing was in an unfamiliar alphabet, which she presumed must be Polish, and although she could understand spoken Polish fairly well, she still couldn't make out exactly what the man was saying. He kept repeating the same phrase over and over again and smiled expectantly at her. Finally Baba understood that he was demanding to be billeted at the house. She shook her head and tried to push the door closed. She had her granddaughters in the house – she couldn't let a strange, foreign man come and stay, however polite he appeared! But the Pole stuck his boot by the door jamb and told her firmly that the orders had come from headquarters and she had no choice but to let him stay.

The visitor was a gentleman and a general in the Polish army. It appeared that the Poles had spied an opportunity to take back the Ukrainian territories that had once belonged to them. As a state of anarchy prevailed across the land, with so many conflicting, confusing and fragmented armies chasing one another across the plains, Polish troops had been pushing their way eastward for several months and now they had occupied Pavolitch. As foreign invaders, the Poles were supposed to be our enemy, but, just like during the German occupation a couple of years earlier, we greeted their arrival as a blessing. The Poles didn't hate the Jews like the banda did and we felt safe from the pogroms with a general in the house. He kept to himself and always waved away any food that Baba offered him with softly spoken thanks, a gentle "*spacibo, spacibo*"[1] escaping from beneath his walrus moustache. He had started speaking to my grandparents in Russian even though Baba would actually have understood him better in Polish.

The general was a surprisingly sensitive man for a soldier.

"I feel guilty for every man I've killed on the battlefield," he told my grandfather one day. "Killing is wrong, but I have to do my job." Zayde became quite fond of the gentle general and offered him books to read, which he always returned when he had finished without leaving a single mark, folded page or dirty smudge. He had a great appetite for books and we soon discovered that the other Polish soldiers knew him as the Teacher. Many of them were illiterate and the Teacher gave them lessons in reading and writing. In the four months that he lived with us, I caught a glimpse of him only rarely. Even though he was a gentleman, Baba made sure that we girls were kept well out of his way. And some of the Teacher's visitors weren't nearly as cultivated as himself.

"Where are your lovely granddaughters, eh?" visiting soldiers would probe Baba when they came to the door to see their general.

"My granddaughters are much too refined for a beast like you!" Baba scolded. It sounded like she was joking with them, but in truth she was terrified that they might rape us. So we were exiled to our bedrooms and weren't allowed downstairs when the Poles were around.

One evening, the Teacher went to the main synagogue to make an announcement before Friday prayers.

"I am appealing to you on behalf of the Polish army," the Teacher began. "We will be staying with you just a little while longer and we want to

---

1. Thank you (Russian).

ask for your assistance. Many of our men lack uniforms. We will shortly
be going into battle and we are in desperate need of jackets. We are asking
you, as brothers and sisters, if you can help us by making us five hundred
jackets by the end of next week." The prayer hall filled with chatter as men
turned to one another to check that they had understood correctly. The
women on the balcony above stifled their giggles. The Poles had helped
us by providing some respite from the pogroms and so, in return, the Jews
of Pavolitch began stitching uniforms for the occupying army. From old
women with gnarled hands and dim sight to young girls who had never
sat still for so long at once, all stayed up night after night sewing by the
light of candles and oil lamps to ensure that the jackets would be ready
on time.

I was a member of a sewing group that had met once a week before
the Civil War started. We began to assemble again, now stitching coarse
Polish army uniforms rather than embroidering the delicate linens of our
own trousseaux. Some of our number no longer joined us and it was best
not to ask why. I knew that a few had managed to escape to the West, but
pogroms had taken others. And listening to stories about those less lucky
than ourselves was too harrowing and only served to make us realize how
vulnerable we all were.

The jackets were finished just in time for the Bolshevik advance and,
all of a sudden, the whole of Pavolitch became a battlefield. The Poles
attacked from our side of the lake while the Bolsheviks fired back at them
across the water. My grandfather sent us up to an old friend of his who
lived on the hill, beyond the lake, to keep us out of the way. As I scrambled
up to safety, I could see the action unfolding below as if I were watching
a battle scene from some terrible onstage tragedy from a seat high up in
the theater. I could see the Polish unit advancing and firing, tiny soldiers
stumbling and falling, retreating and advancing again, to a background
of bangs that sounded, from where I was standing, as if they were made
by toys rather than real weapons. The Bolsheviks were clearly gaining
ground and I wondered which one of the little model soldiers below was
the Teacher. Perhaps that was him – leading the Polish retreat back in
the direction of Popilna. Or maybe he was one of those lying injured or
killed. We would never find out. From that day on the civil authorities in
Pavolitch were Bolshevik and my grandparents never saw or heard from
the Teacher again.

Naftula's Escape

IN THE summer of 1920, all the yeshiva boys were called up to go to war. The new soviet Red Army was beginning its first offensive to try to spread the doctrine of world revolution, starting with Poland, on our doorstep. Only weeks after the Poles had abandoned Pavolitch to the Bolsheviks, the Red Army was chasing them back to the border and they wanted Naftula to help. He was just sixteen when he received his military papers.

Even in his teens, Naftula remained as calm and softly-spoken as he had been as a little boy and his years at the yeshiva had removed any opportunity for him to toughen up with the local youths. He had never spent his summers running around the dusty streets and getting himself dirty like the other boys did. That would have been too undignified for Naftula. When in Pavolitch, he had attended synagogue with his father three times a day. I used to itch with jealousy when watching the two of them walking together, talking animatedly about Talmudic logic and other things I couldn't understand. I had envied Naftula for his close relationship with Tata and also feared that my beloved brother might slip away from me into his own religious world – a world that I could never be part of. Even before he had left for yeshiva, he already seemed to prefer spending time in the prayer house to playing with his sisters. Unlike Tata, he had never been asked to help my grandfather in the warehouse. Nobody had even considered that Naftula might inherit the family grain business. However proud Zayde was of his enterprise, his first-born grandson was made for the Talmud. He would be a rabbi or a teacher one day.

The idea of Naftula going off to war was as unreal as the sun failing to

rise in the morning or the snow not falling in winter. Baba threw away the
letter calling for him to present himself at the local army headquarters and
vowed that no grandson of hers would fight for the Bolsheviks – or anyone else for that matter. Naftula remained at the yeshiva, coming home to
Pavolitch only at Sabbath and for high holidays. During one of his visits,
a knock at the door sent my grandmother into a panic. It was a neighbor
who had heard through the grapevine that the local militia was rounding
up all the young men for the army. The plaited valedictory candle had
just been lit, marking the end of the Sabbath, and Naftula was just about
to return to Skvira. Immediately his travel plans were cancelled and he
was sent to the back of the house. He wasn't to set foot outside, not even
to pray. Nobody but Baba was allowed to open the door.

My grandparents sat up late with Naftula that night formulating a plan.
Most important was to find somewhere safe for my brother to hide in case
the police came to the house. The warehouse seemed to offer the most
promising solution. Mounds of grain had begun to rebuild in the months
since the banda had left us in peace and my grandfather set about organizing a hiding place where Naftula would be completely invisible. He
would be swathed in empty sacks then covered over entirely with grain.
A tube poking out by the wall served as a breathing apparatus. Naftula
practiced installing himself in the spot over and over again until he could
do it in half a minute or less.

The very next morning, just before dawn, the dreaded moment came.
Even drowsy with sleep, Naftula was able to make himself invisible in
moments. By the time my grandmother opened the door, he was hidden.

"My grandson isn't here," Baba told the militia. "He's at the yeshiva.
He went back to Skvira last night once Sabbath was over." She held her
breath for a moment before continuing, "Come in and look for him if you
like."

Three militia men entered the house. We girls were chivvied out of bed
and into the kitchen, still dressed in our nightclothes, so that they could
search all the rooms. When they headed into the warehouse I had to look
away lest the fear on my face should reveal Naftula's secret. A minute
later they were gone. A wave of relief washed over me. My brother remained hidden a little longer in case the men should return and the rest
of us sat around the kitchen table, our heads in our hands, none of us able
to speak.

From that moment on we all became even more cautious about whom we talked to and any knock at the door would send Naftula scurrying to the warehouse to hide. My grandmother's state became one of perennial nervous panic. For ten days we lived with the fear that the militia would arrive on our doorstep and demand to take Naftula away with them. Only Naftula himself seemed to remain calm. He had an unshakeable belief that God would protect him and never seemed to understand the serious danger he was in. The weather was warm and humid and, while the rest of us enjoyed the sunshine and relative peace, taking our books or our sewing outside, Naftula grew paler and thinner, sitting in the back room studying his *Gemara*.

Of course, even Baba realized we couldn't go on like this forever and that the authorities would catch up with Naftula one day. We had already learned from the grain requisitions of the Bolsheviks' ruthlessness and knew the consequences could be dreadful if we continued to deceive them. My grandparents had been sending coded messages to all our relatives asking for their advice and a plan was coming to fruition. The only way to save Naftula from the army, they resolved, was for him to go and join our great-uncle Menachem Mendl and his family in Canada. Our cousin Nochum in Makarov was in the same dilemma and the two young men would travel together. Nochum was more worldly wise than my innocent, God-fearing brother and my grandparents hoped he would help Naftula overcome the numerous hurdles that he was bound to come across during his illegal voyage to the Free World.

My grandfather planned the trip meticulously. The two young men left Pavolitch in a rickety carriage at dawn on a bright summer morning. The carriage was pulled by two handsome chestnut horses; they were a little on the skinny side, but the best that Zayde was able to hire, and their coats shimmered in a steamy haze as they sped from the town. The crossbar connecting the carriage to the horses was reinforced by the blacksmith, leaving a hollow tube that my grandfather stuffed with as many banknotes as he could, poking them into the hole with his stubby fingers.

Every couple of days or so a telegram arrived, written in a special code Zayde had developed before Naftula left. The telegrams marked his progress westward and we plotted his course on a big, cloth-backed map. But little more than a week into his voyage, the telegrams stopped. Had he made it to Trieste already and onto a ship? None of us really knew how far away the exotic-sounding port really was, for our map didn't go that far, but it seemed remarkably quick progress. Or had he been caught by the militia and forced to join the advance on Poland? Or was it something worse? We all hoped against hope that the lack of news was a good omen and that soon we would hear of my brother's arrival in Canada. Weeks passed. Every day we waited expectantly for news. And then, at long last, a telegram finally arrived. I watched every movement of Zayde's expression as he opened it. The seconds seemed like minutes. Eventually my grandfather spoke.

"He only got as far as Kishinev. He was robbed. We have to send him more money." Baba crumpled into a chair while Rachel and I stared at one another stunned. He had been gone over a month and he was only in Kishinev!

Naftula's naivety and his eternal belief that God would protect him made him an easy target for thieves and vagabonds. But little did anyone expect that trouble would come from a member of his own family. His cousin Nochum had stolen all the money that Zayde had scrabbled together and hidden in the hollow crossbar, and crept off in the dead of night, filching Naftula's ship pass and even his shoes as he went. Naftula was left with nothing but the clothes on his back and his Canadian entry permit, arranged for him by Menachem Mendl's family in Winnipeg. He had set off with no transit visas or passport – the Soviet passport system didn't even exist yet – and his guardian had left him stranded in Kishinev. Poor Naftula, he had only ever been trained in the Talmud. No boy could have been more hopelessly equipped than he to deal with finding himself alone, destitute and on the run from the Red Army.

When she had recovered her senses, Baba immediately set about preparing a parcel of food to send to her grandson. She dipped a loaf of bread in some beer to stop it from going moldy and sent me out to look for meat. It was still a rare luxury and we were lucky if we ate meat once a month. But, for Naftula, no expense was spared. I came home with a goose and Baba stuffed the meat into the bird's long neck and packed it together with the beer-soaked bread and some money.

Kishinev was in Bessarabia, which was nominally independent from Russia, but nobody my grandfather asked was sure exactly where our country's borders lay – since the war, all the maps were out of date. Zayde wasn't convinced that Naftula would be safe in Kishinev. He quickly dispatched a telegram telling his grandson to get to Romania at all costs.

Money was too precious for him to keep us regularly updated of his progress, but eventually Naftula wrote that he had made it to Romania. There, at least, he was definitely safe from the Bolshevik recruiting officers. Back home, Baba, Rachel and I wept with relief, finally releasing the fear and dread that had been welling up inside us since Naftula's hurried departure over six weeks earlier. But the tide of worry soon began to rise again as the weeks continued to pass, the first snows began to fall and still we heard nothing more from him. Baba banned me and Rachel from talking about our brother lest we provoke the Evil Eye and, as the cold nights drew in, a heavy feeling of gloom descended like the evening darkness over our house. It wasn't until the following year that we finally heard from Naftula again. Having wandered from village to village, offering lessons in reading and writing in return for food, he had finally reached Trieste. There he was working as a stevedore trying to raise sufficient funds to buy his ticket. Somehow the depth of his faith had helped him to survive and in a few weeks more he would be on a ship bound for Canada.

Hunger

MY GRANDFATHER'S house was colder and darker than it had been when I was little. Fuel and kerosene were hard to find, so the stoves and oil lamps remained unlit. Even candles were precious and had to be used sparingly. Zayde paced around the house like an animal in a cage. He had recovered from his ordeal at the hands of Denikin's men, but that didn't make him any less grumpy. Now that he was feeling better he didn't know what to do with himself all day. His business associates had all vanished. The railway station at Popilna, where he used to spend his days, was in a state of war, repeatedly attacked and bombed and rebuilt; several sections of line were blocked by trains that had been stopped by snowdrifts or run out of fuel. Some of the railway cars had become bastions for robber bands or fugitive refuges. Only the armored trains continued to criss-cross the country without fear of disruption.

Traders had stopped congregating at the station to find out prices and execute deals years ago, when the war started, and now it had become a place of dread for all but the bravest. Nevertheless, desperate men and women continued to gather there and force themselves aboard the infrequent trains to undertake terrifying journeys in search of food. The Bolshevik government had introduced harsh requisitioning targets that the newspapers called War Communism and some peasants had taken to ripping up their crops rather than harvesting them only to have them taken away by government agents. Even here, in the Breadbasket of Europe, grain was hard to find. Nevertheless, every now and again, people would arrive at our door, some having travelled for hours by train or by sled, hoping to exchange a pound or two of wheat or millet for a pair of shoes, some warm, knitted underwear, or other goods they could use for barter.

My grandfather's warehouse was almost bare, but he never turned anybody away. He accepted whatever goods he was offered and gave what he could in return. Slowly and tentatively, even though he was by now an old man and lacked his former vigor, he began to build up his business again. I was grateful that Zayde had something to occupy himself again and more so that his new supplies spared us the dreadfulness of black-market bread. People said that flour made up only five percent of the loaf; the rest was a revolting blend of dried potato skins, mashed up soldiers' coats or even dirt and mud from the road. It stuck to the roof of the mouth and trying to cut it with a bread knife was a wasted effort – you needed a saw! Even so, if someone was unwise enough go out in the street holding a piece of bread, children would steal it straight from their hands.

Ukrainian black bread was almost impossible to find and who could afford it when it cost sixty rubles a pound? Before the war even a white loaf was just fifty kopeks. The Bolsheviks were trying to introduce a standard exchange rate: one pound of flour would be worth exactly one pound of salt. But at the market a pound of salt was trading for two pood of flour, equivalent to seventy-two pounds!

Sugar was more precious still and could rarely be purchased even with a ration card. We began sucking our tea through a lump of sugar like peasants, keeping each little cube for several days and guarding it ferociously. Cooking oil, too, was increasingly hard to come by, so my grandmother fried our meals in cod-liver or sometimes even castor oil, despite the fact that it made the food taste foul. For many, fried potatoes became the staple meal even though the potatoes available were often frozen, rotten and slimy. If they couldn't get potatoes, people would eat millet cooked in plenty of water to form a liquid gruel. It tasted like boiled-up socks, but they ate it nevertheless, for such is the power of hunger. We even heard once that a horse had collapsed in the road at the other end of town and died from exhaustion. Within moments it was surrounded by starving scavengers hacking off chunks of meat.

The trunk containing my grandparents' valuables had already been dug up and much of Baba's silverware had been sold to pay for food and fuel. Besides, who would buy silver now? The best one could do was to exchange a silver candlestick for a bundle of Ukrainian karbovantsy, which people had in bales, but were worth virtually nothing. Only Kerensky rubles could be used to buy food, but that type of money was hard to come by. In fact, paper money hardly operated at all.

Finding enough food to feed a family was becoming a full-time occupation. Many goods were rationed and any that weren't had become impossible to find. We hadn't seen pickled herring since Denikin's army left and, once the lake froze over again, there was no fresh fish to be found either. Meat and dairy produce were terrifically expensive, or otherwise unavailable altogether, as people had barely enough to feed themselves let alone sufficient to keep cows or chickens. The price of a pail of milk had increased almost daily ever since the summer of 1918 and it now cost almost as much as a horse. Eggs were equally precious and, even if my grandmother did manage to buy half a dozen from a trader, chances were that four of them would be rotten and spread an evil stench when she cracked them open.

Officially, trading was forbidden and occasionally Red Guards raided bazaars or set up road blocks to catch those travelling to buy or sell goods. But the Bolsheviks couldn't stop all the weekly markets held in towns and villages across the land that kept the population alive. With my grandparents now old and weak, I believed it was my duty, as the eldest of the children still living at home, to find food for us all and enable us to avoid the indignity of eating rotten potatoes and watery kasha. I planned to start travelling to the trade fair in Kiev, held every other Tuesday, in search of goods that I could bring back to Pavolitch to eat or sell. Although fearful of what my new role might entail, I knew I had to do it. I still needed to prove my worth to the memory of my father, even though he was no longer with us. I felt an urgency to vindicate the death of Hertzl who was killed as he came to save me. And I wanted to demonstrate that I was every bit as good as Sarah. She might be at the university, but it was time I showed what I could do, too.

For my first trading trips, my grandfather weighed out ten pounds of dried peas and ten pounds of dried beans that I put into sacks in a woven basket that I carried on my back. Zayde's old balagula was no longer around, but often I would catch a ride on a sled with one of the other drivers that ploughed the route between Pavolitch and Popilna. If not, I trudged the twelve versts along icy roads to the train station on foot. Before I began my fortnightly trips to Kiev I hadn't been near a train station for years. During the war, sensible people had avoided them at all costs; they were terrifying and off-limits. Battles had been fought around railway junctions and, even though the Bolsheviks had by now consolidated their command in the area, Makhno and his black-capped anarchists continued to raid trains and villages near the railway, throwing Jews out of carriages or shooting them point-blank.

It was still several years before regular services were to resume; there were no timetables and no carriages for passengers. It wasn't possible to just buy a ticket and climb aboard. In fact, officially, ordinary people weren't allowed on board at all. Trains appeared whenever their cargoes of goods or troops were ready. This meant sometimes they travelled through Popilna to Kiev or Odessa three times a day and other times it was more like three times a week. Every so often they stopped at our station, but on many occasions they didn't.

If the train didn't stop, I had to leap aboard while it was moving and cling on for dear life until I had the chance to find a better spot: on a footplate between carriages, perched on top of a freight car or crouching in the corner of an empty wagon. Thankfully the trains travelled slowly, but still I was terrified the first time I jumped onto a moving wagon (just as I was, many decades later, when I first stepped onto an escalator). But if one does something often enough it becomes second nature and so it was with trains. I never lost the dread and fear, but I learned how to leap into the doorway of a freight car, to aim for the gap between the wagons or even, if the train was travelling slowly enough, to crawl in between the wheels and work my way up to the carriage roof.

The most terrifying part of the journey was arriving in Kiev. The station was the most awful place I had ever encountered. It consisted of dozens of makeshift wooden huts that reeked of urine and crawled with rats and lice and all sorts of lowlife who had found their way to the city: refugees, smugglers, gypsies, deserters, the homeless and the destitute. Not only were traders at risk of being attacked and robbed, but officials were known to offer bribes to informers and, in return for a hunk of bread or a handful of rubles, any of these people could report me to the authorities for dealing in contraband goods – and then heaven knows where I would end up.

So, to avoid the risk, I threw myself off the train before reaching the station and gave the whole area a wide berth. Jumping off was much worse than boarding the train in the first place. At least in winter deep drifts of snow lay either side of the train tracks creating a soft bed to land in. But when spring arrived, the embankments were piled high with blackened slush, which towered above deep puddles that I had to try to avoid. And later, in summer when the ground was hard, I came home spotted with inky bruises where I had hit the ground.

Whenever possible, I would leap off the left side of the train. I found that, as long as I was careful to avoid any rocks or other objects that could cause injury, I could roll out as the train was moving and my momentum would keep me flipping over like a pancake until I came to a standstill as the train screeched away toward the station. Sometimes, though, it wasn't possible to jump off to the left if a crowd of people was gathered there, or worse, an official. Or there could be an embankment or a cluster of trees that made it too dangerous. Then I had to spring onto the tracks to the right of the train and remain crouching or lying until the train had passed over me before getting up and moving on.

Very occasionally I would have the luxury of stepping off the train in a conventional fashion just as I might have done in the days before the war: I had made friends with one of the coal men who worked the route.

"I've got a daughter of my own, must be just the same age as you," he told me. "Hoping to marry her off next year to a fellow who'll look after her. I don't want her riding on the trains like you – it's no life for a young lady!"

In return for a couple of potatoes or a few rubles, he would let me scramble aboard and stand on the footplate where it was warm. He wasn't on duty very often – I think he was sent all over the country – but, when he was, he would take my hand and help me down the steps as if I were a lady in a silk dress carrying a parasol rather than a sack of beans. I would also find out from him when the train would be heading back in the direction of Odessa saving me hours of perilous waiting. For the return leg, I stopped at a railway goods yard seven versts from the main Kiev station and here my coal man would haul me up as the train slowed to a crawl. Even when he wasn't working, I would wait at the goods yard for the train home rather than hang around anywhere near the station. In addition to the other perils, anyone boarding a train in Kiev was likely to be asked to show a travel permit and, of course, I did not have one.

Kerensky Rubles

I HAD RARELY visited Kiev before I began trading at the market. What struck me most was the grime in the air. The whole of this vast, bustling city seemed to be filled with smoke that billowed from factories and countless chimneypots. A heavy mist settled above the river in the lower parts of town where most of the Jews lived. Even after dark, when Pavolitch came to a standstill, Kiev was still full of life. Black-clad lamplighters with long poles lit street lamps just as the many-storied buildings were melting into the darkness, the gaslight shining in their windows like multiple pairs of eyes. On my first visit Sarah met me a safe distance from the station. She introduced me to Shaya, her boyfriend, and together they showed me the sights of Kiev: the grandeur of Khreshchatik, the great central boulevard; the glittering, golden domes of the Pecherskaya monastery; the opulent Brodsky synagogue. All the time Shaya grilled me on my opinions of the city. I didn't tell Sarah, but I found his questions and the determination in his eyes quite terrifying.

I couldn't linger too long. I was visiting on business. Traders and peasants travelled sometimes hundreds of miles to come to the Tuesday fairs in Kiev. The marketplace thronged with scores of people, old and young, some illiterate peasants, others clearly well educated and once prosperous, all carrying on their backs sacks filled with whatever goods they could find to sell or barter. They were known as bagmen. I avoided talking to the other traders as much as possible. Throughout my childhood I had been kept hidden away from the men who came to trade with my grandfather; now I was among them and I found the whole experience distasteful.

Dirty lads in coarse jackets stood in pens surrounded by horses and cows whose ribs showed beneath their taut, scabby coats; country bumpkins held up skinny ducks or scrawny geese by their ankles; walnut-skinned old women in flowered headscarves hugged icons, crosses or kettles, flogging the last of their precious possessions for food to keep them alive for another day, another week; some, in their desperation, were even trying to exchange old Easter cards for a pinch of salt or a spoonful of tea. Enterprising young wives sat in front of low tables neatly arranged with jars of plum jam, pickled tomatoes or gherkins; ragged waifs wandered around selling cigarettes; and the occasional shifty-eyed man walked up and down the rows of tables week after week with the same jacket or pair of trousers hanging over his arm.

Inflation was by now out of control. Eggs cost six hundred rubles apiece; milk was fifteen hundred. A chicken was worth millions. Instead, many people reverted to a barter economy with no exchange of money. They gave what they had in return for what they needed. Sometimes they had to undertake several trades to end up with the goods they wanted. For example, if somebody needed to buy potatoes, and the potato seller wasn't interested in what they were offering, they would sell their wares to somebody else in exchange for, say, a chicken, then swap the chicken for a sack of potatoes. All kinds of arguments broke out between the vendors over how much corn a pumpkin was worth or the exchange rate between onions and flour. There were no official prices and everybody would pitch in with a noisy opinion.

Even in money transactions it was a challenge to work out how much to charge. Money and food were both so precious that nobody wanted to pay a fair price, but nobody really knew how much it was reasonable to ask, or even what sort of money to use. Mostly people still dealt in Kerensky rubles, which had been issued after the fall of the tsar. But every opposing side in the Civil War had issued its own currency and each refused to recognize notes printed by its adversaries. The Bolshevik government had circulated money, too, and the further away from Moscow or Petrograd you lived, the harder it was to know what was good money and what was not. Lots of people didn't trust the Bolshevik currency believing that it wasn't real money, that the regime wouldn't last. Nobody was entirely sure what all the different types of notes should look like and, as forgery was rife, it was almost impossible to be certain whether notes were genuine or not.

To add to the confusion, despite prices sometimes doubling from one week to the next, rather than designing new bank notes in higher denominations, the printers stopped cutting the sheets into individual notes. To buy a cabbage worth a thousand rubles, people exchanged whole pages of twenties and forties. I couldn't carry my money in a purse anymore – I needed a sack! After a good day's trading, I would come home with enough sheets to wallpaper a whole room. It was very hard to imagine that just a few years earlier, taking a forty ruble banknote to the market had been pointless; bread had cost a handful of kopeks and sellers turned away anyone proffering notes for which they could never find sufficient change.

My grandfather insisted that I accept only reliable, solid Kerensky rubles for my wares. Kerensky's lofty status among the Jews meant that, even four years after his demise, many still believed that only a banknote bearing his image could be relied on. All the money I made, I took back to my grandparents.

In addition to the Tuesday fairs a smaller Jewish market was held every Thursday in the Podol district of Kiev near the river. Occasionally Haskl accompanied me to the pre-Sabbath market hoping to buy some food that his wife could cook for the holiday. I was still as fond of Haskl as I had been as a little girl. I felt safe with him by my side and he carried my basket of goods with such ease that it could have been filled with feathers. On one occasion I helped Haskl pick out some potatoes that didn't look too moldy and a small cabbage. I pulled out a concertina of forty ruble notes. But the peasant woman behind the stall shook her head.

"What's wrong?" I asked, unfolding the sheet so she could see the hundreds of rubles I was offering her.

"That money's no good," she replied. I turned to Haskl who looked as shaken as I was. "They're saying Kerensky rubles aren't legal tender anymore," the woman continued. "I'm only accepting Bolshevik money."

Haskl may have suffered a physical deformity, but what he lacked in looks and stature, he made up for in guile. With his help, I managed to exchange the old money for whatever goods I could buy from the few traders who still believed that Kerensky rubles were worth keeping. Haskl and I returned to Pavolitch that night with sweet-smelling tobacco stuffed into little newspaper pouches and tins of a special type of fish that was only available in Kiev. In Pavolitch they should fetch a good price. But Zayde was livid when I showed him what I had bought.

"Are you mad, girl?" he shouted. "Kerensky money is proper money! These Bolsheviks won't last. What use are fancy fish and tobacco when we need to buy food to eat and shoes for our feet? If you want to be a trader, at least choose a proper commodity – like grain!" He roared with laughter at my crestfallen face then stormed out slamming the door behind him.

The next day Zayde was kept busy with a continual stream of customers arriving in search of grain. It was 1921 and the Bolsheviks had abandoned their requisitioning program under the policy of War Communism, which had caused so much misery and widespread starvation. Now, thanks to what the newspapers called Lenin's New Economic Policy, traders like my grandfather were able to resume their business. Peasants had returned in greater numbers after a four year interlude and, although activity was limited and volumes much reduced compared with the days before the October Revolution, Zayde busied himself once again with commerce, which seemed to bring him back to life.

And all of a sudden business was booming. The klet hadn't seen so much activity for years. First through the door that morning was Moishe, an old acquaintance of my grandfather's who had come all the way from Fastov, fifty versts away. From Skvira and even Berdichev buyers arrived and took away with them as much grain as Zayde could sell them. Nobody else was allowed in the warehouse when my grandfather was doing business, but Baba was called in when a transaction had been finalized and collected the money in the front pocket of her apron. When the pouch was bursting with sheets of Kerensky rubles and could hold no more, she locked the money away in a drawer. All day she went to and from the drawer until it was so full that it barely closed. I stayed in the kitchen and watched my grandmother bustling to and from the klet. I knew better than to venture into the warehouse myself; if Rachel, Baya or I went anywhere near it when customers were around, Zayde would chase us out with a stick, threatening to beat us around the head. He said it was because he hated men gawping at us.

"You see, nobody else is worried about Kerensky rubles, Pearl," Baba told me after the tenth customer had departed. "We haven't had so much money for years!" She showed me the apron with its pocket stuffed full.

"But that's just it, Baba. We never have this many customers. Don't you think people might be buying the grain because they know Kerensky money is worthless and they want to get rid of it as soon as they can?"

Baba gave me a clip round the ear and sent me packing. "Your grandfather's not a fool and nobody around here takes him for one. Now get out!"

When the warehouse was bare, and the last of the customers had disappeared, Zayde went to the drawer and began counting how much money he had made. My grandmother told him what I had said. He looked thoughtful for a moment then shook his head seriously.

"No, I don't believe it. After all, it was Moishe who came in first. I've known Moishe a long time and I can trust him. He wouldn't deceive me," said Zayde. That evening he set off for the synagogue with a spring in his step, delighted at the upturn in his fortunes. But when he returned an hour or so later, he was crestfallen.

"I've been duped, Pessy Tochter. They've taken advantage of an old man. Perele was right and the money's worthless. I may as well burn it." It was as close as Zayde ever came to apologizing for anything.

All day I had been worried about the Kerensky money that was pouring into our house and had spent my time hatching a plan. We needed to find a place where nobody yet knew that the old rubles were now worthless. I studied the railway map and decided that Kozyatin would be a good bet. It was far enough away that nobody knew me there and was further from Kiev than Pavolitch. My grandmother didn't want me to undertake such a mission on my own and insisted that her nephew Zillig accompany me. Zillig was a soldier home from Poland on leave. He was tall and stocky and Baba knew he would look after me.

Before dawn the following morning the two of us set off for Popilna to await a train. The summer was drawing to an end and as we marched up and down outside the station, we clapped our hands together to keep out the early morning chill. While we waited, a young man approached us, a friend of Zillig's. We didn't tell him why we were headed for Kozyatin, but I think he guessed what we were up to. Dozens of people were making for the trains, all journeying away from Kiev to dispose of any worthless currency they had in towns and villages that might not yet have heard the news. Zillig's friend told us to look out for a fellow called Gomberg in Kozyatin. We would recognize him by his round glasses and pointy nose, he said. He was a fellow Pavolitcher and, if we mentioned the friend's name, he would help us in whatever way he could.

Thankfully we didn't have to wait much more than an hour for a train

heading in the right direction. It even slowed down and stopped at Popilna, so there was no need to run alongside it and jump aboard. When
travelling alone to Kiev I had always avoided the empty freight cars. They
were often haunted by shadowy figures of drunks or gypsies and I was terrified of being robbed, or worse. But with Zillig I wasn't scared. Nobody
would dare touch me. So I leant against the wooden carriage wall, while
Zillig stood in front of me, his arm outstretched and his hand against the
side of the car to support himself and protect me from the gaze of other
travelers. As our journey would be taking us in the opposite direction
from Kiev, I didn't know the route and relied on Zillig to tell me which
areas were safe, when I should crouch down to make myself invisible, and
at what point we needed to jump off.

It was late morning when we arrived in Kozyatin and we came across
Gomberg straight away. "If you've got any Kerensky rubles, go straight to
the market and spend them. It's up the hill there, to the right. Then get
out of here as quick as you can," he advised us in a sharp whisper.

We nodded sagely and set off for the market at a trot. The poor people
of Kozyatin accepted our stacks of rubles with glee. We bought a sack-full
of salt and more plums than our bags could hold. We were hungry by
now and ate some of the plums greedily as we wandered around the market taking care not to drop a trail of stones that the stallholders we had
tricked could use to trace us. And we still had plenty of money to spend.

I spied an old lady at the back of the market standing behind a pile of
shawls. They would be light and easy to carry. The shawls were beautifully
soft, but rather plain and, despite their obvious high quality, I couldn't
see them attracting much interest among the women of Pavolitch, let
alone Kiev.

"Do you have any colored ones?" I asked her.

"Oh, yes, my dear. I've got plenty more at home, but I can't leave the
stall now to go and fetch them. If you come back next week, I'll make sure
to bring some with me then," she said.

I tried to look my most innocent as I explained that I wasn't sure I
would be able to make it next week. We agreed that Zillig would stay and
watch the market stall while I went back to the woman's house to look at
the other shawls. It wasn't far and she talked all the way there.

"They're very good shawls, my dear. I make them myself and they'll last
you many, many years. I've still got the shawls I wore when my boys were
babies. Nice pretty ones I've got at home, too, you know, but there's not

much call for them these days. The red ones would look beautiful on you with your big dark eyes. They'd show off your color lovely." I let her talk as I struggled silently to keep up with her. She may have been old, but she walked briskly, with the ease of someone accustomed to physical activity.

When we reached the woman's house, she told me to give the door a push and go in. It creaked open and I let out a gasp. Inside, two enormous, burly soldiers were sitting at the table drinking vodka. They looked rough and unkempt. I stood stock still not knowing whether to enter or turn and run. They know what I'm up to and I've fallen into a trap, I thought, as the two men turned to me and stared.

But the old woman pushed past me with a broad smile. "Don't be scared of my boys!" she laughed. "They may be big and important-looking in their uniforms, but they're as gentle as lambs really. Aren't you boys?" She went up to the table and gave each of the men a noisy kiss on the cheek then scolded them: "Now scam! Get out of here, can't you see you're scaring the girl?"

True to her word, the woman had several brightly colored shawls strewn around the room. Some weren't finished yet, but I picked out several that I liked and handed over my sheets of Kerensky rubles.

"Thank you so much, my dear. I don't think I've ever sold so many in one week, let alone one day. You've made me very happy, dear, you really have." We hurried back to the market where Zillig was waiting. I called my goodbyes to the shawl-seller and grabbed Zillig by the arm to pull him away.

"Let's get out of here," I whispered.

I half-ran-half-walked back to the station feeling more guilty with every step about what I had done. Part of me wanted to rush back and tell the woman to spend the money I had given her as quickly as possible. But I knew I couldn't. She had been so warm-hearted, so maternal toward me. And, as a girl who had been brought up without her mother, those were qualities I appreciated. I felt truly awful for deceiving her.

It took forever to get home from Kozyatin. The hours we spent waiting at the train station were agonizing. I kept looking around nervously, constantly fearful that someone would place a hand on my shoulder and drag me back to the market to face the traders I had defrauded. My mind kept going back to the old lady with the shawls and I hoped she would have the sense to spend her money quickly.

"You have to relax, Pearl. Don't look so nervous or people will get suspicious," Zillig cautioned. I tried to do as he advised, but my heart was pounding as loudly as heavy footsteps and my mind kept tricking me that someone was running after me. I felt sure everybody around me could hear it, too.

At last, as the sky was beginning to darken, a train bound for Kiev arrived. It would have to go past Popilna whether it stopped or not. Zillig found a windowless carriage where he thought we would be safe. Several soldiers were inside and they stared at me as we entered. The floor was strewn with straw, but there were no benches. Zillig piled up a little bed of straw for me and told me to lie down and get some sleep while he watched over me and our prized purchases. But how could I sleep? My mind was still racing, my pulse throbbing, and although Zillig tried to shelter me from the gaze of the soldiers, I could feel their eyes boring into me like nails. And besides, the straw reeked of horse manure. Zillig was trying to act tough, but I knew he was nervous, too. He could barely keep still and looked up at the doorway constantly, as if he expected a figure to appear there. To an outsider, the movement of the train would disguise the fact that his right leg jiggled continuously, as if he had a nervous twitch in his hip.

Finally, we arrived at Popilna in the dead of night. The train didn't stop so Zillig jumped off with our sacks of salt and plums, then I leaped off into his arms with the shawls flapping around me like a multi-colored bird. Even though it was so late the area around the station was still buzzing with people. They crowded around us firing questions:

"Where have you been?"

"What did you buy?"

"Are Kerenskys still good?"

"What have you heard?"

But Zillig and I walked straight through the rabble, avoiding looking into the dozens of pairs of eyes that followed us and saying not a word to anybody. I had no idea what time it was, but I could barely keep my eyes open during the long trudge back to Pavolitch. The sky was already starting to brighten by the time we reached the double-fronted house. I crept inside silently, and fell gratefully into my bed, more than twenty-four hours after I had left it, and as the pent-up emotions of the day drifted in clouds around me, I cried myself gently to sleep.

I awoke around midday, still feeling guilty about deceiving the vendors at the market in Kozyatin, fearful even now that someone would come after me, hurl abuse at me, beat or arrest me. But if I hadn't exchanged the worthless money for saleable goods, where would that have left us? My grandfather would have given away his entire stock for nothing and we would be destitute. Now it was every man for himself. Zayde's supposed friend Moishe from Fastov had proved that: rather than deceiving a stranger as I had done, he had defrauded a man he had known for years. Nobody could afford to listen to his conscience anymore and do only what he thought was morally right. We just had to make sure that our family survived, and if others suffered as a result, then so be it.

Over the days that followed, I slowly exchanged the salt, plums and shawls that I had bought in Kozyatin. Baba made most of the plums into jam and I sold three jars for a scraggy chicken, a shawl for a few pounds of corn, a small bag of salt for a box of tea. I bought things we needed to feed ourselves, foodstuffs that Zayde could sell in his warehouse and goods that I could take to Kiev and exchange.

People got to know me at the Ukrainian market in Pavolitch, held after church every Sunday, as well as at the Jewish market in Kiev on Thursdays, and around the ramshackle wooden huts near the station in Popilna where the bagmen congregated. But I kept to myself by avoiding talking to the traders unless strictly necessary and shunning eye contact. They called me the *Pritza*, the Lady, because I refused to carry a sack over my shoulder like a bagman and instead carried my wares in my grandmother's woven baskets.

After pouring scorn on my earlier trading foray in Kiev, sneering at me for bringing home tobacco and boxes of fish, Zayde recognized that I had inherited some of his skills and could be a successful trader, too. I was a businesswoman now and at last I was starting to prove myself. I would be the one to ensure my grandparents, sister and cousins survived and, in doing so, I would demonstrate that I was every bit as good as Sarah, just in a different way – and that our neighbor Hertzl hadn't died for nothing. Once all the goods I had bought in Kozyatin were either sold for new Bolshevik money or exchanged, I began my new career in earnest: I started going on the *yarid*.[1]

1. Fair (Yiddish).

The Yarid

LITTLE HAD I realized on that terrible night when I returned from the market in Kozyatin that it would mark the beginning a new stage in my life, one in which fear and danger were to become my constant companions. I learned on which days each week all the towns and villages in our area held their markets. There was always something going on somewhere. Every day I rode the railways like a hobo, buying and selling, bartering and exchanging. My travels took me further and further afield. I started with places close to Pavolitch: Popilna, Kozhanka, Skvira and Ruzhin, then to Berdichev and Vinnitsa to the west, Odessa way down south, and even Kharkov far away in eastern Ukraine. Journeys could take several days and I survived with almost no rest for nobody slept when they travelled with merchandise, always fearful of unknown dangers and wary of the people around them.

If pickings had been rich in the last few days and I had plenty to sell, and if my destination wasn't too far, Rachel, or occasionally Mendl, would come with me to help carry my wares. But usually I travelled alone. Rachel hated the yarid and only came when I forced her.

"I don't see why we have to do this," she would whine. "The family could get by without the yarid." She lacked my sense of duty, my need to prove my worth, and she wasn't as tough as I was. She railed against the cold and the lack of sleep and she found the whole experience terrifying. Mendl, on the other hand, enjoyed the adventure. For him, the yarid wasn't a matter of survival, but a game in which we scored or lost points depending on our degree of success. And he loved leaping out of moving trains. But Mendl was just ten years old and Baba would only let him come on short journeys.

Each day I rose early, filled my basket with whatever goods I had accumulated, hauled it onto my back, and headed along the road to Popilna. The station wasn't as dangerous as the one in Kiev, but still it was no place for a woman to wait on her own. You never knew what kind of thieves and hoodlums could be hanging around there waiting for a chance to steal money or food like vultures circling in search of easy prey. As more and more Jews started going on the yarid, a group of Jewish men from Pavolitch clubbed together and renovated a ramshackle hut near the station to use as a waiting room, or even a hostel. Here we would congregate until a train arrived. With trains running so erratically it soon became my second home. Sometimes I would stay there overnight, even for two or three nights if the trains had stopped again: frequently they would grind to a halt in the middle of nowhere, having run out of fuel or, as the year wore on, been caught in snowdrifts.

However noisy the chatter of voices in the hut, it was impossible to miss the shrill whistle of the steam train as it wheezed toward the station. As one we jumped up and ran outside, kicking earth over the embers of the fire as we left. From all directions people sprinted to the railway as if drawn by a magnet. Even if the train stopped at the station, I wouldn't climb aboard there. It was too dangerous. There were too many people hanging about, predators who could attack, steal or report me. Instead I would head a few yards further up the line and wait for the puffing hulk of the engine to reach me.

Dozens, sometimes hundreds, of men and women piled onto the trains at each station. Often I recognized faces and knew where people were likely to jump off. Sometimes there were so many bodies on the trains that it seemed half the population was on the move. But no sense of solidarity existed among those riding the railroad. Boarding the train was a battle, and it was each person for himself. Nobody ever offered a hand to someone being left behind unless they were related. Everyone was wary of everyone else. Nobody spoke and nobody smiled. Our means of travel was illegal and so was our trade; you never knew who might be an informer, a bribe-taker, even a murderer. I kept to myself and neither told anyone where I was going, nor where I came from.

Once aboard, each found his own little spot to nestle in. As far as possible, I still avoided travelling in freight cars. I once heard of a girl from Kiev who was raped in broad daylight when she was travelling in a freight carriage. Unless it was piercingly cold, I would hurry onto the roof of the train to one of my most coveted spots. Being small I could nestle into a niche between the timber that was transported endlessly from one side of the country to another. There I could make myself almost invisible and the lofty position afforded me a good view of any dangers lying in wait. On a sunny day it could be quite pleasant, lying back on a cargo of timber, watching the clouds shifting across the sky and the birch trees swaying to the rhythmic clackety clack of the wheels.

Occasionally I even felt safe enough to allow my mind to drift into day-dreams of better times: childhood days when there was always enough to eat, listening to my great-grandfather Akiva's stories and munching poppy-seed cookies. On a particularly bright and cheery day I might even dare picture a hopeful future. Eventually, maybe, we could all join my great-uncle Menachem Mendl in Canada. Naftula had reached Winnipeg by now and had a job in a retail store. How I longed to see my beloved brother again! But even if we were never to be reunited with Naftula, life couldn't always be this difficult. The hardship had to end one day. It was clear by now that the tsar and his family were dead and there could be no return to the persecution of the past. But surely Communist power couldn't last long – or could it? Perhaps one day when life gets easier I might fall in love like Sarah, even have children of my own . . . I floated away again.

Of course once the snows arrived it was deathly cold on the roof and the wind gnawed through my bones. I would wedge myself as deeply as I could between the logs or planks, but this didn't stop me from shivering. As the winters passed my old coat – once so fashionable – became more and more tatty. Its fancy double seams, hand-stitched by the best tailor in Berdichev, gradually came loose and through them the chill penetrated like icy fingers.

Sometimes the train roof became very crowded. Accidents and arguments were inevitable. I remember the first time I saw one of my fellow travelers fall off a railcar. He was a young lad, fifteen at most. One minute he was picking his way over the logs trying to get to the next carriage where a friend was beckoning. The wood was slippery with hoar-frost and when the train braked suddenly, he was gone. I don't know whether he survived. From where I was sitting it was impossible to tell, but I never saw him again. At least once a month I saw someone fall. Often they were being careless or reckless and I was confident the same fate would never befall me. I was always extremely careful when I moved around the top of the carriages, slithering on my stomach like a snake. Nevertheless I made sure never to tell my grandparents what I saw. They worried enough about me as it was. And if Rachel was with me I would try to distract her if I could.

Rachel was less hardy than me and suffered dreadfully from the cold. One bitter night we were travelling back to Popilna together, huddling under a pile of sacks.

"I'm freezing, Pearl, I can't move my toes," she moaned.

"Stamp your feet," I told her, but it was too late for that. She could barely stand. Rachel had made the fatal mistake of falling asleep. I covered her feet with sacking and kneaded them with my hands, but it was no good. I hauled her off the roof and into one of the containers that had been used to transport salt from Odessa to Kiev and was now returning empty. It was only marginally warmer and I sat down in a corner taking Rachel's feet in my lap. When we finally reached Popilna it was dark and the train didn't stop. It slowed to a crawl for the station master to signal to the driver that the track was clear. It was imperative that we leap off before the train sped up again, but by now Rachel was hardly able to move at all. I had to push her off the train into the darkness before jumping myself. Thankfully we found a balagula to take us back to Pavolitch and Rachel fell straight into bed. Baba refused to let her sleep in case she never woke up again, forcing her to sit up and drink hot tea while massaging her frozen feet. No remedy, compress or bandage seemed to make any difference and for a whole year afterwards Rachel could only hobble.

As well as the risk of falling and the terrible cold, for Jews travelling on the trains there was the added danger of falling into the hands of unsavory Ukrainian travelers. As the Bolsheviks' power consolidated, the old resentments re-emerged. It was awful to watch a group of Ukrainians surround a poor Jewish traveler, snatch his bags and boot him off the train. Even worse was when Makhno's anarchists organized a raid on one of the trains. They were some of the fiercest anti-Semites of all and I was much more fearful of being caught by Makhno than I was of falling off the roof. Kozhanka was the first stop after Popilna on the route to Kiev and it was one of the anarchists' strongholds. As we slowed down through Kozhanka station I would keep very still and quiet, trying to make myself even smaller than I really was. Makhno's black-hatted brigade frequently stopped the trains and turfed off any Jews they found as if they were discarding pieces of litter. They didn't normally come onto the roof, but sometimes they would fire their guns in our direction. Even after I heard that Makhno had been defeated by the Communists and fled, I still breathed more easily once the train had passed Kozhanka.

I had become so good at making myself go unnoticed on the trains that I was often able to listen in to the conversations of others without them knowing. Information about which goods were available where was valuable and traders tried to keep it to themselves. But I was small and quiet and could squeeze into tiny gaps where I often picked up tit-bits of whispered news that I could use to my own advantage. One day I overheard a young man telling his companion that he had bought caustic soda in Berdichev. Caustic soda was a precious commodity – it was used for cleaning and even to make soap. The next day Rachel and I set off for Berdichev armed with a map that my grandfather had drawn us showing where the Hager family lived, relatives of my great-grandfather Akiva's brother. I remembered them from my childhood trips to Berdichev, but our relatives had lost touch since Akiva died shortly after the outbreak of war.

"Just go to the street and ask anyone you see. Everyone knows the Hagers and they'll point you to the house," Zayde said. "If there's no train home, I'm sure they'll let you stay as long as you need."

But Berdichev had changed dramatically since the days of our happy childhood outings there to visit the dressmaker. We bought the caustic soda and found the Hagers' house without difficulty. It stood dark and menacing. The outside walls were lined with black soot and several window panes were missing, leaving dark, gaping holes in the brickwork like a face with no eyes. The whole street was eerily still and Rachel and I both felt a chill skim over us. A pogrom had taken place here over two years earlier. It appeared that all the Jews had been burnt in their homes or murdered in the street. Nobody was left to rebuild the houses, replace the windows and wash off the soot. The whole area had become a ghost town; dark, sinister and silent. Our relatives had surely perished. I turned and fled, oblivious to the burns from the caustic soda that was corroding my basket and singeing my skin. Rachel shambled after me moving as fast as her still tender feet would allow.

My back took some weeks to recover from the caustic soda burns and the bulky woven basket I carried irritated the raw flesh. With the pain adding to the cold and fear, I dreaded my trips to market more than ever.

Black-market Gold

FOR MONTHS my grandparents had been accustomed to asking their acquaintances in Pavolitch for small commissions that I could fulfill for them at the markets.

"Tobacco, as much baccy as you can get."

"Sweets for the children."

"More sugar to make the tree-bark tea taste less bad."

"Cigarette papers – newspaper's not the same!"

One day an old friend of my grandfather's made a more curious request: "Could you see if you can sell some gold for me". If I could trade gold rather than bulky, heavy commodities, I could hide it in my clothing and wouldn't have to carry the basket that was rubbing so painfully against my acid-burnt back. Besides, I was fed up with hauling heavy loads. I was small and thin and the goods I traded could be so awkward to carry.

And so I became a black-market gold dealer. My grandparents collected coins, rings, medals, jewelry, any gold that family, friends or acquaintances still had. Young women gave earrings and bracelets that they had been saving for their wedding trousseaux, mothers offered medals awarded to their dead sons for their bravery, wives even gave up their wedding rings. All these goods were given to my grandparents on trust and hidden in secret compartments that Baba sewed into my tattered coat.

I took the gold hundreds of miles away, to Kharkov. The journey was murderous. Once I had jumped off the train in Kiev I had to work my way across to the other side of the jumble of stinking huts that made up the main station and leap aboard a train heading east. The trains were a different design from those travelling between Kiev and Odessa and they offered no means of climbing onto the roof, nor even inside the carriages.

Instead I perched on the wooden boards that ran across the wheel axles. There was very little space. The icy wind whistled straight through me and the noise of the wheels on the tracks was almost deafening, but these tiny platforms were in great demand. Hands clawed at me and clung to my arms as bagmen piled onto the boards and held onto whatever they could in a desperate attempt to stop themselves from falling off. Occasionally, with a sinister howl, the train would jerk or brake fiercely and somebody tumbled from the platform. It would have been almost impossible not to fall under the wheels.

Even if the train didn't stop, it took all day to reach Kharkov. More often it stopped repeatedly in the middle of nowhere, the endless miles of woodland revealing nothing of our location. But I never dared jump down to stretch my legs; it was too risky. There was no timetable to indicate when the train might move again and, besides, I was fearful of losing my precious spot above the wheels. If I gave it up, the other travelers might never let me back on board. At the end of each journey I thanked God that I was still alive.

Once in Kharkov, through a complex network of contacts, I was introduced to some shady dealers who asked me to follow them to the back of the market. I was almost shaking with nerves the first time I stepped behind the brick wall that separated me from the other market traders who might have offered some protection. The men were gruff but brisk, well dressed if not well mannered. They inspected my goods meticulously then handed over hard currency in return. I hid the money away carefully in my secret pockets before stepping back into the marketplace. Most people in Pavolitch wanted Polish money in return for their gold, in the belief that it would be more permanent than the numerous transient Russian currencies that had circulated over the last few years. Many had found themselves left with now worthless tsarist, Kerensky or White Army rubles, or Petlyurist karbovantsy, and still didn't trust the Bolsheviks' notes.

I didn't feel any safer on the return journey from Kharkov. My heart seemed to skip several beats at every stop and I held my breath as I made my way across Kiev station, my eyes alert and watchful for police agents or informers. Whether I was trading in gold or foreign currency, my punishment would be the same. If caught, I would have been shot on the spot.

*

One evening, after I had just returned home from a particularly tiring trip, we heard a knock at the door. It was dark already and my grandmother peered out tentatively. It was one of our Ukrainian neighbors.

"Pani Pessy, can I come in?" she asked, already shouldering her way through the door. Baba opened her mouth to greet her, but before she could say a word a torrent burst from her visitor's lips.

"Pani Pessy, I have just returned from Popilna where I saw your grand-daughters doing the most dangerous thing. I don't know how you can allow it! Pearl jumped right off the train while it was still moving. And my husband said he saw Rachel do just the same. They'll kill themselves playing that game. You must put a stop to it at once!"

Baba called us in. "Is this true?" she asked with a frown.

My grandparents had no idea what I went through each and every day to provide the food that Baba put on the table. I nodded.

"There is no other way, Baba," I told her. "I have been doing this for three years, and I haven't injured myself badly yet. If we are going to eat, I have to jump off the trains. They don't always stop!"

I heard the murmur of my grandparents' voices continuing long into the night. At breakfast the next morning, they announced their verdict.

"You're to stop going on the yarid, Perele. If we can't eat meat, we'll have potatoes. And if there are no potatoes, well, we'll find something else to eat. God will provide for us." I looked from one serious face to the other and saw their love and concern etched into every deepening wrinkle.

"Hertzl didn't die just so that we could all starve to death ourselves," I told them. "I don't like jumping out of trains. I don't like taking gold to Kharkov. I hate it! I'm terrified every moment of every day that I'm away from here! But it's my duty to you. You have looked after me all my life and I owe it to you to provide for you because you couldn't do yourselves what I have been doing for these last three years. That's the end of it. We will get through this."

But deep in my heart, where I hid my most secret feelings, I was grow-ing less and less confident that we would get through it. For three long years I had been travelling across the plains selling, buying, bartering, hiding on train roofs, crouching above wheels, freezing half to death and being terrified to the same measure. I was exhausted and I could see no way out. How many more years could I keep this up? Zayde was growing older and visibly weaker. Baba seemed to be shrinking by the day. And Rachel had spent a year barely able to walk as a result of my occupation. In the freezing snows of late 1923, my strength finally gave out. I could take it no more.

The previous day, as usual, I had jumped onto the train as it passed Popilna and hidden among the timber in the last wagon. It was particularly cold – minus thirty degrees at least – and I shivered as I tried to wedge myself among the snow-covered planks to shelter from the wind that was humming through the wood. The frost was so severe that I felt it burning my nose and cheeks. I pulled my hat down further over my ears and wound my shawl tighter around my head and shoulders so that only my eyes were showing. I wasn't travelling too far, only to the market in Fastov where I had heard that salt was available. But the marketplace was quiet; traders were few and far between. No doubt the weather was keeping most people indoors. I had no luck tracking down the salt, but I knew I faced several hours' wait before a train would be heading back toward home. I dejectedly wandered around the market trying to keep warm.

All of a sudden the sky darkened as a cavalry of clouds rode overhead from the north. It was as if dusk had fallen from one moment to the next even though it was only midday. The wind bellowed and started to lift the powdery snow from the ground and swirl it round like a vortex.

"Come away! You can't risk staying here in this. Pack up your things, everybody, and I'll take you back!" called the lone balagula who was hanging around waiting for a fare. Most of the traders had come from a settlement a few versts distant from Fastov. They hurriedly bundled together their wares and jumped aboard the balagula's horse-drawn sled. I had no option but to join them. The horse was old and struggled before the weight of so many passengers. But every one of us knew that if we left somebody behind, he would not last long. Already I couldn't see a thing. All the tracks through the snow had been obliterated and it was impossible to tell where the road was. But the driver knew the area, I thought, as I pulled my shawl over my eyes and wriggled my feet to keep the blood pumping.

We seemed to have been moving for an hour at least. My tongue had frozen inside my mouth and the cold was making my head hurt, but I was sure our destination couldn't be far. I lowered my shawl for a moment and glanced around at the other passengers, all huddled like motionless lumps of sackcloth. I prodded the woman next to me with my elbow. She didn't move. My shallow breath turned to ice on my shawl and my eyelashes were sticking together. I had lost all sensation not just in my hands and feet but in my arms and legs as well. I had never been so cold in all my life. I knew that if I stopped praying I would die. "Please, God, let us arrive somewhere soon; please, God, let the driver not be lost; please, God, let the driver still be conscious; please, God; please, God; please . . ." But we had surely lost the road and must be travelling across open fields. The miserable horse was clearly in difficulty, snorting and tossing its head as it struggled for breath through ice-clogged nostrils.

Suddenly the world turned back to front and became shrouded in a cloak of white. The driver had accidentally turned the sled into a snow-drift.

"Get up! Get up!" he yelled. He didn't admit to being lost, but insisted we all get out and move around before we freeze to death while he lashed at the horse and pulled the vehicle out of the drift.

"Just keep in touching distance of the sled!" he warned. I hauled myself upright and almost toppled straight over as if my feet had fallen off the end of my legs. Tentatively I moved them and after a few seconds I was able to jump up and down without falling, clapping my mittened hands in front of my face to try to revive my circulation. Some of my fellow passengers were not moving and those of us that were able dragged them to their feet and shook them. We were all still alive.

The snow continued to fall not in flakes but in sheets all around us. After a minute or so we set off again into the endless universe of white. Just as I was beginning to give up all hope, I heard the unmistakable sound of dogs barking. The driver jerked his head, too, and we headed in the direction the noise was coming from. In fact the dogs were just yards away from us, but we couldn't see them until they surrounded us. We had reached a small hamlet. We were saved.

Thankfully a Jewish lady lived nearby and when she heard the news that a group of market traders, including a young Jewish woman, had been lost on their way back from Fastov, she welcomed me into her home. She put a pan of potatoes on the stove and heated up some broth. Slowly, achingly, my body eased its way back into life. I stayed in that house all day and all night gradually recovering.

By the time I arrived back in Pavolitch the following morning my grandparents had given me up for dead. They had spent the night pacing up and down unable to go to bed, let alone sleep, as the storm swirled around the double-fronted house. When I wasn't back by nightfall they feared I must have frozen to death. Baba started and turned pale when I walked through the door as if it were not me, but rather a ghost of her granddaughter that had stepped into the house. I hurried straight past her without even stopping to tell my story and entered the kitchen where I wrapped myself in blankets, lay down on the big, brick stove and burst into a furious fit of tears. The hunger and cold, the responsibility of supporting both grandparents and my sister and cousins, all had become a burden that was too great for me to bear. After my hours stranded in the blizzard, frozen to the bone, blinded by the snow and unable to get home, I realized that I had to escape. I had cheated death too often for a young woman of my years.

"I would rather spend my life breaking stones with an axe than go through that again," I told Baba when I was calm enough to speak. She wept silently as she stroked my puffy cheeks. That evening I wrote a letter to Naftula and one to my great-uncle Menachem Mendl in Canada. I begged them to do whatever they could to get me and the rest of our family out. In the Soviet Union it was just too difficult for us to find the means to live.

A Journey

ORGANIZING THE papers and legal documents to leave the Soviet Union was a long process of endless waiting, of signing forms and hoping for letters to arrive. I was to go first and the rest of the family hoped to follow. At last, after six impatient months, I was ready to go. Zayde gave me the last kopeks he had to finance my journey. I feared for him and Baba, for how they would survive without me. But Rachel was with them; although she hated the yarid, she could find food for them if need be. Whenever I voiced my concerns, they shook their heads adamantly.

"You've done enough for us, Perele. You have your chance now – just go."

"But how will you get by?" I asked over and over again. The reply was always the same: "God will provide."

My grandparents gave me their souls so that I could escape to Canada, and I owed it to them as soon as I arrived to try to gather enough money to bring them over to join me across the great ocean.

After all my years of travelling illicitly on goods trains, it felt miraculous to sit in a carriage with a group of other Jews all heading to Canada, too, and not feel fearful of what might happen to me on the journey. All the transportation was organized by agents for the Canadian authorities. I had my travel pass and my journey was legal and sanctioned. At each stage our group was to be met by somebody who would explain to us what to do next. None of my fellow travelers was from Pavolitch, but they came from towns and villages that were familiar to me from my long train journeys across Ukraine.

From Kiev the train brought us to Moscow, the capital since 1918. It was the first time I had set foot outside the lands that used to make up the Pale of Settlement and I was overawed by the crazy, multi-colored onion domes and startling golden cupolas rising above the river, the wide boulevards and vast squares. There was plenty of time to look around as I had to spend several days in Moscow queuing and re-queuing at the Canadian Embassy for my entry visa and organizing transit permits for all the countries I would have to pass through before I finally arrived in Canada.

I wandered around and around Red Square and the Kremlin marveling at the richness of the colors; I walked under the elegant arcades of Petrovka and gazed across the great squares surrounding the Bolshoi Theater and Pushkin's statue. I had never been a "tourist" before and the experience was somewhat unnerving. This city was now the capital of the country in which I had lived all my life, yet it didn't feel like my country. The capital of the lands I knew was Kiev; Moscow was most definitely foreign. I didn't even understand the language and felt lost and vulnerable whenever anybody spoke to me. I gathered together in my head all the words of Ukrainian and Polish I knew, jumbled them together with my scant spattering of Russian and tried to make myself understood.

The next train took us west to Vitebsk where we changed carriages to travel the next few miles to Polatsk. Here we were herded like cattle into a delousing station. Never have I felt so humiliated. Along with the rest of the women, I was separated from the men of our party and taken to an empty, white room, where a stocky woman with a harsh voice and gigantic arms forced us to undress. I removed my coat and dress and stood waiting in my underwear and stockings.

"Everything off, ladies. Take everything off," the woman called out. I didn't want to remove my underwear in front of all these strange people so I kept it on. It was a mistake. I was soon spotted and, with her huge hands, the woman tugged at my straps and pulled at my buttons until I was as naked as the day I was born. Our clothes were bundled away to be cleaned while we were forced to take cold showers in a communal wash room, and to scrub ourselves with hard, yellow soap that made my skin itch. Then we were given scratchy gowns to wear until our own clothes were returned to us. When I was finally able to pull my dress over my head again I experienced a wave of nausea. The stench of the powerful washing detergent was overwhelming. Over the next day or two I repeatedly had to stop myself from gagging until the smell wore off.

Next we continued westward by train to the border of newly independent Latvia and beautiful, medieval Riga, with its cobbled streets, synagogues and bustling port. Here I picked up money that Naftula had wired to me from Canada and sent back to my grandfather all that remained of the cash he had given me for the journey. I had spent very little, knowing how badly my family would need every last kopek that Zayde had insisted I take with me. Finally, we took another train for the short journey to Libau[1] where we were to board the ship. Beside the port was a decontamination center. Once again we had to undress and this time our clothes and hair were checked for lice.

As I was clean, I was allowed to board the next ship, which arrived in port the following day. A great gate opened and I walked through to meet my freedom. But anyone who was classed as unclean had to stay in Libau's decontamination center for several days, or even weeks, until their bodies were free from lice and a new ship had arrived to take them away. They remained in numbered compartments, sleeping in rows like sick people in a hospital, enclosed by high, brick walls and separated from the world by barred windows. The group I had been travelling with for the last week disbanded with just a handful allowed onto the boat with me and the rest remaining in Libau, languishing in a sense of hopelessness as the gates closed again behind the chosen few.

I had never been on a ship before and I found the movement of the waves beneath me unsettling. The floor sloped first one way then another, tipping me against walls and railings as I walked. The journey across the Baltic was to last the best part of the three days and I wondered how I would survive the churning sickness in my stomach and the unsteadiness on my feet. I soon learned, however, that when the sea became rough, it was best to head to the deck and watch the waves breaking against the bow of the ship. The movement was mesmerizing and my nausea soon dispersed. Watching the waves, I spent hour after hour thinking about the family I had left behind and the world I had escaped. Now that I had left the Soviet Union, life seemed suddenly brighter, the smells sweeter and, for the first time in many years, the future was within my grasp.

At each port of call traders boarded the boat, selling food and home-made goods: black bread, pickled cabbage, fried potatoes, plump chicken

1. Now Liepaja.

legs; I hadn't seen such a feast in years. I wasn't sure if it was kosher, but I tried to put the question out of my mind and savor every mouthful. At the same time, I wept for Zayde, Baba, Sarah and even Rachel; I had been her guardian, her constant companion, ever since she was born and we had never been apart for more than a few days before. Even in Makarov, when we had been parted from the rest of the family, Rachel and I were together. Often my little sister had felt like a burden; being five years younger than me, she needed constant protection. But now I missed her continual presence.

I looked forward, too, to being reunited with Naftula, my dear, sweet brother, and with Feter Mendl and Mima Bluma and my cousins. I was just a girl when they had left Pavolitch for Winnipeg. How different would their lives be now? And what would await me in Canada, a country I couldn't even begin to picture in my imagination? All I knew about Winnipeg was that it was even colder in winter than Pavolitch. But what would the people be like? How many Jews were there? Did they have synagogues? And how were Jews treated by the other races that lived there? These questions buzzed around my head as we skirted the Baltic coast to Kiel, through the canal to the Dutch frontier and south to Belgium. At last we disembarked and I found myself swaying and unable to walk straight after three days at sea. Once again we were decontaminated and deloused before the final stretch of my journey across Europe to reach England.

London was a city I had dreamed about: a distant land of kings and queens. But rather than the golden carriages I had imagined, we were met at the dock by a cattle truck and transported across town like animals. Despite the disappointment, shame and mortification I felt, I looked out from my moving cage at majestic buildings – houses fit for princesses – that lined the wide avenues leading us to a railway station so grand it looked like a palace. It was springtime and the rows and rows of trees that colonnaded the streets were bursting into leaf, full, just like me, of anticipation for the life awaiting them. Everything felt clean and fresh and joyful.

What a shock, then, to arrive a few hours later in grey, smoke-clogged Liverpool. A cold, stinging rain was beating down as we were herded into a kind of barracks that was grimy and rancid. The walls were streaked with dirt and the atmosphere was grim and threatening. We stopped in a dark room lined with filthy wooden benches. I chose to stand. Nobody told us how long we would be staying, nor what we should do next, and I felt sick at the idea of spending a night in this smelly place. Thankfully, though, my stay lasted only a couple of hours. Just as I was getting used to the gloom and the stench, I was called up to board another boat. It seemed much too small to take us all the way to Canada and it was only when we arrived in Glasgow that I realized what was happening. In Glasgow we transferred to a much bigger ship that was to take us across the ocean.

How terrible were the long days and nights that followed, rolling and swaying with nothing outside but the churning ocean and an entire universe of endless grey fog. The ocean was much rougher than the European waters and the moans and grunts of the two women I shared a cabin with did nothing to ease my own sea-sickness. Our cabin was at the front of the ship and rose and fell discordantly, slapping the waves with an almighty bang. On deck the wind was ferocious, but better the cold and gales than the smell of vomit below. I ate barely a morsel and counted down the days until our eventual arrival in distant Halifax, Nova Scotia: three dreadful weeks.

More than a month after leaving Pavolitch I had finally made it to Canada. But my journey wasn't over yet. In Halifax we were transferred to the train station for the journey to Montreal, then divided into groups. Mine boarded another train bound, finally, for Winnipeg. From the window I watched in awe as the unfamiliar landscapes slipped slowly past. We passed lakes so big I thought they were seas, dense forests of dark trees so different from the pale birches I was used to. The scale was immense. For two whole days I drank in the vast beauty of Canada. As we approached Winnipeg the terrain became bleaker and flatter with less variation than the Ukrainian plains. The soil was uncultivated and now I began to understand why the Canadian government was so keen to invite immigrants to its country, to put this fertile land to the plough. Many, many Ukrainians, and among them a multitude of Jews, had come to Canada in the last thirty years and bought land for next to nothing.

The Family Reunited

THE WHOLE family came to meet me at the station in Winnipeg. There was Feter Mendl and Mima Bluma and all their children and grandchildren and, of course, Naftula. I was ecstatic to see him again. He had changed enormously in the four years since he had left Pavolitch that summer morning in 1920. He was twenty years old. His chest had broadened, his voice deepened and his skin had lost its pallor. Strangest of all, he had anglicized his name and now everybody knew him as Nathan. But he was still the same sensitive, beautiful Naftula that I had always loved and his tender smile was unchanged.

Menachem Mendl's family had been in Winnipeg for more than fifteen years already and most of my cousins had by now made a success of their lives. They had studied at university and become doctors or lawyers or married wealthy businessmen. In Pavolitch Feter Mendl had always been the poorer, less successful of Akiva's sons and now he and Bluma lived in a comfortable house with their high-achieving family around them.

Naftula had been just a little boy when Menachem Mendl left Pavolitch, but when he arrived in Winnipeg, Feter Mendl and Mima Bluma had invited him to stay with them until he had enough money to rent a room of his own. It was ironic, really, that Naftula and I, who had been brought up in a life of comfort, were now reliant on the goodwill of our great-uncle and aunt. Menachem Mendl's family had always resented Berl and Pessy for their prosperity and for bringing their daughters up like royalty. Now their children and grandchildren were thriving and we were paupers.

Nathan, as his friends and colleagues called him, had been working in a retail store ever since he arrived in Winnipeg and I, too, needed to find work as soon as possible. I started off in a fruit shop, which was run by a fellow immigrant from Pavolitch. My job was to sort the good fruit from the bad, sifting through boxes of strawberries and trays of apples and pears. I needed to pay rent on the room I had taken, but, more importantly, I had to somehow find enough money to bring Zayde and Baba and the rest of the family to Winnipeg.

I wept as I lay down to sleep at night thinking about Rachel going on the yarid on her own or with cousin Mendl, who was barely more than a child. I knew that Zayde was growing weaker and I feared that I might never see him again. Once out of the Soviet Union I learned news that I could have only guessed at from the inside: that millions had died from famine in Russia since 1921. Thanks to my trading activities, we had survived that crisis, but I was fearful for the future. If I wanted to see the rest of my family again, I needed money quickly.

When winter came and there was no more fresh fruit to sort through, I moved down into the cold cellar where I spent all day surrounded by scuttling mice and rats, weighing currants and raisins and other dried fruit into one-pound packages and ladling jam from giant tins into jars that would be sold in the shop. I hated the cellar and dreaded going to work each morning. Ukrainian Jews owned most of the stores in Winnipeg and mine was no exception. The boss called me Pritza and laughed at me for complaining about the rats.

"If you don't like working in the cellar, we'll have to find you a job in the factory," he said.

Until then I had drawn the line at working in a factory – it was the lowest form of employment of all – but it couldn't be any worse than the rat-infested cellar. The factories, too, were owned by Jews and the following week I swallowed the last of my pride and landed a job at the Globe Bedding factory where I spent the next few years stitching mattresses. In Pavolitch I hadn't even learned how to sew properly; I could embroider a pillowcase beautifully, but mattresses were another matter. I may have lived like a pritza as a girl, but I certainly wasn't one anymore.

I was amazed just how quickly Winnipeg came to feel like home. I was surrounded by familiar faces and not just those of my relatives. In the streets I recognized people I had known in the past, in a life that was fast becoming a distant memory. Winnipeg was full of Pavolitchers; there was even a Pavolitch synagogue where almost every worshipper was familiar. Names and faces I had forgotten over the years came flooding back. How strange, I thought, that I hadn't noticed all these people disappear from my life over the last twenty years, yet here they all were, carrying on just as they did back home, but half way across the world. I was reunited with some less-welcome characters from the past, too, for it wasn't just Jews who had made their way to Canada in their thousands. Winnipeg was home to hundreds of Ukrainians who had brought with them from the old country all the tensions and resentments of the Pale. They snubbed me in the street and refused to frequent what they called the "Jew stores".

Even the weather in Winnipeg was familiar. The warm summer months were followed by a brisk descent into winter. Although outside it was just as cold as during the worst Pavolitch snows, the houses were more sturdy and better insulated. And there was enough wood to light fires in all the rooms. I had forgotten what it was like not to feel a permanent chill throughout the long winter months. Even in the bleakest times, the stores remained well stocked. I thought back to the years of cold and hunger in Pavolitch and wondered how we had all survived. And as for my trading trips across the country, they seemed like a nightmare from another lifetime entirely.

Now that I was settled in my new life and had a job that enabled me to save a little money each week, I became more determined than ever that the rest of the family should be able to join Naftula and me. I missed my grandparents terribly, especially Baba. They had been devoted to us our whole lives and here we were, separated by thousands of miles. So in 1925, a year after my arrival, we prepared to bring the rest of the family to Canada. My grandfather had been busy with the necessary documentation his end, and Naftula and I scraped together all we could to buy tickets. We still didn't have enough money, but Mendl and Bluma made a contribution, too, and the rest we borrowed on credit from their wealthy son-in-law Dudi Rusen.

Just weeks before the family was due to leave Pavolitch, one of my worst fears was realized. A telegram arrived informing us that Zayde had died. Everything I had I owed to my grandfather. It was his grain business that had allowed us every luxury as children and had helped keep us going during the long years of war. And it was he who had insisted that I take the opportunity to leave the Soviet Union, even though life for him and the rest of the family would be so much tougher without me. All the childhood beatings with his old leather belt were long since forgotten. Now I remembered only the wilted remains of that once vigorous man and thought back to how he had given me his last kopeks for my journey. Despite his gruffness, his outbursts and his grumbles, I loved my Zayde with all my heart. I felt crushed by the thought that I would never see him again. I reasoned with myself that he would have detested the three long weeks at sea, but I knew he would have been overjoyed to see Moscow and London and, most of all, to be reunited with Naftula, who had always been his favorite grandchild.

As always, Baba insisted that the family carry on as normal and she continued the application process for their emigration. At last, after months of planning and preparation, she and the rest of the family arrived at Winnipeg station. Baba was dressed in black from head to toe. She looked older and thinner than I remembered and I wondered how she had managed to find the strength for the journey. But inside that frail body was a deep well of resourcefulness. She hugged me so tightly and for so long that it felt as if we would be locked together forever. Despite the sadness etched deeply into her face, her eyes were bright with the joy of seeing Naftula and me again. With her were the newly wedded Sarah and Shaya, and Rachel and Mendl. One by one I embraced my sisters and my cousin and my new brother-in-law as unrestrainable tears rolled down my face. There had been times when I didn't think this joyful day would ever come. If only Zayde had been with us to share it. And, as it so often was back in Pavolitch, my family was accompanied by Haskl, the hunchback. Haskl had always been like a favorite uncle to me and I was as overjoyed to see him as I was the rest of the family.

We all rented a large house together and, except for the hole where Zayde should have been, our family felt more united than at any time over the last ten years. We could finally live the life we had dreamed of, that we had hoped Kerensky might be able to offer us back in Pavolitch. Instead we had had to journey across a vast ocean to achieve it. Sarah was at home with us again and, although he didn't live in the same house, Naftula was nearby. Only Baya was missing. She had stayed behind in the Soviet Union. Having already distanced herself from her family over the years, she moved to Kiev as soon as she was old enough. Now she was studying engineering at the university and was soon to be married.

Except for Baba, we all went out to work so that we could pay the rent and return the money we had borrowed for my family's passage. All our earnings were given to Baba at the end of the week. She acted as our treasurer and made sure the rent was paid and the groceries purchased. And of course she did all the cooking and baking, replicating the delicious meals of blintzes and knishes, soups and dumplings, liver and gefilte fish that we had enjoyed in our youth. Any earnings left over once the week's bills were paid were shared out so that each of us had a little money of our own to spend.

I continued to work at Globe Bedding and Rachel found a job in a candy factory. Although it was hot, tiring and repetitive, it was a job that in her childhood Rachel might have dreamed about, especially during the hungry years when she always complained that she didn't get enough to eat! Sarah gave private Hebrew lessons to those wealthy enough to pay for them while her husband Shaya taught in the Talmud Torah school, which offered a Jewish education to the children of the poor. Mendl was just thirteen and attended English school where he soon adopted the name Morris and, from that moment on, he insisted that we call him by his new name.

Not long after the rest of the family arrived in Canada, Naftula celebrated his marriage to Bessie Fishman, a pretty young woman from a wealthy family. Like Naftula, Bessie had a beautiful voice and together they would sing all the Yiddish songs we loved from our old life. Bessie's parents were financing a general store to be run by another of their sons-in-law in a town called Oakburn, two hundred miles northwest of Winnipeg. They wanted Naftula to become a partner in the store, too. Of course Oakburn wasn't so terribly far away, but I felt I had only just got my brother back after years of separation and I hated losing him again.

I continued to work for an additional two years at Globe Bedding. The conditions were stifling and I still resented the fact that I had been forced into factory work, which was the most lowly and monotonous of professions. I felt like a robot, clocking on, clocking off, sitting in a line with all the other seamstresses hour after hour, day after day, month after month.

Then, from one day to the next, everything changed. Isador Cooper came into my life. Born Yitzhak Yakov Koopershmit in Mezhurich near the city of Rovno in western Ukraine, Isador was quite a successful businessman in Winnipeg running a trading store beside the Canadian Pacific Railway station. It wasn't love at first sight; Isador wasn't that sort of man. He was small like me, with a round, open face, cropped hair and little glasses, but he endeared me with his warmth, his generous nature and his kind heart. Gradually, nervously, I allowed myself to take the first faltering steps along the path that would lead me to a new, terrifying emotion that I knew was called love, but that I had never before experienced. No man had ever treated me as Isador did, looked at me so tenderly or shown so much interest in the stories I recounted.

I thought back to the dreams I had had back in Pavolitch, when I was riding on the railways from one market to another, nestling between planks of timber in search of shelter. I had known that one day I was bound to grow up and fall in love, but it had been difficult to imagine how such a future could come about. The daily necessities of finding food, keeping warm and somehow finding the means to go on kept my dreams at bay. Now the struggle was over and the future was here and now, in Winnipeg, and with Itzhik (as I called him). In the spring of 1926 Itzhik and I were married. Nine months later to the day our baby daughter was born. The dream was complete. We named our little girl Leah, in honor of Ettie Leah, the mother I had lost half a world away when I was just six years old. As I thought back to my parents with fondness, I felt that at last I really had become a daughter they could have been proud of.

Epilogue

THERE I will leave Pearl to the first flushes of motherhood and catch up with what happened to other members of her family. Her grandmother Pessy lived for two more years after Pearl was married. To my immense gratitude, she at last overcame her fear of the Evil Eye sufficiently to allow herself to be photographed, revealing herself to us as a tiny, bony woman with prominent cheekbones and high arches above her eyes, which gave her a slightly surprised expression. She still covered her hair with a matron's wig, as tradition dictates, right up until her death in 1928.

Babtsy and her family arrived in Winnipeg in 1929. Having fled Khodarkov after the pogrom in 1919, they remained with the parents of Babtsy's husband Moishe and his three sisters in Kiev. As a watchmaker, Moishe was considered a class enemy by the Soviets and was unable to work while his children were initially barred from school as places were available only to the sons and daughters of workers or Communist Party members. Owing to administrative errors, it took two years for the paperwork for the family's immigration to Canada to be finalized. When at last they boarded the ship, Babtsy's mother Leah was refused entry because she was, by this time, blind. The mother and daughter who had always been inseparable were forced to part. Leah stayed behind with her son-in-law's relatives, much to the distress of her whole family. She died in Kiev in 1931.

Babtsy's daughter Marion recalls how she struggled to adapt to capitalist society once in Canada. She was fourteen years old when her family took her away from the Soviet Union, a dedicated socialist and member of the Young Pioneer communist youth movement.

Haskl's wife Batya (Bessie) joined her husband with their two daughters, Yetta and Ruchel (Rose), in Winnipeg once Haskl had raised sufficient funds for their passage. My family and theirs remained extremely close, even after Haskl's descendents moved to New York, where Pearl visited them and fell into Rose's arms like a long-lost sister.

Baya never joined her brother and cousins in Canada. She completed her studies in Kiev and married an engineer; the couple remained childless. Baya stayed in Kiev until World War II when she became a victim of the Nazis. She and her husband were among a group of Jews herded to the banks of the river Dniepr, which divides the city, and forced aboard a ship. It was set alight. There were no survivors.

Virtually no Jews that remained in the former territory of the Pale lived to see the end of World War II. Some, with great prescience, fled eastwards to the Urals or Central Asia before the Nazis reached them, not returning until the war was over. But the vast majority of Jews stayed at home. Many didn't believe the rumors emanating from Nazi-occupied territories. Instead, they remembered the German occupation of 1918 when the foreign troops had kept order and maintained good relations with the Jews among whom they were stationed.

The Nazis completed the job that Denikin's White Army had begun twenty years earlier. They stretched to their logical conclusion many techniques for mass killing that had been used during the Civil War, enabling them to murder Jews in an even more ruthless and systematic manner. Pavolitch became a killing field. In 1941 more than thirteen hundred Jews were shot beside a mass grave dug in the Jewish cemetery. The bodies were jumbled one on top of another. The victims came from many outlying villages as well as Pavolitch, herded to a single spot for ease of slaughter. The gentile population fared badly, too. In November 1943 dozens were rounded up and locked in the basement of one of the old synagogues, where they were burnt alive. Today a memorial marks the spot.

I have no relatives living in Ukraine today. Of Pearl's family in Makarov, only Meyer's two youngest siblings, Avrom and Maryam, remained in the Soviet Union until their deaths in 1970. The older brothers Berl and Moishe had died of typhus in 1919 while sisters Yetta and Bassy emigrated from Ukraine to the United States. Avrom, who worked as a therapist near Kiev, was childless, but much loved by all his patients. Maryam, a doctor, stayed in the city. They both escaped to Central Asia during the war years before returning to Kiev where Maryam's descendents remained until the 1990s. Then, driven away by the dire economic situation and extreme lawlessness of newly independent Ukraine (the husband of one was murdered in 1995), they emigrated from there to Germany. Around the same time the sole remaining descendant of Meyer's brother Berl also abandoned Ukraine for Germany. Moishe's line has lived in Israel for many decades. Pearl visited them there with my father in the 1960s.

Pearl, herself, apart from a brief, unsuccessful interlude in Toronto, remained in Winnipeg until 1956. Her husband Itzhik's business collapsed in the 1930s during the Great Depression and the family was destitute once again. To try to make ends meet, he found work on the railways selling food and other goods to travelers crossing Canada's great expanse. Pearl put her own trading skills to work for a second time by selling matzos to Jewish families for Passover and supplying them with kosher chicken. Meanwhile, her second child, a son – my father, was born in 1932. They named him Meyer, after his grandfather.

A few years later Pearl and Itzhik went into partnership with cousin Morris (Mendl) and opened a restaurant next door to Winnipeg's Tribune newspaper. It acted as a canteen for the newspaper staff and a meeting point for the family. They worked hard and earned a decent living. The restaurant opened before dawn when the printers turned up for their shifts. Rather than the Jewish dishes she had learned from her grandmother, Pearl cooked up a decidedly non-kosher breakfast of bacon and eggs despite adhering to the Jewish dietary laws for herself and her family. During the nightshift, Itzhik and Morris took it in turns to carry large, steel scuttles filled with drinks and snacks up to the newspaper men next door. They stayed in the catering business until the late 1950s and later opened a restaurant beside the federal government offices.

Morris proved to be a keen businessman and soon established his own restaurant next to the offices of the other Winnipeg newspaper, the Free Press. He lived alone, never marrying, in an apartment across the road from his restaurant. There he died of a heart attack when he was in his late forties.

Sarah and Shaya settled in Toronto where Shaya became the principal of a Yiddish school and Sarah a teacher. Later they moved to Chicago so that Shaya, by now a leading Hebrew poet, could take up a post as Professor of Modern Hebrew Literature. They had a son, Shloime – now known as Sol – who became a pathologist at the university hospital in Toronto.

Nathan (Naftula), with his wife Bessie, remained in Oakburn until his death in 1976. He soon bought out his partner in the trading store he ran and continued to work there all his life. Today a memorial is dedicated to him in the town, a mark of gratitude from the townsfolk for his kindness and generosity, for he always offered goods on credit to the needy – even if it left him unable to pay his own bills. His son, Melvyn, had a successful career in the insurance industry and lives in Vancouver.

Rachel married a large, jovial, but dominating man called Leib Coodin and remained in Winnipeg until her husband's death. They had two daughters: Betty settled in Los Angeles while her younger sister Adele is the only one of my father's maternal cousins to live in Winnipeg to this day.

In 1950 Pearl's daughter Leah, now called Lilian, moved from Winnipeg to Los Angeles. Her son Meyer (now Morley) followed in 1955 and the next year Pearl and Itzhik sold their restaurant and joined their children under the southern sun. For a couple of years they ran a restaurant in downtown Los Angeles before Itzhik died of a heart attack in January 1959 at age sixty-two. In September of the same year, Morley moved to England to take up a place at Cambridge University. He never returned to live in North America.

After Rachel's husband died, she, too, followed her daughter in moving from Winnipeg to Los Angeles. Eventually Pearl and Rachel moved into an apartment together in West Hollywood, the only home of my grandmother's that I ever knew. Just as they spent their early years together side by side, they spent their final ones, too. Pearl died in 1988. Rachel outlived her by seven years. Despite the hardships they suffered in their youth, both lived until their late eighties while Sarah, who was exactly as old as the century, battled on into her nineties dying in 1992.

*

My father and I travelled to Ukraine together in May 2005 to visit the towns and villages where our ancestors had lived. Pavolitch – Pavoloch in Russian – exists to this day, now a sleepy village of a few dozen houses. Nothing remains of the double-fronted dwelling that Akiva had built for his sons. It, like every other house in Pavolitch, was destroyed during World War II. The only buildings still in place from my grandmother's era are the mill by the lake where Meyer worked as a bookkeeper and the main synagogue: a square building with painted brick-work and tall, arched windows.

Today it is a museum telling the history of Pavolitch through a series of ill-lit displays, annotated by hand. The curator, Ivan Bubliy, a former language teacher in his mid-eighties, showed us around at a slow, shuffling pace, cocking his head quizzically whenever we asked a question and hesitating while he attempted to dig out suitable answers from the dusty pit of his memory. The museum recounts Pavolitch's early origins as a staging post for the silk and cloth trade, used for storing fabric over the winter until the inland waterways from the Black Sea to the Baltic unfroze. The town's first recorded history was as a Cossack stronghold in the sixteenth century; after countless bloody battles it became a fiefdom of the Polish nobility before becoming part of Russia in 1793.

The old Jewish cemetery had recently been partially restored thanks to donations from descendents of some Pavolitch families who immigrated to Winnipeg. It was the great-grandson of Josef Nathanson – the man who took the custom of Poritz Baskakov causing the demise of Berl's business – who organized the restoration. Many of the headstones were destroyed during the Nazi occupation; we were told that the Germans often used them for road building. Of those that remain, the inscriptions, in Hebrew characters, are worn and a large number are illegible. We did not find the graves of any of our forefathers.

Elsewhere we heard confirmation of some of my grandmother's stories: a ninety-five year old woman in Khodarkov recounted to us her memories of the pogrom in which the Jews were drowned in the river, the same pogrom that Babtsy and her family survived by hiding in the cellar of Moishe's watch shop. And in Andrushky we tracked down the sugar factory, still functioning, that had belonged to Poritz Baskakov. Here we were interrogated at length by the factory director before he would respond to any of our questions, fearful perhaps that we were sugar barons ourselves, travelling to Ukraine with the aim of snapping up cheap commercial assets.

In Makarov the Twersky court was destroyed by the Nazis and nobody knows exactly where it stood. The place where the main synagogue was located is now a rubble-strewn patch of wasteland close to the large, Soviet-style town square. Only a tiny handful of Jews now live in the town, all of them incomers after World War II. The old Jewish cemeteries have been destroyed. The graves of the Twersky rabbis were somehow safeguarded, however, and it seems fitting that their remains should now reside in the vast Jewish cemetery in Berdichev. Thanks to money sent from abroad, their graves are topped with newly hewn, gleaming gravestones of slate and marble and housed in a small, painted mausoleum. They are surrounded by acre after acre of crumbling headstones belonging to men and women who have long been forgotten, generations of Jews whose descendents either escaped to the West or were mown down by Nazi bullets. Now nobody is left to tend their graves.

Likewise, the final resting place of Reb Dovidl of Talna, the patriarch of the Twersky dynasty, is a dirty concrete box housed in an old shack covered with graffiti. It lies at the end of a dingy alley that smells of urine, on the edge of what was once a Jewish cemetery and today is an overgrown wasteland littered with old tires. Today the town is called Talnoye and the (gentile) editor of the local newspaper, a fast-talking man by the name of Andrei Ilych Polishchuk, is spearheading a fundraising effort to have Reb Dovidl's remains interred in surroundings more appropriate to the founder of one of the most revered dynasties of Hassidic rabbis. As my father and I stood beside the makeshift mausoleum, I thought how horrified my forebears would be to see what had become of the grave of this near God-like figure. Once inside, we found the concrete sarcophagus littered with melted wax and fragments of Hebrew prayers written in blue biro, testament to the fact that occasional visitors from Israel or North America set foot in this place to light a candle and worship at the last resting place of their hallowed rabbi. Where the remains of his once famous advisor, Velvele Tallner – my great-great-great-grandfather – reside, we will no doubt never know.

Glossary

baba – grandmother

balagula – coach driver

banda – name used for the various warring parties, or bands, in the Civil
   War

batko – local Ukrainian leader; the literal meaning is "father"

Beth Din – rabbinical court

blintzes – pancakes filled with sweet or savory filling

challah – sweet, plaited loaf served on the Sabbath

dacha – holiday home in the country (Russian)

feter – uncle

gefilte fish – ground balls of fish served in sauce, traditionally eaten on the
   Sabbath

gelt – money

goy (plural, *goyim*) – gentile

Gut Shabbas – greeting meaning "Good Sabbath"

Hanukkah – Festival of Lights, celebrated in November/December

happers – government "kidnappers" who round up children for military
   service

Hassid (plural, *Hassidim*) – sect of orthodox Jewry founded in Ukraine in
   the eighteenth century

heder – Jewish primary school

kaddish – prayer for the dead, part of Jewish mourning ritual

kaluzha – pond or pool

kasha – Russian porridge, usually made from buckwheat

kiddush – sanctification, or blessing, pronounced over a goblet of wine

knishes – small balls of dough filled with meat or vegetables

kolbasa – Russian salami-type sausage

kretchma – tavern

latke – potato pancakes traditionally eaten at Hanukkah

Mazel tov! – Hebrew greeting expressing congratulations or best wishes

melamed – teacher

menorah – branched candlestick used particularly at Hanukkah

mima – aunt

minyan – communal prayer (attended by ten or more adult males)

peyes – side-locks of hair traditionally worn by religious Jewish males

pood – Russian unit of measurement, equivalent to thirty-six pounds

poritz (plural, *pritzim*; feminine, *pritza*) – landowner or member of the
    minor nobility; also used as a pejorative term meaning "oppressor"

Purim – Jewish festival in February/March

rebbe – teacher or rabbi

rebbetzin – rabbi's wife

Rosh Hashanah – Jewish New Year, usually celebrated in September

seder – ceremonial dinner held at the beginning of Passover

shamus – beadle, or synagogue assistant

shkole – Russian secondary school

shtetl – small town or village that is home to a Jewish community;
    diminutive of *shtot*, meaning town

Succoth – Feast of Tabernacles, celebrated in October

Talmud – the book of Jewish law and rabbinic literature; it has two
    components – the *Mishnah* and the *Gemara*

tata – father

tichl – head cloth worn by Jewish women

Torah – the first five books of the Bible; also known as the Pentateuch

valenki – Russian felt boots worn in winter

verst – Russian unit of measurement, roughly equivalent to a kilometer
    or two thirds of a mile

yarid – market

yeshiva – boys' school devoted to study of the Torah and the Talmud

Yom Kippur – Day of Atonement, observed nine days after Rosh
    Hashanah

zayde – grandfather

Bibliography

Aleichem, Sholem. *Tevye the Dairyman & The Railroad Stories*. New York: Schocken Books, 1987.

Allen, W. E. D. *The Ukraine – A History*. Cambridge: Cambridge University Press, 1940.

Antin, Mary. *The Promised Land*. London: William Heinemann, 1912.

Babel, Isaac. *The Collected Stories*. New York & London: Norton, 2002.

Baron, Salo W. *The Russian Jew under Tsars and Soviets*. New York: Macmillan, 1976.

Bulgakov, Mikhail. *The White Guard*. London: Collins Harvill, 1989.

Czumer, William A. *Recollections about the life of the first Ukrainian settlers in Canada* (trans: Laychuk, L. T.). Edmonton: Canadian Institute of Ukrainian Studies, 1981.

Figes, Orlando. *A People's Tragedy: The Russian Revolution 1891–1924*. London: Pimlico, 1997.

Footman, David. *Civil War in Russia*. London: Faber & Faber, 1961.

Fraser, Eugenie. *The House by the Dvina*. London: Corgi Books, 1986.

Greenberg, Louis. *The Jews in Russia: the Struggle for Emancipation*. New York: Schocken Books, 1976.

Heifetz, Elias. *The Slaughter of the Jews in the Ukraine in 1919*. New York: Thomas Seltzer, 1921.

Hoffman, Eva. *Shtetl*. London: Vintage, 1999.

Horsbrugh-Porter, Anna (ed.). *Memories of Revolution – Russian Women Remember*. London: Routledge, 1993.

Hosking, Geoffrey. *A History of the Soviet Union*. London: Fontana Press, 1990.

Howe, Irving & Kenneth Libo. *How We Lived – A Documentary History of Immigrant Jews in America 1880–1930*. New York: Richard Marek Publishers, 1979.

Israel, Gérard. *The Jews in Russia*. London: Charles Knight & Co, 1975.

Klier, John D. & Shlomo Lambroza (eds.). *Pogroms: Anti-Jewish Violence in Modern Russian History*. Cambridge: Cambridge University Press, 1992.

Levitas, Isaac. *The Jewish Community in Russia 1772–1844*. New York: Octogon Books, 1970.

Mawdsley, Evan. *The Russian Civil War*. Edinburgh: Birlinn, 2000.

Nathans, Benjamin. *Beyond the Pale: The Jewish Encounter with Late Imperial Russia*. Berkeley, Los Angeles & London: University of California Press, 2004.

Ratushinskaya, Irina. *The Odessans*, London: Sceptre, 1996.

Rubinstein, Aryeh (ed.). *Hasidism*, Jerusalem: Keter Books, 1975.

Singer, I. J. *Of a World That Is No More*. London: Faber & Faber, 1987.

Singer, I. J. *The Brothers Ashkenazi*. London: Penguin, 1993.

Singer, Isaac Bashevis. *In My Father's Court: A memoir*. London: Penguin, 1980.

Singer, Isaac Bashevis. *The Family Moskat*. London: Vintage, 2000.

Wengeroff, Pauline. *Rememberings – The world of a Russian-Jewish woman in the nineteenth century* (trans: Wenkart, Henry). Bethesda: University Press of Maryland, 2000.

About the Author

LISA COOPER was born in 1969 in Norwich, England. She studied Russian at Edinburgh University, attracted by a passion for languages and a fascination with the country's people and history.

As a student, she spent a year in the southern Russian city of Voronezh. Armed with nothing more than an old address dating from the 1960s and a family tree, she managed to make contact with cousins in Kiev, who introduced her to a web of relatives she knew nothing about. The experience helped breed an interest in both family history and Ukrainian history.

A Forgotten Land was originally conceived as a dissertation for a Masters degree in History at University College London, and is based on a series of recordings made by her father in the 1980s of his mother – Pearl – talking in Yiddish about her early life in Ukraine.

Sidetracked by the fascinating story her grandmother's tapes revealed, she abandoned the degree and set about turning her work into a novel based on her own family's lives and experiences.

She lives in Cornwall, south-west England, with her husband and two young children, and works as a journalist. This is her first book.